GREAT POST COLD WAR AMERICAN THINKERS

ON INTERNATIONAL RELATIONS

Gilbert Doctorow

ISBN: 145376447X
ISBN-13: 9781453764473

TABLE OF CONTENTS

FOREWORD

The fall of the Berlin Wall twenty years ago, the overturning of Soviet controlled regimes in Eastern Europe and ultimately the collapse of the Soviet Union itself were epoch making events.

It was obvious at the time that the peoples in the newly liberated Soviet space, in particular those living in the Russian Federation, were totally disoriented. Not only did the economic, social, and political landscape around them change, but value systems were overturned. What yesterday was black had now become white, and vice versa.

What many of us did not appreciate at the time was how fundamental changes in the political environment also affected thinking in the West, on the "winning" side of the Cold War. Military planners and foreign policy professionals were left in confusion. What would the new security risks be now that Communism had been dispatched? What kind of armed forces would be needed? What about nuclear proliferation?

The general public, it now appears, was also quite hungry for a vision of the future, for fresh understanding of the challenges to come. Indeed, the disorientation may have been more severe in the West than in the East. In Eastern Europe and the Former Soviet Union, there was an 'off-the-shelf' model ready to replace the defunct model of Soviet Communism: free markets, parliamentary democracy, association with the European Community and partnership with the former enemy across the Atlantic. In the West, there were uncertainties of a different nature. The bipolar world was dead. What would replace it?

And so an asymmetrical pattern of intellectual life set in: Eastern Europe and Russia abandoned ideology, rushed wholeheartedly into national ideas that boiled down to 'get rich quick,' generating contented strata of *nouveaux riches*, while the United States entered a phase of navel contemplation, search for identity and reconfirmation of ideology. An America that was once self-defined by its pragmatism and common sense approach to problem solving led the way in the search for new big ideas.

You are about to read a collection of essays on the writings of ten of America's most influential thinkers on international relations from the post-Cold War period with a view to how they addressed the questions about the present and future on everyone's minds. Some are professional futurologists. Others improvised to deal with the unexpected.

This volume is intended for use by undergraduates and graduate students, as well as for non-specialist readers, and this is reflected in the construction of the review articles. I try to set out the essential thesis of the respective authors before exposing it to critique, so that this book does not presuppose the reader's prior familiarity with the works in question.

In approaching my material I have placed the accent on considering the methodology of the authors under review. I did not bring particular erudition to the task of writing these critiques. I approached the authors in the manner of the oriental martial arts, applying their own inertial force against them. Where possible I did a logic check, drawing out what a peer review or skilled editor should have picked up.

In the spirit of full disclosure, I inform the reader that I approached the masters of International Relations bringing with me the intellectual baggage of an historian. While interdisciplinary approaches to area studies have long been the vogue, critiques of methodology across disciplinary lines such as I offer here are, admittedly, not common. However, as the reader will quickly realize, when political scientists are not applying deductive reasoning from abstract philosophical principles to reach their conclusions and policy recommendations, they very often are mining history for 'lessons' or case studies to prove their point. In the spirit of reciprocity, I will use the same lever in what follows to push back.

The result of close scrutiny is not always flattering. Works which were intended primarily for scholarly readers may come out better. Those which were more directed to the general public often come out bruised.

In all cases, contemporary political analysis or futurology is by nature written in great haste, since the shelf life of such books is expected to be quite limited. Haste may compromise scientific merit. The partisan agenda of the authors also is at odds with the notion of scholarly detachment.

Given the occasional severity of my remarks, some readers have raised the question of my sincerity in characterizing these authors as 'great thinkers.' Allow me to state unequivocally that I have the highest respect for the intellectual capabilities of all the authors presented here. As we shall see in the given works under examination, their books yield many pleasant surprises, making the journey into their worlds so rewarding What may be questionable is their receptivity to realities which contradict their preconceptions, in short, their honesty with themselves as well as with us and their ethical compass. Let the reader decide.

As the format is a book review, the question will possibly arise - why review books which first appeared ten or twenty years ago?

To that I reply that these major contributions from some of the country's best theorists and practitioners of international affairs have become classics. They are currently in print and are likely to remain so for years to come. The earliest among them have turned from being works potentially shaping the future to works which have shaped the past and present. As with any history, you return to it to pick out the causal lines which were unclear to most of us at the time but which have, over time, become salient. Elements in the books which presented great interest to readers when these books were first published and touched off professional disputes due to their topical nature may have receded in importance. Other elements that were passed over by reviewers back then may now, in light of events within the United States and the world, well merit discussion.

Some of the works which we shall examine in this book were written by young conceptual thinkers who were taking their first steps in the public marketplace of ideas; others were late works by senior statesmen and scholars who had decades of writings in their portfolios. In the latter case, my intent is not to trace the evolution in their thinking, instead to take only their works published in the period under examination and to connect them with the debate hanging in the air at the time.

I open with a look at the writings of Francis Fukuyama, who began the debate over the future of the post-Cold War world with his stimulating and controversial *End of History*. The challenge to the foreign policy Establishment of a world without conflict implicit in Fukuyama's first major work was taken up by his former graduate studies adviser at Harvard, doyen of the American political science profession and master of futurology, Samuel Huntington.

His *Clash of Civilizations* gave comfort to those who needed something to worry about and penetrated the consciousness of a global public thirsty for a new paradigm in international relations.

We will examine next several books written in the 1990s and new millennium by America's two leading scholar-practitioners in the field of international affairs from the period of the Cold War, Zbigniew Brzezinski and Henry Kissinger. We shall be interested to see in what ways the new age changed their views of what was required of American statecraft. Did the end of the Cold War mean indeed an end of the associated mentality? Is what they wrote new wine in old casks?

In Leslie Gelb and Joseph Nye we have two further long-time Establishment figures whose works under examination here dealt with both the changing international landscape and changing U.S. government management of foreign policy in the George W. Bush era which made them both outsiders.

We turn next to two academics whose writings are basically addressed to their peers in the profession, Stanley Hoffmann and John Ikenberry. Their works on the theory of international relations reviewed here are delivered at a higher level of abstraction, though they are clearly responding to changes in the political environment off campus since the end of the Cold War. Professor Hoffmann belongs to the same generation as the practitioner-scholars already mentioned. Professor Ikenberry represents a younger generation and may be said to be in the prime of his career, with speaking engagements and appearances on learned panels which attract the attention of the general public.

Finally we will move out of the classroom and into the street to see what a couple of widely read intellectual-polemicists have been saying about U.S. foreign policy in the post-Cold War world. These are the prominent Neoconservative writer Robert Kagan and the polymath academic Noam Chomsky, who is probably the best known American 'dissident' writer on U.S. foreign policy to audiences around the world and also enjoys considerable readership of his prolific writings within the United States.

It bears mention that there is a commonality to the 10 authors presented here which, though unintended when they were chosen, afterwards became fairly striking: in the course of their careers all but one, namely G.

John Ikenberry, has had an affiliation with Harvard University, whether as a student, resident fellow or professor.

Though they have their differences, which we will highlight, these 'apples' also did not fall very far from the tree. Apart from their institutional link-up, these independent minded and individualistic authors nearly all place themselves along a divide between 'realists' and 'idealists' which gave tight focus to their debates. Thus, I contend that what I am about to present is not merely 10 prima donna authors, but an important part of the tableau of American intellectual history in the period 1992-2009.

How did I come upon precisely these 10 authors? Admittedly, it was partly a process of trial and error as I expanded my list outwards from the most obvious and inevitable names. I was also assisted by some expert help from the sidelines. The scope of my search was influenced considerably by a conversation I had with Andrew Bacevich, Professor of International Relations and History at Boston University, in June 2009. Some further tips and comments were offered by Professor S. Frederick Starr of the Paul H. Nitze School of Advanced International Studies, Johns Hopkins University. Obviously, responsibility for any omissions or wrongful inclusions in the list of 'great thinkers' rests solely with me.

The essays appearing in this book were first published as blog articles on the portal of *La Libre Belgique*, a middle-of-the road French language newspaper of Belgium. In the conversion from blog postings to chapters, I have edited the text to achieve as consistent an analytical approach to the subject matter as possible without altering the conversational tone. I am hopeful these essays will provide the reader with both a guide and incentive for reading the authors under review with better appreciation of the achievements and limitations of the genre.

Francis Fukuyama

from *The End of History* to *After the Neocons*

Published in the year which saw the collapse of the Soviet Union and the apparent worldwide triumph of liberal democracy and free markets championed by the United States, Francis Fukuyama's seminal work *The End of History and the Last Man* (1992) was the stone tossed into the water which created ripples of debate over what sense to make of the end of the Cold War which reverberate to our day.

In light of his remarkably good timing, which foreordained high interest among the general reading public as well as among foreign policy professionals, it is easy to overlook the fact that the author's underlying thesis came out still earlier, in 1989, somewhat in advance of the most dramatic events it eventually explained, in the form of an essay entitled "The End of History?" The article appeared in the low circulation foreign policy magazine *The National Interest* published by a founder of the Neoconservative movement, Irving Kristol.

The positioning for publication of the article was by no means accidental since Fukuyama at the time held similar political views to his editor and his argument that history had reached its final resting place not in Socialism but in the democratic capitalism created by the French and American revolutions was highly supportive of the Neoconservative world view. The fact that his contention was at the time of its writing in 1989 still more tentative than demonstrable (hence the question mark) was no handicap in the mind of the ideologically driven publishers.

By contrast, the book rode a wave of events proving its thesis and came to play a major role in bringing Neoconservative ideas into the mainstream of American political thinking during the 1990s.

Thesis

There is a compelling logic to the composition of *The End of History* which must command respect. The book opens with a description of the liberation wave spreading around the world in the previous two decades as authoritarian regimes of the Right and totalitarian regimes of the Left gave way to liberal democracies. This started in Southern Europe, moved to Asia and Latin America and culminated in Central and Eastern Europe with the collapse of Soviet Communism.

Fukuyama presents a table showing the rise and fall in the number of democratic states around the world at regular intervals since 1790. The current wave marks a high point in the trend. The fact that it has occurred in so many different countries with very different traditions suggests that we are witnessing the operation of universal laws and that perhaps the 19th century Positivists were right, that history is moving in a directional manner towards liberal democracy as the highest form of human society.

Fukuyama is challenging the mood of pessimism over the human condition which dominated the 20th century under the impact of its unfathomable irruptions of evil, the Holocaust and Stalin's Gulag. In light of the new dawn of liberty now rising, he tells us that these were aberrations of irrationalism. They must not deter us from seeing the dominant trend, which has moved once again to the foreground.

The task he sets for himself in the book is to explain the march of humanity towards liberal democracy and free markets. For this he relies mostly on abstract argumentation, reasoning with his reader, walking him through a variety of possible causal factors before settling on those with greatest persuasiveness. Indeed we are treated to a masterly exegesis of 2,000 years of political philosophy beginning with Plato and pausing to reflect on Hobbes, Locke and Hume, Rousseau, Montesquieu, Kant, Hegel and Marx, among others.

As Fukuyama tells us, liberal democracy and free markets have two chief causal factors propelling them. They are intertwined in what might be likened to the DNA double-helix,

First, there is natural science, which advances in a unidirectional manner and brings progressively greater material wellbeing to mankind. It is rational and as it advances leads to industrialization, urbanization, bureaucratization – in a word, a *modernization* that spells convergence in the economic organization of societies across the globe. The most productive expression of this economic mechanism pushing history is liberal capitalism, which brings in its wake the creation of an educated population and relatively prosperous middle classes, the agents of political liberalization.

However, the economic causal factor is not in itself sufficient to explain the shift to rule of law, recognition of freedoms and participation in political life which characterizes liberal democracy. The driver here is an irrational component, the universal human yearning for recognition as was described by Hegel in his dialectics.

Drawing further on points in Kantian and Hegelian theory, Fukuyama tells us that it is in the nature of liberal democracies to get along with one another peaceably. The closest possible approximation of satisfying human yearnings, material and immaterial, has been achieved and with this war and revolution have been vanquished

The antagonisms and conflict assumed to drive relations between states by the Realist school of international affairs that goes back to Machiavelli are not relevant to relations between liberal democracies. Their only remaining application is to relations among non-liberal states and between them and the community of liberal democratic states. Here military power is the decisive determinant.

Given that liberal democracy is advancing around the world, that history is indeed directional and all states are set on the same road, some ahead, some behind, the future will ultimately be one in which conflict between nations entirely disappears.

METHODOLOGY

In this essay I will not challenge Fukuyama's thesis that we are at the dawn of a golden age. That has been done by a succession of his peers and several of the outstanding works in this genre will be examined separately in later chapters.

I must say, however, that the line of attack on Fukuyama's book is typically focused on his reading of empirical data on the world we presently live in rather than the correctness of his abstract reasoning and his interpretation of the writings of the classics of political philosophy.

It seems appropriate to me to set out below what none of Fukuyama's sparring partners has bothered to call attention to: the author's very particular methodology in *The End of History* and how it drew upon his education and personal strengths.

How do you provide a new paradigm to a drastically changing world in a matter of months or even a few years? This is something which Fukuyama did and he achieved it the only way it can be approached – by drawing upon pre-existing models to match approximately what he saw around him. His achievement was that of a magnificent synthesizer rather than original thinker. He must be complimented for the boldness to take his audience straight where his discoveries led him, to reason with his readers and not lecture them in the manner of a senior professor. This is the sign of a young mind who still takes very seriously the world of ideas.

The principle source of Fukuyama's ideas on the causal factor driving liberal democracy is Hegel as interpreted and popularized in the 1930s by the French-Russian philosopher Alexandre Kojève. The very notion of an 'end of history' - a global, universal social and political order towards which all humanity is striving - was posed precisely by Hegel and so frames the intellectual investigation Fukuyama pursues in his best-selling opus.

While getting his undergraduate degree in philosophy at Cornell, Fukuyama was a student of Allan Bloom, who in turn had studied under Kojève. It bears mention that these gurus also helped to shape the thinking of another iconic figure of the Neoconservative movement, Paul Wolfowitz, who was Fukuyama's boss in a number of his government posts, as I note below.

Although it is common practice among political scientists writing in the field of international affairs as well as other sub-fields to show off their knowledge of the classics *en passant*, it is remarkable that a book intended to give immediate and practical meaning to the dramatic events shaping the global political landscape and to inform decisions of policy-makers in foreign and military affairs is argued almost entirely by abstract reasoning drawing on the classics of political philosophy. It is still more remarkable that the young author with such striking intellectual credentials as philosopher was at the time making his living in policy analysis within the State Department and in the country's leading think tank, the RAND Corporation, dealing with regional security issues in the Middle East, European military-political affairs and other nitty-gritty.

Fukuyama took his undergraduate degree in the classics at Cornell in 1974, then spent a year at Yale in the Department of Comparative Literature, and finally earned his doctorate from Harvard in political science, where one of his advisers was Professor Sam Huntington, the doyen of American political scientists whose own best known work, *The Clash of Civilizations*, was in many respects a riposte to Fukuyama's *End of History*.

Fukuyama's Ph.D. dissertation was on Soviet foreign policy. Sovietology was considered a very solid preparation for U.S. government service in the intelligence and foreign policy areas during the Cold War. His first career positions were in foreign policy analysis – in the think tank RAND Corporation and in the State Department's policy planning departments.

SUCCESS BREEDS COMPLACENCY

The End of History was enormously successful with the general public and went through numerous print runs and translations into foreign editions. Foreign policy professionals could not ignore it. Whether they acknowledged Fukuyama's challenge by name or not, the heavy hitters in the foreign affairs Establishment felt compelled to respond to his well reasoned prediction of calmer international waters ahead now that the ideological divisions over social and political systems had been resolved in favor of free markets and liberal democracy. Articles and volumes were published attempting to disprove this optimistic scenario and to justify hyper-active American leadership in what was said to be a still very dangerous world.

Within the narrower world of Neoconservatives, Fukuyama's book was taken up as a key scholarly justification of their convictions and for stepped-up political activism to serve as history's own agents of change in the ever expanding march of democracy. He became a paid-up member in good standing and proceeded to take his place in the New American Century think tank. Beginning in 1997, he was among those calling for the overthrow of Saddam Hussein.

Fukuyama's new celebrity status propelled his academic career. From 1996-2000, he held a professorship of public policy at George Mason University just outside Washington, D.C.. He was then recruited by Neoconservative leader and senior statesman Paul Wolfowitz, for whom he had worked at the US Arms Control and Disarmament Agency and later at State Department to join the Johns Hopkins University in Baltimore where Wolfowitz was tenured professor and dean at the time. Fukuyama became the Bernard L. Schwartz Professor of International Political Economy at the Paul H. Nitze School of Advanced International Studies (SAIS) and in due course was made director of the International Development Program within SAIS.

It goes without saying that Fukuyama was inducted into the mainstream Council on Foreign Relations. In addition, among many honorific and advisory positions in the American scholarly community, he assumed a position on the Board of Trustees of the RAND Corporation and on the Board of Governors of the Pardee RAND Graduate School co-located with RAND Corporation headquarters in Santa Monica, California which confers doctoral degrees in public policy analysis.

In rapid order, Fukuyama published a succession of books as well as numerous articles. A sort of cult developed around his name and he was engaged in public exchanges with challengers from all quarters

In considering Fukuyama's career and writings in the 17 years since the publication of his seminal work *The End of History*, what we see is a demonstration of how brilliant youth becomes complacent, empty but enormously successful middle age. Fukuyama moved out of his field of core competence, political philosophy. Exploiting his guru status and drawing upon his talent as synthesizer and popularizer, he has written extensively in domains where he is summarizing the works of others, with greater or lesser understanding, and adding little or no value.

Whereas one might view his 1995 opus *Trust: The Social Virtues and the Creation of Prosperity* (1995) as dealing with economic and philosophical issues abutting those his *End of History*, that hardly can be said for later works including *Our Posthuman Future: Consequences of the Biotechnology Revolution* (2002) about how biotech advances could threaten human dignity or *State Building: Governance and World Order in the 21st Century* (2004) where Fukuyama brings no great expertise or new ideas to justify taking his reader's time.

Meanwhile, early in the first term of President George W. Bush, Fukuyama's political allegiances underwent a marked transformation as he witnessed to his dismay the brutal implementation of Neoconservative principles he had long supported in the abstract.

As from 2002 he became increasingly disillusioned with unilateral armed intervention. In 2003 he voiced his opposition to the Iraq War and he called for the resignation of Donald Rumsfeld as Secretary of Defense. Going into the 2004 presidential elections, he said he could no longer support George W. Bush and made a break with the Neoconservatives.

Once a Neoconservative, Always a Neoconservative

Fukuyama gathered his thoughts on where the Bush administration had gone wrong in its foreign policy and published a new major work in 2006 entitled *After the Neocons. America at the Crossroads* (2006). Here he sought to sketch a way forward for those who, like himself, understood that the term Neoconservative would be forever linked with the failed policies of the Bush administration and yet who were unsympathetic to the alternative approaches of *Realpolitik* in the Kissinger tradition or to liberal multilateralism, the belief that international law and institutions could ensure order in our turbulent world. He described his new path as "realistic Wilsonianism" and offered readers a foretaste of what it would consist of.

This is all a credit to Fukuyama's ability and willingness to face up to unpleasant realities, to revise his political affiliation accordingly and to risk the wrath of his intellectual comrades in arms by venturing into apostasy. But what he managed to produce in *After the Neocons* is not necessarily a credit to his standing as creative thinker. Indeed, the book rings hollow.

In *After the Neocons,* Fukuyama once again leaves the area of his core expertise of political philosophy. Here he presents himself as an expert on nation-building and institutional development. He spends more than half of the book summarizing the findings of genuine specialists in these fields and does not appear to give us something original of his own.

The main contribution of the book is precisely his account of the history of the Neoconservative movement and his lengthy explanation of why he parted company with it. This accounts for perhaps a third of the text.

Fukuyama spells out the fundamental ideas of Neoconservatism which attracted him and traces how their practitioners started going astray after the victory over Communism in 1992 which vindicated their thinking, pushed them into the mainstream and gave them new authority to take charge of American foreign policy. At a time when others were seeking to move America from a war footing to peace-time economy to reap the benefits of the victory over Soviet Communism, the Neoconservatives were calling for a more militarized American posture abroad and for using the country's position as the sole remaining super-power with ever less constraint to pursue their transformational agenda.

The Neoconservative principles which set them apart from the traditional Right-Left divide of American politics were, firstly, priority concern for democracy, human rights and the belief that the internal policies of states matter because regimes which treat their own people badly cannot be trusted as partners by other states; secondly, the conviction that US power can be used for moral purposes; thirdly, skepticism about international law and institutions being able to maintain order in our unruly world; and lastly, an aversion to social engineering, which is what nation-building is all about.

During the first term of George W. Bush, after the September 11th terrorist attacks caused a switch in priorities from domestic concerns to the 'war on terror,' these principles underpinned the writing of a new National Security Strategy in 2002 with its justification of preventive warfare and the will to proceed on a unilateral basis when international institutions refused to provide legitimacy for American actions. The result was a constellation of wrong-headed policy decisions made worse by the incompetence of the Administration in executing those policies. Thus, we had the exaggeration of the threat posed by Iraq's alleged Weapons of Mass Destruction, the prosecution of war without cover of legitimacy from allies and the international institutions generally, the failure to foresee the needs of pacifying and reconstructing Iraq, and the resultant insurgency which made a mockery of the President's early claims of success for the mission.

The net result of all the damage to America's standing in the world coming from its alienation of traditional allies and from the misdeeds as well as inefficacy of its occupation forces was that the good name of Neoconservatives would be forever tarnished by the wrong-headed and inept actions of the Bush Administration.

In setting down all this, Fukuyama necessarily moved against people who had backed his intellectual development and his career, none more so than Paul Wolfowitz, who as Deputy Secretary of Defense was one of the leading architects of the invasion of Iraq in 2003 and a prominent defender of the policy of benevolent hegemony by the United States.

Fukuyama was shocked to see that his erstwhile comrades were in denial over the failures and called for staying the course in Iraq, stood by Israel when it pursued similar misguided military action in Lebanon and were calling loudly for solving the conflict with Iran by yet another military intervention.

Fukuyama decided that the excesses of Bush-ite Neoconservatism could be interred with its bones and the noble principles of the movement could and should be resuscitated under a new name and within certain clearly defined constraints dictated by pragmatism.

This 'realistic Wilsonianism' would carry forward the notion that regimes matter, that the United States must prioritize relations with fellow democracies and encourage respect for human rights and rule of law around the world. But it would be more pragmatic, and not seek mindlessly to impose democracy by destabilizing friendly but authoritarian governments or transforming unfriendly states at the point of a gun. It would appreciate the need to invest in institutions to facilitate nation building. It would curb U.S. unilateralism and seek legitimacy for U.S. engagement in world affairs through an assortment of multilateral organizations.

Based on the composition of its membership, which includes virtually all sovereign states without regard to the nature of their regimes, Fukuyama takes for a given that the United Nations is hopelessly flawed and irreparable. And he concludes that legitimacy for U.S. actions has to be sought elsewhere, with first attention given to NATO, the alliance of similarly minded democracies which had served just this purpose so admirably in the 1990s for intervention in the Balkans.

Of course, the dilemma of the Bush Administration as it prepared for its attack on Iraq was precisely the lack of unanimity within the NATO Council, where several of its closest allies, namely France and Germany, were unconvinced of the threat posed by Iraq and of the need for military action.

What Fukuyama proposes now is a key trade-off whereby the United States would in future abide by NATO resolutions and give up unilateralism. In exchange, NATO decision making would be streamlined, going from unanimity to weighted votes or to a smaller directorate.

With respect to decision-making procedures within NATO, Fukuyama's proposal seems reasonable at first glance. He argues that unanimity is no longer justified in a coordinating body which at the time counted 26 member states (today 28). However, all this ignores the real dynamics of NATO deliberations, where the United States has traditionally dominated discussion and where European members typically submit to majority will and avoid conflict. In practice, if such unanimity is unachievable it is only because the motion under review is highly controversial and possibly fatally flawed. 'Streamlining' decision-making means consolidating an American *Diktat* over the organization and finally represents almost no concession by the United States to the views of its allies. Meanwhile, when push comes to shove, Fukuyama insists the U.S. must 'keep on the table' the option of acting unilaterally if absolutely necessary, however hard this is to reconcile with the aforementioned trade-off of freedom for legitimacy. .

In any case, Fukuyama sees a world order resting on much more than one or two key institutions. He gives favorable mention to Princeton professor John Ikenberry and the notion that the post-World War II world order framed by an array of US-dominated international institutions like the World Bank and the IMF has served admirably to prop up American world preeminence. He goes on to assert that still other less obvious international arrangements taken altogether ensure order in the world. These range from longstanding associations such as the WTU and the ISO to more recent entities like ICANN, which oversees the worldwide web. And moving still further out in the concentric circles of international structures, he points to the codes of multinational corporations as providing essential glue binding together our world order. It is in this realm that Fukuyama goes off the rails and shows a remarkable lack of judgment. To be blunt, his citing ICANN and similar non-state entities as model instruments of world order is frivolous. Moreover, the notion that conflict resolution can be based on ad hoc hobbling together of 'coalitions of the willing' is highly contentious.

While the theoretical framework for a new world order put up by Fukuyama is flawed, the practical recommendations he makes for correcting U.S. foreign policy going forward are generally constructive. He calls for dramatic demilitarization of foreign policy and shift of attention to encouraging good governance and political accountability in problem areas around the world. This is all very welcome coming as it does from one of the fountainheads of Neoconservatism.

Unfortunately, as with the streamlining of NATO, Fukuyama lacks the courage of his convictions and admits exceptions which vitiate the rule. In this case, he tells us that preventive war and regime change via military intervention cannot be abjured entirely, that what is really needed is a much more strict definition of the circumstances in which they are permissible than the Administration's definition set out in 2002..

My conclusion is that despite all his distancing himself from the odious policies and personalities of the Bush White House, Francis Fukuyama remains very much a Neoconservative. He and his erstwhile comrades in arms have exchanged mutual insults, to be sure. But to anyone standing to one side, their rancorous debates are like brawling between Mensheviks and Bolsheviks once upon a time. Looking on from the outside, they all looked like Commies whose attempts at building their utopia cost great human suffering and were doomed to failure. Today Fukuyama and his opponents in the Neoconservative camp all look like values-based ideologues of the American empire.

In this book, Fukuyama speaks in favor of the continued U.S. hegemony and insists that American power is critical to world order. His greatest fear is that the rejection of Bush-ite Neoconservatism due to its excesses and incompetence will lead to America's turning in on itself and failing to fulfill its necessary mission. Yet the requirements Fukuyama himself sets for success are as unachievable as the Soviet utopia - that the hegemony be directed at creating only public goods rather than serving narrow American interests and that it enjoy the enthusiastic support of a people who do not share the imperialist ardor of the Neoconservative avant-garde. All of this suggests that ultimately the ideals of his 'realistic Wilsonianism' will lead to tears.

In *After the Neocons*, Fukuyama announced he was launching a new international affairs journal to promote the cause of 'realistic Wilsonianism.' The eminent names listed on the editorial board of *The American Interest* include John Ikenberry and Zbigniew Brzezinski, showing that, like Neoconservatism, the movement Fukuyama is now promoting cuts across the Democratic-Republican divide in American politics. As publisher, he is to be congratulated for attracting very serious contributors and for framing debates on its pages from diametrically opposed positions. In this regard, the editorial oversight is more professional and less tendentious than that of *Foreign Affairs* magazine, for example. However, it is also clear that to get space in *The American Interest* it does not hurt to pay court to the vanity of the publisher as Philip Auerswald and Zoltan J. Acs did in the opening article "Defining Prosperity" of the May-June 2009 issue, framing their investigation into the impact of the worldwide economic meltdown on the principles set out in Fukuyama's 'classic essay' of 1989, "The End of History?"

In saying all this, I am doing nothing more than bringing out the human foibles of a thinker who, as a young researcher, changed the landscape of American political science discourse by his remarkably well timed and well argued description of a new paradigm to inform foreign policy. That achievement ensured his renown for many years to come.

SAMUEL HUNTINGTON

THE CLASH OF CIVILIZATIONS - PART I

At his death in 2008 at the age of 81, Samuel Huntington, professor emeritus of Harvard, embodied the political science and international affairs Establishment in the United States.

During his 58 years of teaching undergraduates and graduate students at Harvard, he shaped the thinking of several generations of American scholars and practitioners of foreign policy. He twice chaired the university's Government Department and was for 12 years director of its Center for International Affairs. On the national stage, he served as president of the American Political Science Association. His presence was also felt in Washington, where under President Carter he was coordinator of security planning for the National Security Council and in the 1980s was a member of the Presidential Commission on Long-Term Integrated Strategy.

However, it was as a thinker and writer, rather than administrator and teacher that Samuel Huntington made his greatest mark in the world. As his colleague at Harvard, economist Henry Rosovsky commented: "Sam was the kind of scholar that made Harvard a great university. People all over the world studied and debated his ideas. I believe that he was clearly one of the most influential political scientists of the last 50 years." His friend Robert Putnam, a professor at Harvard's Kennedy School called Huntington "one of the giants of American intellectual life of the last half century."

Huntington was the author of 17 books and 90 scholarly articles. Many of those articles were published in the country's most widely read and prestigious journal on international politics, *Foreign Affairs*. At the end of this two-part essay, I will comment on several of the articles which Huntington addressed to fellow professionals and which justify the view that scholarship can produce serious recommendations which statesmen ignore at their peril. However, most of what follows concerns another side of Huntington's writing which is less flattering but has been far better known to the general public.

Of all of Huntington's works, it was his 1997 book *The Clash of Civilizations* that gave currency to his name around the world. The book followed from a 1993 article of the same name (but modestly followed by a question mark) which appeared in *Foreign Affairs*. The spur to write the book came when the magazine told him the article had generated more reader interest than anything they published since the 1940s. For its part, the book continued to make waves in the same way. It was ultimately brought out in 39 languages.

As with so much else, uncanny timing had much to do with the book's success. It captured the public imagination upon its appearance by providing a road map to the future in a world still left disoriented by a Cold War that had ended just 5 years earlier. After 9/11, it took flight anew, providing insights into the new world shaped by Islamic terrorism.

The book received encomiums even from those whom Huntington treated dismissively in it. The edition I read has on the cover two attention-getting citations.

Kissinger: "one of the most important books to have emerged since the end of the Cold War"

Fukuyama: "The book is dazzling in its scope and grasp of the intricacies of contemporary global politics"

From its very first edition, *The Clash of Civilizations* profited by holding up a mirror to many peoples around the world and telling them what they wanted to hear. Huntington seized upon the various claims to uniqueness made by spokesmen for non-Western "civilizations" and served them up as scientific fact.

And though he is disparaging of elites in the book, it is precisely elites in various parts of the world who found elements in this book, which had become conventional reading worldwide, that they could use for their own purposes. Speaking in terms of Huntington's analytical framework became one more proof of urbanity, even if the outsiders reworked the particulars to suit their own identity. As just one typical example that I can cite, at his 24 September

2008 meeting with the Council of Foreign Relations in New York, Russian Foreign Minister Sergey Lavrov spoke precisely in "civilizational' terms and argued, in the Huntington tradition, for acceptance of a multipolar model of international relations as opposed to the unipolar model of the Bush administration. I must note parenthetically that unlike Huntington, Lavrov placed Russia alongside the United States as one of the two subgroups of "European civilization" – but that does not undo the Minister's mark of respect to an intellectual icon of his hosts.

Given the celebrity and widespread admiration for Huntington and his master work, what I am about to undertake in the present essay may appear to be a folly or an act of hopeless presumption. However, I am firmly persuaded that *The Clash of Civilizations* is poor scholarship which is weakly argued. Its foundations are faulty and, in the end, given the sophistication of the author, I am forced to conclude that it is intellectually dishonest. The theoretical framework Huntington deployed was not new. Indeed it had been abandoned by earlier generations of scholars precisely because of its obvious shortcomings and for the impossibility of the tasks it set.

I am emboldened to proceed by some whistle-blowing of the past directed at Sam Huntington's academic credibility. I draw the reader's attention to a devastating critique of some of Huntington's best known work dating from the 1960s and 70s written by Yale mathematics professor Serge Lang: "A Case Study: The Huntington Case" within *Challenges* (Springer-Verlag New York, 1998).

Lang focused on Huntington's methodology. Among many separate examples of pseudo-science in Huntington's work, he exposed what he called 'cockeyed' research techniques and bogus mathematical formulae which Huntington had used in *Political Order in Changing Societies* (1968) to demonstrate that South Africa was a 'satisfied society.' The book in question was considered a classic work of American political science well into the 1980s and was required reading in many university courses.

As a consequence of the controversy surrounding Lang's assertions and the nature of the defense various scholars and university administrators offered on Huntington's behalf, Lang concluded that there was a certain complicity of the academic community and political science establishment in avoiding passing negative judgment on its own or even exposing doubtful work to open peer review.

Some accused Lang of engaging in a vendetta, and he felt obliged to explain in what context his 'personal' or even *ad hominem* remarks about Huntington were relevant to judging the scholar's competence. The proof that there was sufficient merit to Lang's assertions is that he successfully campaigned twice, in 1986 and 1987, against Huntington's election to the National Academy of Sciences. The scandal received national coverage in the newspaper of record, *The New York Times.* .

We all have our limitations coming out of our professional training, and I will make no secret of my own. I approach Professor Huntington's work from the perspective of an historian. My critique is that of the historical craft to the art of futurology that Huntington popularized in the post-Cold War period.

The *Clash of Civilizations* is an enormously rich work, presenting a vast amount of information from societies and events all over the world. Some of this material is fascinating and unexpected. However, nearly all of it came from secondary sources and its informative quality is beside the point. What Huntington personally contributed was a new/old paradigm for interpreting the international landscape, and that is where the problem lies.

Huntington applied himself and some researchers to the huge and, I submit, unachievable task of providing a theory encompassing and attempting to explain and predict all of international affairs. It would be hopelessly boring to the reader if I were to begin to take issue with the myriad separate points of observation and generalization in his book. It would also violate my principle of 'minding one's knitting' and preferably speaking out only when your own research and professionally informed opinions give you the right. Instead what I offer here is pointers to the methodological failings that vitiate Huntington's work and erase the distinction between scholarly objectivity and unsupported prejudice.

THE CONTEXT OF THE WORK'S APPEARANCE

As I mentioned in my preface, the fall of the Berlin Wall, the overturning of Soviet protégé regimes in Eastern Europe and ultimately the collapse of the Soviet Union itself dramatically changed the international landscape and left the general public in the United States and other Western countries fairly confused about what would come next. Into this void, Francis Fukuyama entered in 1992 with his pioneering work of futurology and philosophical speculation intriguingly entitled *The End of History*.

Under the sway of Positivist logic, Fukuyama predicted calmer times ahead as the world's nations progressed along a unique track leading to democratic governance and market economies. The culmination of this universal process would be an end to armed conflict, since, *a priori*, states so organized do not go to war with one another.

Given the controversy that Fukuyama unleashed, it is curious how Huntington deals very briefly with Fukuyama's theories in the opening chapter of *The Clash of Civilizations*, placing his opponent's ideas among three other then current attempts at making sense of post-Cold War international relations. However, it would be no exaggeration to say that *The Clash of Civilization* was a riposte to Fukuyama, who alone was identified by name. Huntington's entire opus was directed precisely at overturning the notion of universality of societal, political, indeed "civilizational" trends.

Huntington was also in a rush. Like Fukuyama, he rummaged past historiography and came up with the anti-positivist theories spun out by Oswald Spengler and Arnold Toynbee in the soul-searching pessimism of the *fin de siècle* period, in the case of the former, and in the face of loss of an entire generation of the nation's best and brightest to an irrational war effort, in the case of the second. Huntington served up to his readers a multipolar, multi-civilizational world in which the glory days of the West were well behind it and the future spelled some accommodation with rising non-Western "civilizations" that were acquiring an ever greater share of the demographic, economic and military power of the world.

HUNTINGTON'S OBJECTIVE AND HIS 'SELL-BY DATE'

Though written in laymen's language accessible to the general public, Huntington's *Clash of Civilizations* was directed primarily at policy makers in Washington, whom he offered a new paradigm, a road map to the future. By the terms he set for himself, the validation of the book would be its practical, predictive value.

As of the present, the outstanding case speaking in favor of Huntington's perspicacity was his stress on the conflict with the Muslim world whose military aggressiveness he called out. Yet, one would hardly have had to subscribe to his multicivilizational explanations to arrive at the same prognosis. Western, especially US policies in the Middle East, the support for repressive regimes and the one-sided interventions in the Arab-Israeli, Palestinian-Israeli disputes unquestionably have fed the recruitment and formation of radical and terrorist groups in the region.. All of this was known to specialists and non-specialists alike. There were entirely sufficient causal factors present to have caught the attention of those responsible for strategic intelligence in Washington.

I will not begin to address all the other trouble spots around the world raised by Huntington in his book Suffice it to say that the predictive results of his theories in all the cases he produced have been very mixed so far.

There is either a touching naivety or an unpleasant measure of deceit in Huntington's presentation of the historical craft as a hard science that can deliver practical findings to be verifiably proven in controlled and repeatable experiments. It is a profound misconception that he shares with a number of other diploma-bearing advisers serving up the 'lessons of history' to governments the world over

It speaks in Huntington's favor that he had a greater measure of self-detachment and modesty than other dealers in futurology. . In the foreword to *The Clash of Civilizations*, Huntington states clearly that any paradigm in political science has a sell-by date, a validity that is limited in time. About his own road-map, he acknowledges it would have been invalid in 1950 and will likely be invalid in 2050. By contrast, Fukuyama failed this reality check egregiously in claiming precisely to have found the ultimate theory explaining the *end* of History

But was Huntington justified in giving his own theories a 50 year lease on life? Whereas Fukuyama took the events of the preceding twenty-five years, namely the replacement of rightwing authoritarian regimes in Southern Europe and Latin America and the collapse of the Soviet Union in the year before his book was completed as the sample base by which to project an explanation of where the world was headed, Huntington took a sampling coming primarily from the two or three years before his writing, looking to state formation amidst the rubble of the former Yugoslavia and the former Soviet Empire, as the basis for a total revision of Fukuyama's projection and for recalibrating the trajectory to target of world history. He saw a 'civilizational' struggle in what were patently traditional nationalist movements of ethnic groups for identity following release from external constraints of Communist overlords, all spurred on by self-aggrandizing politicians.

Just as consumer electronics have in recent decades experienced ever shorter product cycles, it seems the same can be said today about new *Weltanschauungen* of our political scientists. In a way, futurology as practiced by Huntington and Fukuyama presents the same task that the corporate world addresses every year when preparing the Business Plan. Yet in major corporations each year the exercise entails a rolling adjustment to take into account the new inputs of the past year and to recalibrate the five year targets, sometimes dramatically. Then quarterly adjustments for presentation to the Board within the financial year further attenuate the predictive value of the Plan.

So the question arises: is it justified to spin out complex, all-encompassing theories to guide budgetary allocations for national defense and diplomacy when there is no annual, not to mention quarterly, review of basic assumptions. The scope for validity of futurology is as limited as our imaginations in general.

And how limited all of our imaginations are becomes painfully clear towards the end of Huntington's book when he presents a scenario for a future WWIII arising from conflict between the United States and China. These puerile musings would be more suitable to some over-excited undergraduate than to a very senior professor at Harvard. The generation of video game quality algorithms may or may not make sense in Pentagon think tanks, but do they deserve a place on the Harvard campus and should they be promoted by the reputed intellectual leaders of the nation?

SAMUEL HUNTINGTON

THE CLASH OF CIVILIZATIONS - PART II

The indictment:

1) The flawed foundations of Huntington's thesis: Toynbee and "civilizations"

As I have mentioned, the unique contribution of Professor Huntington in *The Clash of Civilizations* was to resuscitate historical theories developed by Arnold Toynbee that had long fallen out of favor. He then attempted to fit the world events of his day into this Procrustean bed to demonstrate their predictive value.

At the start of his book, Huntington justified resurrecting Toynbee to draw a roadmap to the future by pointing to an extensive literature on civilizational theory which already exists. But then in the university library one will also find stacks lined with volumes on phrenology and spiritualism. Quantity is not quality.

Putting aside the 'hem line' issue of changing intellectual fads which could sweep aside any given theories for some time regardless of intrinsic merit, the greater fact is that the "history" deployed by Toynbee never enjoyed the support of mainstream historians in its heyday. In particular, Peter Geyl and Hugh Trevor-Roper were credited with dispatching Toynbee's reputation among professionals epistemologically once and for all.

However, let us put aside the reputation of the well from which Huntington drew his water. Instead let us consider for a moment the major sticking points of his own creation, namely Huntington's definition of civilizations.

Huntington could not avoid dealing with the obvious fact of ever greater contact among peoples and circulation of ideas in the modern age leading to convergence of the external features of societies the world over in what is called globalization. He had to address directly the issue of whether it remains appropriate to speak of civilizations, as opposed to a single universal civilization. This is, after all, the nub of the dispute he has with Fukuyama, who insists that the world shares the same values today, even if local governments find temporary excuses not to apply those values at home.

Huntington's response was that the seeming convergence reflects just the trappings of modernism and that universal values are shared only by a superficial stratum of "Davos culture" elites around the world who are unrepresentative of the basic mass of the population in their own societies. Thus, when the process of democratization takes hold, even the elites have to bury their Western ideas and manners, and we can see the underlying differences in values that define "civilizations."

Huntington's cavalier treatment of elites raises as many questions as it answers. Who, after all is Huntington if not *la crème de la crème* of American elites? And how deeply in the American public do you have to go before you find that respect for *habeas corpus* and the other values that Huntington cherishes dries up and cedes its place to concern over economic and physical security, where most peoples around the world are truly indistinguishable?

I contend that with the exception of extraordinary times such as arise every few generations, history was and is made precisely by elites, and the fact that they share common values is of decisive importance, as Fukuyama argues, rather than merely decorative, as Huntington chooses to believe.

The definition of civilizations in Huntington really comes down to the definition of *Western Civilization*, since the other six or seven he presents are defined primarily by their being *non-Western* and only to a lesser extent by the content they each are said to have. .

Toynbee defined civilizations chiefly by religious attributes. By contrast, in Huntington religion – meaning Catholicism or Protestantism - is just one of the eight criteria which he says together constitute the unique patrimony of the West.

There are two odd cards in his deck of the defining elements which might be considered cultural: the presence of European languages and the Classical legacy, which generously includes Greek philosophy and Roman law, a nod to the humanities but not to the arts.

Otherwise, the remaining five determinants of Western Civilization offered by Huntington all relate to political structures and practices. This is understandable coming from a political scientist but why must the rest of us put up with such parochialism? Indeed, it is an absurdity to define a civilization and not speak about Culture with a capital C, and I will come back to this point in a moment.

The geography of Western Civilization as defined by Huntington is taken straight out of Toynbee and includes all of the weaknesses of the source. Essentially the West means Western Europe as it was at the end of the Roman Empire.

By extension, this formula embraces the former colonies of Western Europe where the same set of 8 criteria took hold. In this context, the case for devolution into what Huntington calls "Latin American" and "African"civilizations is arbitrary and contentious.

By this formula, the West explicitly excludes Russia and the Balkans, which Toynbee and now Huntington set aside as a distinct "Orthodox" civilization. This very artificial separation leads Huntington to pursue many counter-intuitive conclusions that become, quite frankly, an embarrassment today, such as his proposal for ousting Greece from the European Union and NATO since it falls on the wrong side of the civilizational divide.

However, if we return for a moment to a more commonplace understanding of civilization that includes, nay is built on Culture, then the exclusion of Russia from the West presents another major problem: stripping away Russia's contribution to literature, painting, the plastic arts, drama, classical music and dance over the past 150 years would leave our libraries, museums, concert halls and theaters vastly depleted. Only a hopeless dogmatist can deny the reality of our common civilization.

And to those who say that removing modernism exposes the civilizational gap between regions of the world that are at odds today on the level of international politics, I would urge them to read Salmon Rushdie's magnificent response in his 2008 novel *The Enchantress of Florence*. There are definitely issues that can be more efficiently as well as more enjoyably resolved following the parabolic of artistic truth than the plodding and sometimes misguided works purporting to be scholarly truth.

2) The sources

It is no accident that Huntington does not provide us with a bibliography, only Notes. A bibliography would show a reflective attitude to his sources, which I fear was largely absent when he wrote *The Clash of Civilizations*.

The Notes reveal Huntington as an encyclopedic but promiscuous reader. Nearly everything cited in the book can be categorized as a secondary source, that is to say the work of generalizers.

The problem comes from the impossibility of the task he set for himself in devising a 'one size fits all' paradigm to explain nearly all international events everywhere *and also* predict the future. But then again, his aim was to serve Washington policy makers pretending to lead the world. I contend that the ultimate objective of having credible policy guidelines to judge every local dispute worldwide is unrealistic.

Since Huntington could in no way possess first-hand knowledge of all the subject matter he deals with given his ambition to cover all time and all space, he was in no position to judge the objectivity of these authors or their tendentiousness. His "primary" materials are today's media: reports in CNN, *The Economist*, *The Boston Globe*, *The New York Times*, and the like.

We can note his particular liking for *The Economist*, which may be called the American snob's newspaper/magazine of choice. Though its literary style may be superior, *The Economist* shares all the flaws of its more plebeian American counterparts, *Time Magazine* and *Newsweek*: no attribution of authors for most content and a seamless blend of fact and opinion. If you happen to have an expert opinion, you appreciate at once its prejudices and deficiencies.

The way Huntington has spread himself thin is revealed in his treatment of Russian history, among other subjects. What he presents as a thousand years of Russia in *The Clash of Civilizations* could charitably be described as a comic strip.

To be fair, all that he says about Russia falls squarely into line with what Zbigniew Brzezinski and other fervent Cold Warrior scholars with first class Ph.D. degrees from American universities have been saying for years. Often the most vocal among them have roots in Poland, Hungary and other front-line nations positioned as the historic defenders of Western civilization against Russia. In ethnic enclaves, you will find the guy on the next bar stool ready with the same kind of generalizations as Huntington delivers *ex cathedra*. But it is nonetheless disappointing for such prejudices to be given respectability by senior academics at Harvard.

3) The nature of Huntington's argumentation: the dangers of spending too much time lecturing undergraduates

When he wrote his work in 1993, Fukuyama's professional career had been as a writer for a corporate think tank. His intellectual output was set down on paper and his task was to furnish convincing analysis and still more convincing argumentation for his conclusions. One of the most impressive aspects of *The End of History* is the author's frequent time-outs to consider and dispatch alternative interpretations of the phenomena he is describing. There is in all of this an openness and intellectual honesty that one has to respect.

By contrast, when he wrote *The Clash of Civilizations*, Huntington was a senior professor with long years of experience lecturing undergraduates. He was a world-renowned authority with many publications under his belt. That very success and that experience as lecturer made him a 'coddled' rather than self-questioning scientist. He dispatches the opposition in a dozen or so pages at the very start of this 320 page book. Otherwise he delivers his rules on "civilizational" relations very much in the manner of Moses and the graven tablets he brought down from Mt Sinai His truths often are derived from statistical correlations, like the methodology of public health researchers, while he largely ignores the mechanics of causality

It may be *lèse majesté* to say this, but Professor Huntington was clearly making up these rules as he went along. He occasionally acknowledges contradictions to his generalizations, such as the American intervention on behalf of the Muslims in the civil and regional war of Bosnia-Herzegovina that was raging when he wrote his book. This assistance of the preeminent Western power clearly left Huntington dumbfounded. But he spoke of it as if it were a casual anomaly. He never considered whether other analytic frameworks, other "paradigms" might better explain such phenomena.

His very selective presentation of facts calls into question his integrity. For example, he uses the reign of the colonels in Greece as a demonstration of traditions coming down from its Orthodox civilization, from being on the wrong side of the tracks, so to speak. But he is totally silent about Salazar's Portugal and Franco's Spain, for whom the political culture was no better or worse than in pre-democratic Greece. Of course, it is nice to see an American historian of certain religious persuasion not feed us the Black Legend about the slothful Spaniards. However, one can hardly ignore the several hundred years of Muslim Moorish dominion on the Iberian Peninsula (securely "Western") when you speaking loquaciously about the Ottoman Turks on the Balkan Peninsula or the Mongols in Russia ("Orthodox)"as Huntington does.

Huntington's rush to include the Baltic States in the frontiers of Western Civilization entails swallowing a heavy dose of 'captive nation' propaganda and ignoring a lot of historical facts. How can he choose to remember the 20 years of their independence between two world wars and turn a blind eye to the 300 years when a large part of this territory was under Russian rule for reasons that include dynastic alliances as much as military conquest? How can he ignore the demographics, which in the case of Latvia mean that nearly 40% of the population is in fact Russian today?

Huntington's civilizational generalities very often are self-characterizations of the people he is describing. He restates as his own discovery the Japanese insistence on being treated as a *sui generis* culturally, racially and, yes, why not, civilizationally. Similarly Huntington takes the Muslim fundamentalists at their word and allows them to speak on behalf of the nearly one billion co-religionists whose lay or secular sympathies, whose societal and cultural patterns are very diverse across the globe. In the end, Huntington becomes a mouthpiece for the most irresponsible political actors and a disseminator of sensationalism. This is the kind of faulty 'intelligence' that should not drive a national foreign policy, least of all America's.

4) Mind over matter

Like Toynbee, Huntington largely ignores economics as a driver of the historical process and determinant of what we see around us today. Economic issues never got much attention on US campuses due to the prevailing intellectual predilection for mind over matter, for free will over determinism. With the crash of Communism and with it of Marxism, economics got further marginalized

The only objective factor shaping our world which Huntington chooses to honor is demographics. Yet somewhere in his gut, he tacitly also accepts the link between the rise of middle classes and the demand for greater political participation and recognition. This comes out of his advice to American policymakers on how to deal with resurgent China at the very end of the book.

Huntington's political agenda

Just as the science fiction movies of the 1950s and 60s were only partly about entertainment and mostly about politics, so Huntington's *Clash of Civilizations* has an agenda buried in its seemingly dispassionate and academically neutral wrapping

The positives

Among the "good," humane points of the book that come out at the very end is Huntington's recommendation that Americans accept "civilizational" diversity abroad and not to try to force their values down the throats of the Islamic and Chinese worlds, the "civilizations" which are seen to present the greatest challenges in the century ahead.

He tells us that the notion of the universalism of Western values is 'false, immoral and dangerous.' Furthermore, the necessary and logical consequence of universalism is imperialism. And it must be stressed, that in Huntington's mind, 'imperialism' was still a pejorative concept.

In terms of practical policy, Huntington specifically urged the United States to break with its longstanding tradition of opposing the emergence of any regional hegemon in Asia and accept China's growing exercise of that role. His words with respect to Europe were more nuanced. He advocated acceptance of a Russian sphere of influence in its near-abroad at least to the southeast, meaning its hinterland in Central Asia

Curiously, Huntington went to great lengths in this work to describe America's own worldwide hegemonism. He related in detail the critique of the West found in Islamic literature, the allegations of double standards and rank hypocrisy in US foreign policy. He pointed out the corruption of vocabulary and thinking underlying such everyday terms in the media as "the world community." He explained carefully and in a seemingly detached way what is called 'American exceptionalism.' At the same time, Huntington never condemned the Pax Americana and purported only to identify it and explain it.

The negatives

A negative message of his political agenda comes out in the last fifteen or so pages of the book when he urges America to accept its identity as the standard-bearer of Western, meaning Christian civilization, to reassert confidence in its values, even if they are not universalist, and to bury all thought of relativism and of bringing the multi-civilizational world into its own borders: "A multicivilizational United States will not be the United States; it will be the United Nations."

Huntington presented his opus as a clarion call for North America and Europe to rise to the challenge of the clash of civilizations, and to give a new lease on life to the West one century after its relative decline in terms of demography, economic and military weight had become apparent.

But the tools he proposed for doing this were certainly not adequate to the dimensions of the task. With respect to the architecture of international relations, Huntington's vision never went beyond the familiar. For him the "the premier Western institution" was NATO and he called for its expansion to the east. Reading Huntington's backward looking recommendations, one might conclude that genuinely usable roadmaps to the future will have to await the emergence of fresh cartographers

* * *

Writing in the January/February 2010 issue of *Foreign Affairs* magazine, Princeton professor of international relations G. John Ikenberry said of Sam Huntington's original essay "The Clash of Civilizations?" that it 'set off a decade-long debate about culture and identity in world politics.' Indeed, the essay and the book which followed are a key frame of reference for political science theoreticians and pundits up to the present. Huntington's paradigm has been praised and cursed by commentators of every political persuasion. In this respect, the work is unavoidable reading whatever one may think of its intrinsic merits.

As is usually the case with political science treatises, nearly all readers have judged the work by where Huntington's feet were pointed: were his characterizations of the international scene and his policy recommendations likely to direct the general public and its political leaders in a constructive or in a dangerous path? And in this matter, opinions have been divided.

An excellent introduction to these considerations appeared in the year of the book's publication. See the March/April 1997 issue of *Foreign Affairs* magazine, "The West: Precious, not Unique: Civilizations Make for a Poor Paradigm Just Like the Rest" by G. John Ikenberry et.al. This round table was a response to a 1996 article by Huntington in which he set out a condensed argumentation of the clash of civilizations, but it serves to highlight the professional controversy over Huntington's civilizational thesis in general.

I especially direct the reader's attention to the closing remarks of one of the commentators, Bruce Nussbaum, then Editorial Page Editor at Business Week:

"The best thing that can be said about Huntington's thesis is that it provokes. The worst that can be said of it is that it might provide pseudo-intellectual ammunition to nativists everywhere seeking justification for ugly thoughts and uglier deeds."

This remark clearly relates to the idea Huntington set out in the concluding chapter of *The Clash of Civilizations*: that the United States was facing a threat to its national identity coming from academics and publicists promoting multiculturalism and subcultures at the expense of its Western (European, Christian) traditions.

Actually the issue may be said to have been a constant in Huntington's thinking going straight back to the 1993 article which was expanded into *Civilizations*. In a defense of his paradigm appearing in the November/December 1993 issue of *Foreign Affairs* entitled "If Not Civilizations, What?" Huntington spoke about the dramatic rise of Hispanics in the U.S. population and the threat this posed of a *clash of civilizations* within the country. Indeed, one can reasonably ask whether Huntington identified his new paradigm for the world on the basis of his observations of cultural/civilizational tensions within the United States, or whether he identified the risks within the United States on the basis of the clashes developing in the world at large.

Huntington indulged his *idée fixe* by devoting an entire book to the phenomenon of the massive Latino, principally Mexican immigration to the United States and its implications for the country's unity: *Who Are We? The Challenges to America's National Identity* published in 2004. A shortened version of this thesis came out in *Foreign Policy* magazine on March 1, 2004: "The Hispanic Challenge." Here Huntington described in detail the phenomenon of non-assimilated, Spanish speaking populations becoming the majority in cities and whole regions, particularly in the American Southwest, contiguous with Mexico, to whom this territory belonged until the mid 19th century American wars of conquest. Huntington called for re-affirmation of the country's Anglo-Protestant heritage. Though he remained professional and fairly objective in his presentation, some readers have viewed the book as xenophobic if not bigoted, and the controversy simmers in anti-Huntington notes published in the blogosphere.

Against this background of provocative stands by the staid professor on topical issues and his practice of pseudo-scientific methodologies in his best-selling works from the 1960s through the 1990s which some criticize as incompetent or deceitful, the fact remains that Harvard's Sam Huntington also produced some very insightful essays on domestic and international politics which would place him among the most level-headed as well as most experienced commentators on the American national stage in the 1990s.

I have in mind especially two articles which appeared in *Foreign Affairs* magazine which are pertinent to our present concerns since they address directly the question of how the end of the Cold War affected the United States and its formulation of a foreign policy to deal with the new international landscape. The interesting common feature in them is the absence of all scientific pretense including the syntax of neutrality. Huntington shows his hand in these papers and comes very close to using the first person singular

In the opening pages of 'The Erosion of American National Interests' (*FA*, September/October 1997), Huntington gives us a piquant remark for American policy makers from Academician Georgy Arbatov, long-time director of Moscow's Institute of the USA and Canada, and adviser to Russia's President Gorbachev. The quote dates from the late 1980s, as the Cold War was winding down. Said Arbatov, "We are doing something really terrible to you – we are depriving you of an enemy."

Huntington concurs. After the demise of the Soviet Union, the United States was left with a vast military potential without any clear purpose for its use: "This…has led the American foreign policy establishment to search frantically for purposes that would justify a continuing U.S. role in world affairs comparable to that in the Cold War."

But the problem runs deeper, calling into question America's sense of identity. Huntington tells us that the four decades of the Cold War provided the United States with a unifying cause, and that in the years since the vulnerabilities of national unity had been exposed. The nation's 'Northern European, primarily British, and Christian, primarily Protestant' cultural foundations were put in jeopardy by the prevailing political correctness of multiculturalism. Meanwhile, the second pillar of national identity, the so-called Creed of democracy, equality, liberty, limited government, was under stress due to inventions of the civil rights era such as affirmative action. Moreover, Huntington notes that a political ideology such as the 'Creed' is in itself insufficient to hold together a multiethnic society like America's. He points to the implosion of the Soviet Union in 1991 as an example of what the country might undergo.

However, the reason for his concern over the disappearance of a national identity is less speculative and much more immediate. By the manner in which he has set up the problem to be solved, Huntington implicitly appears before us as an exponent of the *realist* school of diplomacy in which foreign policy should defend the national interest. He is telling us that without a clear and commonly accepted national identity for which Americans are ready to sacrifice their wealth and their blood, foreign policy has become incoherent. In Huntington's words, it is now 'particularistic' – serving the demands of commerce and clamorous ethnic-based lobbyists.

More than ever before, American foreign policy has become a function of the domestic political equilibrium. For the moment, the domestic consensus is clear: "that American national interests do not warrant extensive American involvement in most problems of the world."

Huntington calls upon the foreign policy establishment to accommodate itself to these new realities by trimming the ambitions for American 'leadership.' He ends the essay with a pointed message to fellow political science professionals:

"…instead of formulating unrealistic schemes for grand endeavors abroad, foreign policy elites might well devote their energies to designing plans for lowering American involvement in the world in ways that will safeguard possible future national interests."

In his essay 'The Lonely Superpower (*FA*, March-April 1999), what was implicit is now made explicit. Two years after Kissinger published his *realist* manifesto in the form of his master work *Diplomacy*, Huntington had all but abandoned his eccentric *civilizational* paradigm to explain current international affairs. Instead he laid a wreath before the signers of the Peace of Westphalia and now presented a consistently realist analysis of the *balance of power* in the world.

His message to the U.S. foreign policy establishment this time was that the brief interlude of a *unipolar* world following the end of the Cold War was now history, and that unilateral American management of international relations, the exercise of its alleged *benign hegemony,* was no longer possible. Instead the world had moved on to what he called 'a strange hybrid, a uni-multipolar system with one superpower and several major powers.' The distinguishing feature of the new system was that America needed to attract the active cooperation of the other major world powers if it were to achieve any of its foreign policy objectives.

In the new configuration, the principles of balance of power were operating via the efforts of some of the major powers to form an anti-hegemonic, *viz.,* anti-American bloc. Huntington gives a number of reasons why this had not yet succeeded, among them the special relationships America had established with third tier powers to counter regional dominance of the second tier powers who were the initiators of the anti-hegemonic alliances. .

Huntington explicitly denies the practicability of American hegemony, not only because other world powers now are prepared to resist and so to frustrate its initiatives, but also because the American public does not want it, as revealed by recent opinion polls:

"However much foreign policy elites may ignore or deplore it, the United States lacks the domestic political base to create a unipolar world. American leaders repeatedly make threats, promise action, and fail to deliver. The result is a foreign policy of 'rhetoric and retreat' and growing reputation as a 'hollow hegemon''

The specific policy recommendations which follow from this analysis are all entirely in keeping with what other *realists*, first and foremost Henry Kissinger, were saying at the time. To both liberal hawks in the Democratic camp and Neoconservatives in the Republican camp, Huntington calls for abandoning illusions of America, the benevolent hegemon.. It should turn from unilateral actions and instead apply resources to elicit the cooperation of other powers in the manner of *Bismarckian* strategy.(no credits given to H.K., rather to a lesser known associate in Huntington's own Olin Institute for Strategic Studies at Harvard, Josef Joffe).

Most importantly, Huntington calls for giving priority attention to mending fences with Europe, where strategic interests are buttressed by *cultural commonalities*, which is all that remains of his heralded *Clash of Civilizations* paradigm in this 1999 work addressed to professionals.

In any case, Huntington views the hybrid 'uni-multipolar world' as a transitional phase, which, in time, would be transformed into a genuinely multipolar world where the traditional rules of balance of power operate. Contradicting directly the prejudices of America's Wilsonian idealists, Huntington predicted this would usher in a period of reduced tensions in international affairs. America would no longer be the world's sheriff. There would be community policing, with 'major regional powers assuming responsibility for order in their own regions.' He concludes: "For that reason, the United States could find life as a major power in a multipolar world less demanding, less contentious, and more rewarding than it was as the world's only superpower."

* * *

On balance, what sense can we make of Huntington's writings in the post-Cold War period given the obvious dancing from foot to foot that we see in particular in the period 1997 – 1999?

Two observations come to mind. First, that Huntington himself may have taken the value of all paradigms with a grain of salt and was ready to shift positions when the political environment so justified. Second, that whatever the paradigm, there is a certain disconnect between the theoretical framework and specific foreign policy recommendations being advanced. This is an issue to which we will return in the concluding chapter of this book when we compare Huntington with the other major thinkers in our survey.

Zbigniew Brzezinski:

From *Grand Chessboard* to Obama Advisor, Part One

Zbigniew Brzezinski has arguably been the most influential of all the American foreign policy thinkers in the post-Cold War period. The penetration of his ideas today may be noted in various specific policies of the Obama administration. We see Brzezinski's hand in relentless pressure upon American allies to increase their contributions in men and materiel to the fight in Afghanistan. We see it in NATO expansion to the borders of the Russian Federation, meaning support for eventual membership of Ukraine and Georgia, and the principle that no non-member country may have a veto power over who is admitted to the North Atlantic alliance. We see it in US calls for Europe to admit Turkey into the European Union. We see it in the policy of taking charge of diversification of Europe's energy supplies, the strong advocacy of the Nabucco gas pipeline and a 'Southern Corridor' energy strategy.

Although Brzezinski holds no patent on these ideas, and other centrist thinkers and statesmen have advocated one or another of them for a variety of separately argued reasons, they fit into a global strategy for the post-Cold War period which Brzezinski formulated in the 1990s as he proposed to perpetuate the unparalleled primacy of the United States in world affairs that followed the collapse of the Soviet Union. His unique presentation of the interconnectedness of issues, the persuasiveness of his argumentation, and his staying power – his ability to remain active and influential in Washington whatever the administration – set him apart.

Brzezinski's career goes back more than four decades before the collapse of the Soviet Union. He was the consummate Cold Warrior and one of the major tasks in this essay will be to determine to what extent his thinking after 1992 marked a break with his strategic concepts before the new age, to what extent it is new wine in old bottles.

Brzezinski's first calling has been scholarship and university teaching. He took his doctorate at Harvard, writing a dissertation on the national minorities in the Soviet Union. Nearly all the foreign policy thinkers I am examining here are professional political scientists, but Zbigniew Brzezinski is virtually the only career-long Sovietologist, He is surely the scholar best equipped to do country risk analysis himself using the tools of a senior intelligence officer. As he moved on to be a practitioner and major actor in international affairs, his writings moved from being scholarly to being genuine primary sources on the issues and the personalities in the news.

In the 1950s Brzezinski was already one of the pioneering describers and analysts of totalitarianism as practiced in the Soviet Union. He worked in tandem with then senior professor Carl Friedrich. From Harvard, he moved to Columbia University where his teaching affiliation spanned three decades, from 1960-89, He headed Columbia's Institute on Communism. Now he holds a teaching post at Johns Hopkins University's School of Advanced International Studies and is a researcher at the Center for Strategic and International Studies.

Among the general public, Brzezinski has probably been best known for his second career as a public servant in Washington. His route to Washington came through his acquaintance with banker and globalist David Rockefeller, who at the time was chairman of the Council on Foreign Relations and was impressed with Brzezinski's writings. When Rockefeller created the Trilateral Commission in 1972 as a center for leading businessmen, scholars and statesmen from the United States, Japan and Europe to gather periodically to promote common interests, he appointed Brzezinski as its first American director. And among the members whom Brzezinski is said to have brought into the Trilateral Commission was then governor of the State of Georgia, Jimmy Carter, who was also impressed by the academic's writings. In the 1976 electoral campaign Brzezinski provided Carter with guidance on foreign policy matters which helped to differentiate the candidate from the Kissinger-Nixon-Ford foreign policy of accommodation with the Soviet Union. This counsel was an influential factor in the electoral results and Brzezinski was brought along to the capital when Carter was swept into power. Brzezinski's most senior position and the time of his greatest prominence was his service as National Security Advisor to President Carter from 1976 -1980.

Although a committed Democrat in terms of his domestic policy preferences, Brzezinski broke with the party repeatedly when he believed its standard bearer was not capable of defending the national interest properly. Following the Carter presidency, Brzezinski went on to serve successive Republican as well as Democratic administrations. He performed various assignments for Ronald Reagan and George Bush Sr., so that he always remained current in his contacts worldwide. During President Bill Clinton's second term, he was especially close to Secretary of State Madeleine Albright, who had been one of his graduate students at Columbia and was later a staff member in his National Security office team. During this period Brzezinski was dispatched on an important mission to Azerbaijan to promote a major oil pipeline and so help implement strategies which he otherwise outlined in his writings. Today he describes himself as one of President Obama's foreign policy advisors.

Among both the general public and specialists, it is common to speak of Brzezinski as the Democratic Kissinger. Indeed there are numerous parallels in their careers. Both leveraged their Harvard doctoral degrees and scholarly credentials to become National Security Advisors. Of course, in the popular imagination, Kissinger had the greater career, since he went on to become Secretary of State, serving both President Nixon and his successor Gerald Ford. As the third ranking U.S. government official, Kissinger had greater public exposure and he reaped greater public recognition, being awarded the Nobel Peace Prize for his role in ending the war with North Viet Nam.

However, the reality of influence on power over time tells a rather different story. With the defeat of Gerald Ford by Jimmy Carter, Kissinger's standing in Washington waned. His consultancy in New York served a prestigious clientele, but his welcome in the nation's capital had worn thin.

This is so because Kissinger's policy of realism, or *Realpolitik* in foreign affairs which was the guideline of the Nixon years, and in particular what his domestic opponents called a condominium with the Soviet Union, plus the opening to the People's Republic of China and a seeming disregard for values such as human rights. These positions earned him the enmity of a broad swathe of American politicians both on the Right and on the Left who considered it cynical and out of keeping with optimistic and high-minded American traditions. Indeed it was these very policies of Kissinger and Nixon which spurred the founding in 1979 of what came to be known as *Neoconservatism* by idealists who insisted that the nation's mission was to win the Cold War in the name of freedom and democracy, not just manage it.

Thus the incoming administration of Ronald Reagan had not much use for Kissinger and his policies, and the Democratic administration of Bill Clinton which followed in the '90s held his legacy in still less esteem.*

Meanwhile, as we shall see, the ideas which Brzezinski put forward in the post-Cold War period were a blend of what passes for patriotic, hard-nosed toughness and assertiveness against authoritarian regimes which the American public on both sides of the aisles has consistently found attractive. Secretary of State Madeleine Albright and many of the high level staff in the Clinton administration clearly shared Brzezinski's thinking on the way forward.

To be sure, even the highly adaptable Mr. Brzezinski was unwilling to stand with the administration of George W. Bush once it veered off on its unilateralist path following 9/11. For those eight years he provided counsel on foreign policy to leading Democrats and positioned himself to once again be an authoritative voice in the inner circles of the next administration.

During all of this time, despite his advancing age, Brzezinski continued to travel widely, staying both informed and relevant. He maintained a freshness of thinking, a readiness to reason with his audience, that suggests a man in his 50s rather than his chronological age.

And yet as he has constantly evolved, remained open to reevaluating his positions every several years in keeping with the changing world dynamics, there are constants in his interests and in his methodology as a political scientist, just as his alter ego Kissinger has retained his own constants from the outlook expressed in his doctoral dissertation on Metternich to his latest recommendations to incoming President George W. Bush in *Does America Need a Foreign Policy?*

For all of these reasons, we will take our time considering Brzezinski's writings. I propose to examine here first his seminal work in the post-Cold War

---

*As Yogi Berra said, it ain't over till it's over.' Right up to this day, Brzezinski and Kissinger are competing for influence over the Obama.administration. See Kissinger's recent prominent role in the Committee for US Policy on Russia which prepared the way for the Obama-Medvedev summit on April 1st and a rapprochement with Russia. Brzezinski has meanwhile spoken out for a much less accommodative policy, though as in the past he supports measures to reduce the respective nuclear arsenals.

period – *The Grand Chessboard* – which came out roughly in the same time period as Sam Huntington's *Clash of Civilizations* and had a worldwide influence that was not dissimilar. The book was translated into 19 languages.

It is not my intention to follow the twists and turns in the positions taken by our prominent thinkers in detail. By the nature of the genre, political science tracts have a relatively short shelf life and the best known authors are often prolific. Therefore we will fast forward from *Chessboard* to his monograph *Second Chance* written a decade later which picks up where *Chessboard* left off and gives a score card on how the US responded to an historic window of opportunity to provide worldwide leadership as the sole remaining superpower. In *Second Chance,* Brzezinski examines in detail the first 3 post Cold War presidencies of George Bush, Sr., Bill Clinton and George W. Bush.

I also propose to draw on his 2008 book *America and the World,* which records conversations with Brzezinski and Brent Snowcroft, his Republican counterpart as National Security Advisor (under George Bush, Sr) responding to questions posed by a moderator, *Washington Post* journalist David Ignatius. This work is useful precisely because the narrative was guided, and Brzezinski was encouraged to reveal more about himself than he allows in his own writings, which tend to be quite impersonal.

What are the questions before us?

First of all, I propose to examine whether Brzezinski is truly the realist, the single-minded defender of his nation's interests which he projects by his austere, soldierly appearance, from the crew cut on down, and by the hawkish yet coldblooded statements he has issued regularly for the past half century. Or are we dealing with a more emotional, possibly less rational personality?

When this question was put to him by David Ignatius in 2008, Brzezinski waffled, saying: "..I don't know whether I'm a realist or an idealist – I don't classify myself...It seems to be that if you're engaged in statecraft, you have to address the realities of power.....but that is not enough. Power has to be driven by principle and this is where the element of idealism comes in...And you try to strike a balance between the use of power to promote national security and interests, and trying to improve the human condition." [*America and the World*, p. 241]

Given the way Neoconservative idealism has held sway in the American foreign policy Establishment during the post-Cold War period with the support of both Republicans and Democrats, it will be useful to pin down Mr. Brzezinski and find the precise balance between idealism and realism in his thinking.

To the extent that he may be an idealist, of what does this idealism consist? In this regard, I intend to violate the conventions of polite discourse for the sake of greater clarity. I will engage in a brief *ad hominem* investigation, asking whether Brzezinski, the idealist, might not just be the great Polish Romantic of our age.

Secondly, as mentioned above, we will consider the relationship between his past conceptual work and his post-Cold War thinking. This means tracing continuity of such formulations as the trilateral concept (US-Europe-Far East) which was meant to promote the centrality of our dealings with allies, the major industrial democracies, and only thereafter to allow us to invest our efforts in developing relations with other world powers. Then there is Brzezinski's handling of the Russian issue which, despite his professions to the contrary, in fact seems to determine his approach to a great many other policy questions including relations with allies.

As with all the thinkers under review, I intend to devote some attention to the methodology of Brzezinski's scholarship. He is not distracted by grand historical, political and philosophical schemes as often is the habit of American political scientists, who like to march us back to Plato and show off their erudition. Brzezinski is more down to earth. When you sift through his works, you uncover his debt to widely held notions of causality: a mixture of economics, demographics and intellectual currents. Indeed, one of the most interesting dimensions of Brzezinski's writings is the interplay of determinism and voluntarism, which is the counterpoint to the strands of realism and idealism in his personality.

The Grand Chessboard: An Overview

The book is both descriptive of the landscape of international relations at the time of its writing in 1997 and prescriptive, offering a very lucid way forward across bilateral and multilateral relations with the world's leading powers based on a carefully reasoned geopolitical strategy.

Grand Chessboard is written in the style of realism – focusing on national interest of the U.S. and the other players. The very image of a chessboard is value neutral and seemingly unemotional. We accept the hierarchical value of the chess pieces as they are conventionally designated in terms of military and economic power. There would appear to be little room for sentimental attachments, no distractions with side issues like the political structures of the nation states and the sources of legitimacy of their elites.

Indeed a blurb from Professor Sam Huntington, doyen of the American foreign policy community, printed on the back cover of the 1998 paperback edition which I read suggests that Brzezinski fully satisfied the expectations arising from the framing of his monograph:

"The Grand Chessboard is the book we have been waiting for: a clear-eyed, tough-minded, definitive exposition of America's strategic interests in the Post-Cold War world. A masterful synthesis of historical, geographical, and political analysis, it is geostrategic thinking in the grand tradition of Bismarck"

The objective of the chess match Brzezinski has prepared for us is for the United States to maintain the status of sole remaining superpower which followed from the collapse of the Soviet Union and the end of the Cold War, enjoying uncontested leadership of the international community.

In a book in which the author reasons at great length and most impressively with his readers rather than lecturing them, perhaps the least argued element is precisely why the United States should strive to maintain its worldwide primacy. Brzezinski addresses this question mainly in the very last chapter of his book, and we will return to it. Let us first examine his general theses on what being Number One means and *how* to stay there as long as possible even in the face of emerging powers in other parts of the world and the necessarily declining relative U.S. power in the decades to come.

Brzezinski tells us that the United States now has greater power than any country accumulated before, a power which might be called imperial, though it differs from empires of the past in a number of significant ways. This is the first truly global empire and one which is domiciled outside of Eurasia, which for the past 500 years has been the center of power. Moreover, the U.S. empire is unique in world history because of the pluralistic, open nature of America itself, which it reflects. It is an empire built not on territorial conquest and direct control but on international financial institutions and regional or bilateral military alliances which the U.S. dominates. For the U.S. to maintain its primacy or hegemony, it must extend and consolidate its position in Eurasia, which is what the book is all about.

The author breaks Eurasia. down into four regions: Europe, in the western extremity; China and Japan in the Far East; and two regions in the middle, Russia and what he calls the 'Eurasian Balkans,' meaning Central Asia, the Caucasus and the northern tier of the Middle East - Iran, Afghanistan and Turkey.

Brzezinski's description of the political landscape on the eastern and western ends of the Eurasian land mass is both judicious and very insightful, drawing on in-depth knowledge of the countries under examination and the dynamics of their interaction both with one another and with the United States.

The Grand Chessboard: Europe

Within his main chapter dedicated to Europe, Brzezinski states flatly that it is America's 'natural ally' and also America's 'essential geopolitical bridgehead on the Eurasian continent.' He highlights the French-German partnership as the foundation for the European Union and guarantor of its continued successful territorial expansion and political integration. He explains the ambitions of these two lead nations, how they needed one another to succeed in the European project, so that America could not choose between them without damaging the common interest.

These facts may seem commonplace for anyone living on the Old Continent, but they carry several important messages to his American readers who have preferred dealing with the Germans and found the French claims on European leadership and their frequent sparring with the U.S. to be irksome. He says it would be profoundly unwise to overlook the constructive role played by France in Europe and even in NATO because they have been unfailingly loyal to the Atlantic Alliance whenever the chips were down. Moreover, the French have played an indispensable role locking democratic Germany into Europe.

For these reasons he urges America to stand back somewhat and let the German-French leaders get on with their tasks. Brzezinski even acknowledges the merit of the French argument for greater democracy within NATO and a less dominant role there for the United States. Second, he insists that Great Britain cannot serve as a vehicle of American influence in Europe because from the signing of the Rome Treaty to our own day Britain has marginalized itself in Europe. Indeed he says the last vestiges of the 'special relationship' with Britain should be scrapped. This teaching is a major affront to the popular image of Britain held by many Americans.

Brzezinski says that it is in America's own interests to support expansion of the European Union since it necessarily extends the U.S. 'bridgehead' in Eurasia. At the time of his writing this meant the ongoing cooptation of the Central European states recently freed from Soviet rule. In his concluding chapter he adds that their joining would not only shore up Europe's eastern flank but would have the added advantage of providing the U.S. with greater leverage within the EU. What he no doubt had in mind was the enthusiastically pro-American spirit of these countries in gratitude for America's role in their liberation, and the dilution of integration efforts so long as the founding EU members were wholly focused on preparatory work to bring candidates up to the high political and economic standards of the Union. All of this would make it all the easier for the U.S. to prevent Europe from becoming a counterweight or challenge to American geopolitical interests too early. In the medium term, he expected that upon the conclusion of this process of expansion and integration Europe could come to be a compatible partner with which the U.S. would share decision making on security matters.

How far should the eastward expansion of Europe and NATO go? In *The Grand Chessboard*, Brzezinski was already looking to the extension of NATO membership to the Baltic States, which was at the time a particularly prickly issue with Russia since, unlike Hungary or Poland, for example, Lithuania, Estonia and Latvia had been constituent republics of the Soviet Union and had common borders with the Russian Federation. It was in this book that he presented the now very familiar notion guiding our present day debate over Georgia and Ukraine:

"The bottom line guiding the progressive expansion of Europe has to be the proposition that no power outside of the existing transatlantic system has the right to veto the participation of any qualified European state in the European system – and hence also in its transatlantic security system – and that no qualified European state should be excluded a priori from eventual membership in either the EU or NATO."

He also answered unequivocally how any disagreements with Russia over this process should be handled:

"If a choice has to be made between a larger Euro-Atlantic system and a better relationship with Russia, the former has to rank incomparably higher to America."

In 1997, Ukraine was still wallowing in domestic corruption scandals and had an unpromising economic future given its concentration in heavy industry - metallurgy and chemicals - which were then out of favor on the markets. From the perspective of a reader today, it is therefore all the more remarkable that Brzezinski placed special importance on the eventual extension of EU and NATO membership to Ukraine, which he expected would become timely already within the period 2005-2010.

This advocacy, which appears now to be almost prophetic, was founded on geopolitical strategic considerations vis-à-vis Russia and a belief in the transformational role for U.S. policy during the time-limited window of opportunity of its ascendancy on the world stage.

The logic of admitting Ukraine to NATO and the EU which Brzezinski adduced in 1997 and has been repeating ever since centers mainly on his belief that Russia will move, as it should, towards Europe and towards democracy only when it is coaxed and, where necessary, coerced by removing its other options, and in particular options feeding its nostalgia for empire. According to Brzezinski, Ukraine, with its population of 52 million, was essential to Russia if it were to maintain an illusion of empire. Defending Ukrainian independence from Russia and drawing it into Europe would have the additional benefit of moving Europe's geopolitical 'pivot' well to the East; failing that, the lot would fall to Poland.

Given the present debate between Europe and the United States over EU candidacy as a consolation for countries like Ukraine or Georgia which are denied membership in NATO due to differences of opinion within the alliance over their suitability, it is very pertinent to consider the logic and the sequence set out by Brzezinski in this very context of expansion. Brzezinski was arguing in 1997 only a one-way linkage: that NATO protection must follow if an EU candidacy were offered [page 84].

In *The Grand Chessboard*, Brzezinski said that it was too early to fix the ultimate limits of Europe, though it had to move beyond Charlemagne's Europe of the Cold War to embrace the territory of the shared Christian tradition, meaning not only the lands once under the Roman papacy but also Byzantium and Russian Orthodoxy. For reasons which he laid out in the separate chapter on Russia and which we will explore shortly, Brzezinski put off the extension of Europe to the Urals for the indefinite future, at least one generation away.*

---

*It is interesting to note that in an article Brzezinski published two years earlier in *Foreign Affairs*, 'A Plan for Europe: How to Expand NATO,' January/February 1995, he specifically adopted Charles de Gaulle's vision of Europe reaching to the Urals as a possible objective for the year 2020. He also foresaw the eventual extension of Europe and NATO into the Caucasus, to Georgia, Armenia and Azerbaijan some time after Russia achieved some form of association or membership in those bodies. No reason was given for that delay.

Zbigniew Brzezinski:

From *Grand Chessboard* to Obama Advisor, Part Two

The Grand Chessboard: The Far East

The most interesting element in Zbigniew Brzezinski's description of the eastern extremity of Eurasia is that he presents us with two great nations, the People's Republic of China and Japan, as the objects of particular American attention. For the co-founder of the Trilateral Commission, the shift of attention away from Nippon is stunning. Whereas in the 1970s it was quite forward looking to make U.S. relations with Japan in some way comparable with its relations with Europe, by the 1990s the meteoric rise of the Chinese economy and world standing and the onset of Japan's decade long economic stagnation were inescapable and Brzezinski hastened to draw the appropriate conclusions.

Brzezinski devotes separate chapters to the two Asian powers and clearly delineates the different ways each can serve U.S. objectives of consolidating its influence in Eurasia.

China, he tells us, has become a major regional power, but is as yet unprepared to play a global role and given the risks to its stability and growth rate in the years ahead in the form of possible social disruption and political conflict, it is difficult to foresee when it may be ready to take on the world.

Brzezinski took a benign view of China's increasing preponderance among its East Asian neighbors. He compared it more to a 'sphere of deference' than a classical 'sphere of influence.' In this regard, like veteran political scientist Sam Huntington at roughly the same time, Brzezinski was prepared to make an exception to the general rule of condemning the emergence of any regional powers which might challenge U.S. dominance. Indeed, he foresaw that if the United States managed relations skillfully, a 'regionally preeminent China should become America's Far Eastern anchor."

He specifically advised against pursuing a policy of containment directed against China, against deviating from the 'one China' policy even as the United States made plain its willingness to counter any attempt at take-over of Taiwan by military force. The objective should be to ensure China had no reason to enter into an anti-hegemonic coalition with Russia and other dissatisfied powers like Iran. In the near term, the U.S. could draw China into a constructive role whereby it assisted America's geostrategic interest by helping to maintain a politically pluralistic Eurasia. This China could perform by competing with Russia for the attention of Central Asia. Its support of Pakistan would also keep India's ambitions under control.

The very fact that China was unlikely to become a global power in the near term meant that the United States could afford to treat it as a 'globally significant player,' meaning inviting it into the G-7 club.

Brzezinski viewed Japan from the opposite standpoint:

"Unlike China, which can seek global power by first becoming a regional power, Japan can gain global influence by eschewing the quest for regional power."

He explains that any hopes which Japan may have had for regional influence were frustrated by the enmity it created among all its Asian neighbors through military conquest and cruel occupation during WWII. Only under an American protectorate, with its own military power kept in check, and with its attention diverted to the global stage, acting in cooperation with its U.S. partners, could Japan be accepted as a citizen in good standing in Asia and play the role it deserved as the world's second largest economy.

Under these circumstances, Brzezinski recommended that the U.S. maintain its troop presence in both Japan and nearby South Korea, that it not press the Japanese to assume greater defense responsibilities in the Asia-Pacific region or to pursue rearmament. The task was to continue to orient Japan towards a global role, close friendship with the United States and regional accommodation with Greater China. "In effect, Japan should be America's global partner in tackling the new agenda of world affairs."

The *Grand Chessboard*: Russia

The Russian Federation accounts for slightly more than 10% of the Earth's surface and it occupies a central, though unenviable position in Brzezinski's political map of Eurasia as a 'black hole.' Russia is where Brzezinski leaves behind his sober methodology of country risk analysis and engages heavily in speculation on how to change the country under study not only to avoid crossing American objectives elsewhere but also to meet an American. definition of what its self-interest should be. This is where his voluntarism, in the sense of will to act as the agent of history, comes to the fore:

"...the immediate task has to be to reduce the probability of political anarchy or a reversion to a hostile dictatorship in a crumbling state still possessing a powerful nuclear arsenal. But the long-range task remains: how to encourage Russia's democratic transformation and economic recovery while avoiding the reemergence of a Eurasian empire that could obstruct the American geostrategic goal of shaping a larger Euro-Atlantic system to which Russia can then be stably and safely related."

The temptation to meddle in the nation-building exercise was surely encouraged by Russia's public search for a new identity, a new national mission statement as it rose from the ashes of the Soviet Union beginning in 1992. Here Brzezinski very capably describes the various options which the Russians considered in the '90s as they looked for a way forward. These were:

1) To reach a strategic partnership with the United States, meaning global co-equality such as the Soviet leadership of Brezhnev had proposed twenty years earlier. However, this was no longer attractive to the United States and in any case, the Russian Federation was now too weak to be such a global partner*.

---

*Brzezinski paused briefly at this point to consider whether the United States had not missed an opportunity with Russia in 1993 by not responding to the hopes of Russia's westernizing democrats and including the country in the process of NATO expansion.. When Yeltsin dropped his objections to Poland's accession to NATO, the question hung in the air. However, he insists that Russia was not yet sufficiently sure of itself and its westernizers were fated to lose out to its nationalists. Brzezinski may be right, but then again we shall never know since the effort to reach out to the Russians was not made.

2) To spread out into the post-Soviet space, or CIS, as a unifying force of the 'near abroad.' But the supporters of this option were divided among themselves over the nature of the future association, namely whether it would be dominated by functional considerations of commercial exchange and consist merely of a 'common economic space' similar to the EEC or entail the resurrection of the Soviet empire under some new unifying principal such as a mystical pan-Slav or Eurasian world view. At the moment restoration of empire was improbable because Russia lacked the strength to impose its will on the 'near abroad' and was also too poor to get its way by force of attraction

3) A counter-alliance with China and other powers directed against the American worldwide hegemony. This was the latest of the fashionable concepts to seize the imagination of Russian statesmen, having been floated by the Yeltsin government in the year when Brzezinski was preparing *Chessboard* for publication. He expected it to fail because it supposed an association of outcasts and for Russia, in particular, held the prospect of being a junior partner.

For these reasons, Brzezinski concluded that Russia had only one viable option available to it as it proceeded with remaking its national identity and finding a realistic international role for itself. This was to modernize socially and politically by aligning with the enlarging EU and NATO. The first step on this path would be to give up its imperial ambitions, and the acid test would be Russia's unqualified acceptance of Ukrainian sovereignty and abandonment of any right of say over NATO's further expansion.

There were a number of important problems with this proposal at the time he wrote it and they have largely remained with us to this day, not least of all that Brzezinski did not name any significant immediate reward even if the Russian leadership were capable of acceding to these demands. At the very end of the book he speaks about enhancing Russia's status with the reward of a seat at the G7, plus the following perks: "a role in the Organization for Security and Co-operation in Europe, further Western financial assistance, improved highways and railway connections." It is hard to believe that Brzezinski was serious about such meager inducements for a country to agree on "a clear-cut abjuration of the imperial past." The reason is obvious: the Americans were in no position to offer Russia a safe harbor of close relationship with the European Union. Moreover, as more and more former Soviet Bloc countries joined the EU and brought their resentments against Russia into the inner counsels of Europe, the prospects for the solution he held out progressively dimmed.

In any case, his prescription is one-dimensional: it ignores the nature of the successor states in the post-Soviet space and their ongoing relations with Russia, all of which militated against the Russians throwing themselves unreservedly into the arms of the EU and letting go of their neighbors. The political and social stability of these states was and remains highly variable, creating some serious security risks for Russia. Their national identities were often being created through anti-Russian slogans, which did not bode well for future inter-state relations. They all have substantial minorities of ethnic Russians who, following the break-up of the Soviet Union, were relegated to second class citizenship, generating massive inflows of displaced persons into the Russian Federation and exacerbating nationalist resentments. There were and remain very significant common industrial projects and economic interests with some of these countries and often major *Gastarbeiter* relations with immigrant non-ethnic Russian labor coming from the former republics

Meanwhile, at the same time that Brzezinski was urging the Russians to seek their future in the embrace of Europe, he was calling for Western measures to ensure 'geopolitical pluralism' in Eurasia by wresting Central Asia away from Russian economic control. At issue were projects to ensure direct access of the energy riches of that region to Europe via Azerbaijan and Georgia without passing through Russia. This was and remains to our day one of the key elements in what has to be described as open economic warfare with the Russian Federation. It is hard to see how this could pave the way for closer Russian relations with Europe.

Still the most remarkable passages on Russia in *The Grand Chessboard* come at the very end, in the chapter entitled 'Conclusion.' This is something of a misnomer, since Brzezinski proceeds to make some recommendations in it which hardly follow from the preceding 193 pages.

Here he suggests that Russia abandon its futile attempts to regain global power status and instead modernize itself by decentralizing its political system and building on a free market. This, he says, will liberate the creative potential of the Russian people and its vast natural resources which have been held back for generations by stifling bureaucracy.

Here, at last, he spells out what he means by decentralization. It is the break-up of Russia into three loosely federated states: European Russia, a Siberian Republic and a Far Eastern Republic.

This was written in 1997 when the results of a five-year devolution of power to the provinces under Boris Yeltsin and of economic shock therapy for the purpose of establishing a market economy on the ruins of state planning were perfectly clear. The relaxation of central controls from Moscow had already led to the development of virtual satrapies in the provinces run by local thugs or demagogues. There were rumblings of ethnic-based independence movements across the land. An energy-rich Muslim republic of Tatarstan was on its way to autonomy just several hundred miles from the capital. Meanwhile the international brotherhood of energy companies had concluded long term contracts for oil and gas extraction under terms very prejudicial to Russia's national interests, and home-grown oligarchs had taken over vast mineral resources in exchange for political support to the Yeltsin regime while draining the proceeds to offshore accounts. Within a year of Brzezinski's publication of his master work, the widely expected bankruptcy of the country occurred and Russia defaulted on its state obligations.

These facts on the growing chaos resulting from decentralization and the likelihood of financial collapse were well known to all serious Western observers at the time when Brzezinski was writing *The Grand Chessboard*, so it is very difficult to accept his recommendations on Russia as having been made in good faith.

However, it must be acknowledged that among Russia's 'westernizing intellectuals,' with whom Brzezinski surely was and today remains in contact, the notion of breaking up the country for the sake of its democratic salvation had a certain appeal at the time, such was their hatred of the Soviet past and wish to ensure against its possible revival. The problem is that such individuals, who often are fluent in English and quick to attract the ear of foreign visitors, were wholly inexperienced in the practical matters of politics and wholly unrepresentative of the country at large.

To be charitable, Brzezinski's taking up and lending his authority to ideas which could only lead to still greater pauperization, disorder and armed conflict on the territory of the Russian Federation, is indicative of the epistemological limits of intelligence work underpinning state-building schemes from some foreign capital even when the master analyst is as experienced in the métier as Zbigniew Brzezinski.

The Grand Chessboard: The Eurasian Balkans

The one remaining region in Eurasia which Brzezinski serves up is what he calls the "Eurasian Balkans" which takes in Central Asia, the Caucasus, Iran, Afghanistan and Turkey. The logic to this designation is that these countries are ethnically heterogeneous with many disaffected minority peoples and like the Balkans in southeast Europe they are unstable and potentially explosive. He provides us with tables to demonstrate the ethnic, religious, linguistic complexities. He sets out in the manner of a good intelligence officer the domestic political issues and the interests of neighboring powers which play out here.

However, Brzezinski's explanation of commonality of these countries as a region is not persuasive One can say the same about large swathes of the world in general where nation states emerged from colonial rule and did not necessarily have a basis in ethnic and linguistic homogeneity or in borders that are well defined by topography.

The true distinguishing feature of most of this region to the South of Russia is vast energy and other natural resources. Its core area is Central Asia, where the various Soviet republics emerged as independent states in 1992. They remained for some time under Russian economic domination because they are landlocked and most pipelines and transportation routes to market passed north across Russia.

In *The Grand Chessboard*, Brzezinski argued the case for their liberation from the Russian embrace....into the waiting arms of the international community:

"America's primary interest is to help ensure than no single power comes to control this geopolitical space and that the global community has unhindered financial and economic access to it. Geopolitical pluralism will become an enduring reality only when a network of pipeline and transportation routes links the region directly to the major centers of global economic activity via the Mediterranean and Arabian Seas, as well as overland."

Apart from Central Asia, the other countries in what he calls the Eurasian Balkans are put there mainly because they can serve as logistics facilitators. They are the territories through which the pipelines would pass, and, in the case of Iran and Azerbaijan, they could also be major contributors to the oil and gas flows heading to Europe from their own considerable reserves.

Brzezinski wants to persuade his readers that these energy projects would bring peace and stability to the region and that possible Russian opposition would be "inimical to regional stability." However, he disavowed any wish to boot out the Russians. So long as Russia did not seek exclusive domination of the region, it would remain welcome to participate actively in the region's development, which could be enriching for all.

It bears mention that around the time he was writing these lines Brzezinski was providing counsel on promoting 'geopolitical pluralism' in Central Asia and the Caucasus to the Clinton administration and he accepted an assignment to assist negotiations surrounding the first major pipeline to realize the task of bringing regional energy resources to European markets: the Baku-Tbilisi-Ceyhan project. It is surely no accident that the senior administration official responsible for Eurasian energy policy at the time, Richard Morningstar, spoke and wrote about the geopolitical objectives then and in 2006 when the pipeline was finally opened in virtually the same terms as Brzezinski.*

The Russian-Georgian war of August 2008 may be said to have resulted in good part from the *carte blanche* security assurances which the United States eventually extended to Tbilisi in recognition of the central role Georgia assumed in the transmission of Azerbaijan oil to Europe per the strategy authored by Brzezinski. And the present day Grand Game in Central Asia over the creation of a Trans-Caspian pipeline linked to the projected Nabucco pipeline which in turn follows the path of Baku-Tbilisi into Turkey is merely an update to the scheme for realizing geopolitical objectives which we find in Brzezinski's 1997 book. Once again Richard Morningstar has been invited by the State Department to act as America's principal emissary to drive the delicate and complex multiparty negotiations to successful conclusion.

Back in 1997, Brzezinski was able to justify America's move into Central Asia by Russia's weakness and inability to regain imperial rule over the region, creating what could be argued was a power vacuum. The United States proposed to play a constructive role by bringing in development funds and raising the general prosperity. In 2009, following Russia's economic and political resurgence and its ability and determination to protect its position as largest energy supplier to Europe from both its own and Central Asian reserves, the activities which Brzezinski advocates appear to be simply brazen meddling in other people's backyard for the purpose of weakening a challenger to

* See my blog article "Richard Morningstar, Letter to a Wayward Classmate," *La Libre Belgique*, 06.05.2009.

U.S. global hegemony. It is at this point that Brzezinski's policies become destabilizing and a threat to the peace.

TRIUMPHALISM AND OTHER FAILINGS

As I mentioned at the beginning of this examination of *The Grand Chessboard*, the author devotes only a handful of pages to explaining why it is desirable and necessary to perpetuate American worldwide hegemony which came about suddenly and unexpectedly with the collapse of the Soviet Union in late 1991.

Initially he contents himself with citing Harvard professor and doyen of American foreign policy studies Sam Huntington: "A world without U.S. primacy will be a world with more violence and disorder and less democracy and economic growth than a world where the United States continues to have more influence than any other country in shaping global affairs."

We have to wait to the very end of the book for Brzezinski to present his own case for American worldwide domination and he does so in a manner which does not allow of contradiction, saying flatly: "Short of a deliberate or unintentional American abdication, the only real alternative to American global leadership in the foreseeable future is international anarchy."

What then are the engines of disorder which can bring about calamity, indeed global anarchy, if America does not take the lead? Brzezinski offers a hodge-podge list of threats including the consequences of population explosion, poverty-driven migration, radicalizing urbanization, ethnic and religious hostility and the proliferation of weapons of mass destruction.

He tells us that without America defending peace and order, Europe may lose its way, and xenophobia fed by high unemployment could propel political extremism. He claims that a genuinely prerevolutionary situation is brewing in Europe. Meanwhile, America's steadying hand is essential to see Russia off to a brighter future in close cooperation with Europe and to oversee the grand accommodation with China among its neighbors in the Far East.

What we have here is scare-mongering on behalf of the favored scenario, continued American world domination. What is missing in this type of intelligence work or risk analysis is a review of alternative scenarios. For example, it is hard to understand why the threats to peace and stability which Brzezinski catalogues could not have been managed at once by a presidium of world powers, whether the narrow G8 or some broader body.

Without explanation, Brzezinski states that a shift to more equitably shared decision making in the world community can begin some time after five years within a twenty year horizon. The strategic partners in this new condominium would be an expanded and politically integrated European Union, Japan and possibly Greater China. Is this schedule dictated by the unpreparedness of the proposed partners or by the unpreparedness of the United States to let go until its own strength declines significantly in consequence of the rise of emerging powers? In a book that is otherwise strikingly frank, this is an important question which is not addressed.

Instead we only get Brzezinski's say-so that America is truly "indispensable" and has to do the job of managing the world as it best sees fit. Thus, in the end, Brzezinski offers us in this book a splendid edifice of reasoning about managing and perpetuating world domination placed atop a foundation of blind faith in the justness of the mission.

En passant, one might also ask why Brzezinski does not raise the question of whether world domination was in the national interest of….the United States. This is no idle question. During 19th century colonialism, though there were obviously beneficiaries in the home country in terms of companies and cadres of administrators, in many cases it was never clear that the net revenue inflow to the imperial home countries exceeded the outflows in infrastructure development and running costs. Brzezinski is interested in geopolitical strategy on chessboards, not in the workaday issues of paying for a vast military establishment which has a greater budget than the defense costs of the rest of the world put together.

Instead what we find is Brzezinski's expression of doubt about the staying power of the American public for reasons of its own lack of seriousness. His remarks about his compatriots have a smack of elitism, as he criticizes them for unwillingness to make sacrifices, for hedonistic life style, concluding that the country is fixated on mass entertainment and social escapism.

Unlike past empires, the Pax Americana is borne by a populist democracy which has no ambition for international supremacy. He cites polls indicating a mere 13% of Americans are pleased that the country is the only remaining superpower while 74% would prefer if the burden of managing the world were shared with others.

Brzezinski wrote *The Grand Chessboard* at the high point in U.S. power and, notwithstanding his reputation for steely reserve, his text is imbued with the triumphalism which held sway in Washington at the time. The overarching objective he is serving, maintaining U.S. worldwide domination, is frequently stated with astonishing lack of embarrassment in a way that borders on hubris. The following succinct statement of strategy is a perfect example.

"To put it in a terminology that hearkens back to the more brutal age of ancient empires, the three grand imperatives of imperial geostrategy are to prevent collusion and maintain security dependence among the vassals, to keep tributaries pliant and protected, and to keep the barbarians from coming together."

In the context of his book, it would be safe to assume that the vassals are the Europeans; the tributaries are the Japanese, and the barbarians are the Russians, Chinese and Iranians. However, regardless of who is who, Brzezinski's terminology is grossly offensive and it is almost as if he never expected these cynical remarks to be read by those he is describing. Yet the book was promoted by his publishers and sold widely abroad, where it laid bare the worst suspicions of many.

Among the countries where Brzezinski's *Grand Chessboard* was most widely read among the educated classes was Russia, and the impact of a book like this by one of America's most reputed and influential strategists should not be overlooked. Ten years after its publication, on 1 September 2008, in a speech delivered at Moscow's elite school of international relations studies, MGIMO, on the occasion of the opening of the academic year, Russian Foreign Minister Sergei Lavrov reminded his audience whence came the policies which led to the Russian-Georgian war three weeks earlier, saying "To us, [post-Soviet space] is not a 'chessboard' for playing geopolitical games."

The disarming frankness of Brzezinski's narrative is such that several of the reviews of the book which one finds on the internet consist of nothing other than clippings of the more bold if not outrageous quotations from the book. It is not without reason that one critic, Scott Thompson writing in the *Executive Intelligence Review*, entitled his article "Brzezinski testifies against himself.' .'.

Zbigniew Brzezinski:

From *Grand Chessboard* to Obama Advisor, Part Three

The onset of contrition

The U.S. presidential election of the year 2000 was in good part fought over the future direction of foreign policy, with candidate George W. Bush calling for a trimming of the sails. Bush appeared to side with a traditional 'Jacksonian' strand of centrist thinking, which had been deeply critical of American military interventions under Bill Clinton in furtherance of human rights and other soft causes. The climate was so propitious to a return of *realism* that Henry Kissinger came out of semi-retirement and published his own volume of advice to the new Prince.

However, the events of September 11, 2001 brought about a cardinal change in the thinking of the President and his security and foreign policy team around a crudely formulated 'war on terrorism.' A new national security strategy was put in place in 2002, setting out the principles of pre-emptive war and unilateralism which justified and explained America's 2003 invasion of Iraq. President Bush put the nations of the world on notice that they were either 'with us or against us,' a theological crusade against an axis of evil was launched, and the hubris implicit in American post-Cold War triumphalism was exposed in a bullying foreign policy which abandoned all pretence at diplomatic niceties and generated enormous ill will towards the country in foreign capitals.

Brzezinski, the realist, rejected the policies of George W. Bush, because they violated the rules of statecraft and his own warnings on the finite nature of U.S. resources and the need to enlist others to maximize the effect of American actions. Moreover, a great many of the specific policy recommendations for managing relations with Europe and the Far East which Brzezinski had advanced in *The Grand Chessboard* fell among the broken china as the

United States prioritized formation of its 'coalition of the willing.' Relations with traditional close allies soured over French and German unwillingness to support a military campaign for 'regime change' in Baghdad without cover of legitimacy from the United Nations Security Council. Secretary of Defense Donald Rumsfeld strove to drive a wedge between squeamish Old Europe and the dynamic and supportive New European states like Poland which generously contributed troops to the U.S. coalition. In the Far East, great pressure was applied to the Japanese to raise their level of participation in other related American military operations (logistics for the Afghanistan effort). Eventually this led to formation of a U.S.-Australian-Japanese axis in the Far East which worked directly counter to the strategic partnership with China which Brzezinski had urged. However, I am getting ahead of events.

Brzezinski was among the minority of foreign policy specialists who came out against the invasion of Iraq both before and after the United States brought down Saddam Hussein. He was quick to appreciate the damage, actual and potential, to his painstakingly designed architecture of international relations and he acted. In 2004 he published his response to American unilateralism: *The Choice: Global Domination or Global Leadership*

As John Inkenberry aptly put it in his review published in *The New York Times* ("Books of the Times" section, March 30, 2004), Brzezinski planted a flag on behalf of the Democratic Party opposition to stand against George W. Bush's vision of security. Ikenberry also indicated that the key contribution of *The Choice* may lie elsewhere than in its conceptual strength, which he faulted. Indeed, I would maintain that the book's real contribution to the debate was linguistic.

As I noted here earlier, in his 1997 master work Brzezinski had imbibed fully the ambrosia of 'primacy,' 'dominance' and 'empire.' Now he learned to watch his p's and q's much better and his language becomes almost, if not quite contrite.

In general, the controversy aroused by the Bush Doctrine shook loose the various strands of conservatism and patriotic posturing which had become almost indistinguishable in the second half of the 1990s. Hard and fast Neoconservatives like Paul Wolfowitz moved to one side, cheering on a benevolent U.S. domination of the international scene in unapologetic unilateralism. Progressive Democrats, on the other hand, now took up Brzezinski's call for American *leadership*, which remains to this day the new politically correct term for consensual hegemony. Meanwhile, Jacksonians and 'realists' remain marginalized as in the two decades before George W. Bush.

Now let us move on to Brzezinski's latest monograph, *Second Chance* which I will supplement with related items from *Conversations on the Future of American Foreign Policy*, published in 2008, in which he is jointly featured with Brent Snowcroft in a free flowing question and answer format.

Both books provide an affirmative answer to the question: can an old dog learn new tricks? From his renown as hands-on fighter in the trenches of Washington and polemicist of note in the past, Brzezinski emerges here as a judicious, insightful observer who is generous in his appraisals of adversaries as well as friends and colleagues – with the possible exception of President George W Bush, whose thinking he obviously does not hold in high regard. Throughout the book, Brzezinski reasons with his reader rather than lecture him.

One reason for the change in mood of his writing has to do with the perspective. *Second Chance* is primarily a work of history rather than futurology or strategizing. It looks back at the past fifteen years since the end of the Cold War and explores how each of the three presidents of this period– George W. H. Bush (Sr), Bill Clinton and George W. Bush (Jr) – responded to the historic window of opportunity to transform the world in circumstances of American worldwide hegemony. *Conversations* is largely a document in the memoir genre of personal recollections.

In general, he concludes that whatever each president achieved in office, none exploited successfully the unprecedented power which the United States enjoyed in the world during their mandates.

Bush Sr was a master of foreign policy when he came to office and succeeded in managing very well the major issues which developed on his watch: the withdrawal of Soviet forces from Central Europe and the peaceful collapse of the Soviet Union beginning in late 1991; and the Iraqi invasion of Kuwait. However, he lacked the vision to move beyond competent management to a transformational role which was there for the taking in both instances.

Bill Clinton acceded to the presidency without any strategy for foreign policy, believing in the benevolent determinism of globalization which would guide the world to a safer harbor over time. In his second term, when Madeleine Albright ran the State Department and Brzezinski's counsel carried some weight, the Clinton presidency was given purpose in foreign policy by NATO enlargement. However, it largely missed any opportunity to bring Russia into a constructive relationship or to bring about a comprehensive settlement in the Middle East as it became bogged down in the president's domestic woes with Congress and the impeachment proceedings against him.

The sitting president imposed self-inflicted wounds on the body politic and set back the cause of American leadership.

Brzezinski explains these developments in terms of the differing personalities, skills and outlooks of the presidents themselves and also in the different strengths and weaknesses of the American people which their policies addressed.

Brzezinski has nearly 20-20 vision looking back into the past. Though I have remarked earlier that he was prophetic in calling out in 1997 certain relatively obscure issues which became very important ten years later such as Ukrainian membership in NATO, this was to a certain extent a self-fulfilling prophecy given that Brzezinski himself was not an idle bystander in some scholarly ivory tower; he himself set in motion the wheels of political expectations which later matured.

I say 'nearly' perfect vision on the past, because there is an astigmatism which must be acknowledged, namely his tendentiousness with respect to continuities or discontinuities of policy under the various administrations. Brzezinski is quick to pick up the continuity between the Defense Planning Guide document of 1992 under George H.W. Bush (Sr.) and the unilateralist, preventive war policies of Bush, Jr. both in terms of outlook and implementers, since the middle level authors of the working draft under the father later reappeared as high Defense Department and National Security Council officials under the son, and its main sponsor, Defense Secretary Dick Cheney, served as Vice President in the administration of George W. Bush.

What he willfully overlooks is the continuities in policy of all three presidents in their pursuit of U.S. hegemony and the proliferating American military interventions abroad during the entire period.

The basic point of the narrative is missed opportunities and a concluding reaffirmation that the United States would have a 'second chance' to fulfill them if its next president learned from the errors of the recent past. Along the way Brzezinski provides a lot of very interesting material answering questions which I posed at the start of this four part analytical article on his post-Cold War thinking.

IS BRZEZINSKI ANTI-RUSSIAN?

First of all, *Second Chance* and, still more, the book of *Conversations* which came out a year later provide very useful information bearing on the author's view of Russia.

One may ask, of course, what is the relevance of that question to his general strategic recommendations for U.S. foreign policy. Zbigniew Brzezinski is very widely traveled and totally conversant with the issues and personalities of most of the world's countries. He also has spent a large part of his professional life accentuating the positive: the need to concentrate on improving America's relations with its main allies in Europe and the Far East or the need to show differentiated and kindly treatment of the East European subject countries in the Soviet bloc rather than dwelling solely on confrontation with and containment of the USSR.

And yet Soviet studies were his core expertise, as is true of the entire U.S. foreign intelligence community in the period up to the September 11, 2001 attacks, and many of his policy recommendations in a great variety of areas have in one way or another reflected his reading of Russia. In the past that was justified by the worldwide standoff of the two powers in a bipolar world. But it is all the more true today, long after the demise of the Soviet Union, when a 'resurgent' and resentful Russia has emerged as the most vocal opponent to U.S. hegemony on the world stage.

So is Brzezinski anti-Russian or not?

We already indicated that his seminal work *The Grand Chessboard* left us uncertain whether his recommendations on the way forward for Russia were delivered in good faith. What do his last two books contribute by way of clarification?

There is in *Second Chance* a fairly lengthy discussion of bad, at times illegal behavior by American and other Western advisors to the Yeltsin government in the 1990s which compounded the problem of theft of national property by the oligarchs. Western malfeasance contributed to the 1998 financial melt-down in Russia ending in default and all of this irrevocably associated the reformers and their Western backers with chaos and pauperization in the mind of the broad Russian public.

In this text Brzezinski is not saying anything which one would not find in "Who Lost Russia?" – the memoirs of his adventures in Russia as speculator and philanthropist during the Yeltsin years published by George Soros in April 2000.* However, Soros later changed sides and has in recent publications decided to pin the blame for Russia's turn to authoritarianism on Vladimir Putin rather than on the misdeeds and meanness of Western governments during the 1990s. It is very much to Brzezinski's credit that he has remained true to the historical record and holds to account the U.S. government under Bill Clinton as well as private American consultants who let down Russia's democrats.

However, at the very same time Brzezinski repeats and amplifies his attention to Russia's 'imperial nostalgia' as the principal impediment to improved relations with the West. I do not deny that such nostalgia once existed, particularly in the early 1990s when the newly created Russian Federation was embarking on a search for its national identity. However, by the turn of the millennium, the question of the national mission statement had long been solved otherwise and without reference to any resuscitation of an empire.

It is disappointing that Brzezinski stubbornly refuses to see the present day reality of Russia. Instead he trots out Vladimir Putin's famous remark that 'the collapse of the Soviet Union was the greatest calamity of the 20th century' as proof of such nostalgia in today's leadership and as an even worse indication about the nature of the regime: according to Brzezinski the phrase means "Leninism-Stalinism has been swept under the carpet and not exorcised."

Because the very same quotation from Putin is regularly used by Robert Kagan and the Neoconservatives generally these days to demonstrate the 'values gap' between the West and Russia and to justify arms length dealings instead of rapprochement, it is worth taking a short time out to consider what Putin's remark truly meant.

---

*See my blog article "George Soros on the Russian Problem: When Sour Grapes Turn Rancid," *La Libre Belgique*, February 18, 2009.

To begin with, interpretation of the phrase need not be literal In the broader sense, the end of the bipolar world following the collapse of the USSR was and remains a 'calamity' for the West as well as for Russia. The American worldwide hegemony and hubris made possible a war of aggression against Iraq and dramatically changed the perception of the United States in the community of nations from peacemaker to the single greatest threat to world peace.

However, there is no need to be too clever about all this. The collapse of the Soviet Union and the removal from power of the Communist Party in the Russian Federation was a nearly bloodless revolution which left both persecutors and their progeny and victims and their progeny on the political and social stage of Russia. In this context of widely divergent and passionately held views about the country's past, present and future, Vladimir Putin's government maneuvered from one side to another, as most any skillful statesmen would, allowing memorials to be built to those who had been repressed and also honoring the institutional traditions of those responsible for the abuses while proceeding step-by-step in consolidating not only Russia's unity of state power but its transformation into a young democracy and market economy.

The legislative electoral campaigns of late 2007 and the presidential campaign of the spring 2008 which gave the Kremlin party control of the State Duma and Mr Dmitry Medvedev the presidency were waged around an extremely modest and achievable platform of improving the daily life of the vast majority of the population and feeling of national pride to the point where Russians would no longer dream of emigrating, would be content to marry and raise children in their communities.

The country's foreign policy under Sergei Lavrov has been built upon the traditional principles of *Realpolitik*, namely the defense of the economic and strategic interests of the nation-state and support for Russian business and private persons abroad. Economic interests include, of course, defense of market share in the growing European energy markets by, on the one hand, retaining its status as predominant customer for gas from its Central Asian neighbors and on the other hand retaining secure transit of its gas through the neighboring countries to the West, Ukraine and Belarus. Neither preoccupation can be characterized as 'imperial' or 'nostalgic' in the sense meant by Brzezinski.

In *Conversations,* Brzezinski expands on the question of Russia's alleged nostalgia for empire. He tells us that Putin wants to subjugate states like Ukraine or Georgia since they are geopolitically critical to its dream of empire. In his view Russia seeks to dominate Ukraine to pursue a Slavic Union and must humble Georgia because it is essential to rule the Caucasus

It is regrettable but I must say that Brzezinski's remarks about Ukraine and Georgia are humbug. No Slavic Union is on the political agenda of the Russian Federation today. Ideologies and big ideas of all kinds are not part of the national program, which is fixated on personal prosperity. And as for the Caucasus, the Russians are clearly concerned to keep the peace in their own republics of Ingushetia, Dagestan and Chechnya, which are indeed critical to their domestic tranquility lest Russia experience the centrifugal forces once again which nearly led to chaos in the 1990s. Georgia has been a distraction and a nuisance at the level of external security only because of American support for an unstable local potentate, Mr. Saakashvili, in defense of oil transit pipelines built across his nation as part of Brzezinski's strategy directed against Russia.

In the years since the completion of the Baku-Tbilisi-Ceyhan which Brzezinski helped to negotiate during the Clinton administration, natural developments within the Central Asian and trans-Caucasus region have done more to establish economic pluralism there than all of Washington's geopolitically motivated meddling. The China factor has been of major importance in changing how Russia deals with its 'near abroad' to the south economically and politically. More recently Iran and Turkey have exercised their own pull on Central Asia as energy consumers. Pakistan and India are looming on the horizon. All are looking after their private commercial interests and none has need of prodding from Washington to act on behalf of high geopolitical considerations under American tutelage.

And as we close out the issue of Russia's alleged 'imperial nostalgia,' it is essential to highlight a lesson of a different sort which is completely in line with realist theory about the behavior of all nation states, whatever their internal social and political structure: all without exception behave 'imperially' when given a chance. It is irresponsible of Brzezinski and betokens double standards not to allow Russia's claims to a 'privileged relationship' with its neighbors of the 'near abroad' and to ignore the revived imperial ambitions of Sweden, Poland, Turkey and other former 'master nations' to Russia's southern and western borderlands.

These are the parties which waged wars over the same flat spaces for centuries until each was defeated by the forces of Moscow. It is simply remarkable how the peaceable, neutrality-loving Swedes rediscovered their rapacious Viking genes once the Baltics were free again for their economic colonization. It is equally amazing how quickly humble Poland took the lead in fomenting the Orange Revolution in Ukraine and championing the cause of democracy in still enslaved Belarus, Imperial Poland entices guest workers from the poorer countries to the East whose highly trained medical personnel and unskilled labor fill the vacancies created in Polish towns by its own brain drain and exodus of plumbers to France, the UK and Ireland. Poland from the Baltic to Black Seas is the revived ambition of Mr Brzezinski's former homeland.

For its part, Turkey unrolled an ambitious campaign of pan-Turkism in the Central Asian republics largely focusing on commercial investments and cultural centers. But the respective republics were at the time preoccupied with their own power struggles and image problems, so that the Turkish approaches bore few fruit and were ultimately discontinued. It is depressing to observe how American advisors in the region today, following the lead of Mr Richard Morningstar, are trying to revive Turkey's allegedly stabilizing mission in Central Asia. My point is simply that Russia's interest in maintaining close, even privileged relations with the countries on its borders should not be an argument against its full integration into the institutions of European security and trade given that the entire region is already an open marketplace for competing forces of attraction.

However, let us move on. The question of whether Zbigniew Brzezinski is anti-Russian was given a thorough airing in *Conversations*. Moderator David Ignatius, whose views are well to the right of center in American politics, nonetheless acted on his best journalistic instincts when he probed several of Brzezinski's policy positions about Russia that strain the onlooker's credulity. [page 172 ff] Can Brzezinski really mean what he says?

Ignatius began by asking about the wisdom of continuing the policy of NATO expansion: "How would we feel if a potential adversary advanced into Mexico or Canada? What should a wise policy towards Russia be?"

Brzezinski insisted that NATO's expansion eastward into Central Europe Soviet Bloc countries had not caused trouble, saying "…by and large, [they] have a much better relationship today with Russia than ever before, Poland particularly. So I don't think the expansion of NATO has been disruptive, quite the reverse." And as for Ukraine and Georgia, Brzezinski said the point was to keep open the option for the future.

Ignatius then had another go at it, asking rhetorically: "Zbig, how many times can you poke a stick in Russia's eye without their fighting back? We've gotten in the habit, through the years of Russian weakness under Yeltsin, of poking them a lot and getting away with it. Isn't that period ending."

But Brzezinski would not be moved. He reiterated the position we saw him set out in 1997 in *The Grand Chessboard*, namely that if Ukraine moved towards the EU and NATO that would prod Russia to do likewise. And Brzezinski also held to the time lines he sketched out a decade earlier: Russia in his view still has to undergo a long and painful evolution towards democracy, so that its joining with the West remained 'a very long range goal.'

These passages suggest that somewhere around 1997 Brzezinski either stopped looking closely at what is going on in Russia and in the neighboring states on its borders or succumbed to self-delusion. The only other explanation, still less attractive, is that he is prevaricating.

Like a bloodhound on the scent, Ignatius later asked Brzezinski what he thought of the Russians generally, to which he received the following stunning response: "..I like Russians. I like to be among Russians. You may be surprised to hear that I fit in very well, and most of them are very warm towards me, because I often dislike the same things they dislike in their own country."

The last remark is a fine clarification of the type of Russians with whom Brzezinski may be expected to meet. They are almost certainly the self-appointed fighters for democracy, people who in the Soviet days would have been labeled 'dissidents.'

Very few Westerners would have wanted to live under a government run by former Soviet dissidents, people who by definition had to be mad to stand up against a totalitarian regime. Their successors today, the human rights defenders and anti-Putin campaigners are not an easy bunch to get along with either as we may read between the lines in Brzezinski's further remarks:

"It's sometimes said that the Russians are among the most saintly and the most evil of peoples at the same time. There's no doubt that some of the human rights activists in Russia are prepared to put everything on the line, to sacrifice everything. They do it with a commitment that is beyond one's capacity to even remotely equal.'

Saintly and evil. Love – hate. Brzezinski went on to round out his impression of Russians in words that are an indictment of his qualifications as objective area specialist:

"And then there's this tradition of insensitivity to suffering, a willingness to brutalize people…I often think that that brutality is the product of the semi-animalistic level of peasant life, which breeds the feeling that you can mistreat animals and that human beings are no different."

Brzezinski simply has no 'feel' for his subject matter. He is taking us to the level of discourse of the chap at the next bar stool. He is also being unashamedly elitist. The only mitigating factor is that further on in the same book he acknowledges that certain 'backward, traditional farming regions' in his native Poland also have 'almost a peasant culture." But there he speaks with the voice of a hereditary petty Polish nobleman.

ZBIGNIEW BRZEZINSKI:

FROM *GRAND CHESSBOARD* TO OBAMA ADVISOR, PART FOUR

Internal contradictions: should an ignorant and hedonistic America run the world?

In these analytical essays dedicated to America's leading post-Cold War thinkers, I do not claim to marshal great erudition or to introduce major new facts to strike down the idols of conventional wisdom. Instead, for the most part, I am merely performing a 'logic check' and searching for contradictions and errors of judgment which competent editors or conscientious collegial readers should have spotted. To put it another way, I am attempting to practice the oriental martial arts approach, employing the energy of a sparring partner to win matches. It is an approach which is all the more justified in the case of Zbigniew Brzezinski who himself cites Sun Tzu [*Conversations*, p. 103]: "The best strategy is to let your opponent defeat himself."

Looking at Brzezinski's latest writings, there is no change in his stress on the need for continued American worldwide hegemony compared to what he wrote a decade ago. In *Second Chance*, he tells us that America plays the role of essential stabilizer and warns ominously that "the most likely short-term alternative to a constructive American world role is chaos." What has changed is Brzezinski's appreciation of serious domestic factors in the United States standing in the way of successful exercise of leadership.

This is not to say that the essential contradiction which vitiates his entire line of argumentation in favor of American hegemony was not present in his *Grand Chessboard* of 1997. In his concluding remarks in that book dealing with America's hegemonic legacy, Brzezinski remarked that the window of opportunity for what he called 'constructive exploitation of global power' might be shortened because the country's populist democracy was not attuned to an imperial role. He pointed to poll statistics indicating that only 13% of Americans were pleased at the notion of the country's standing as sole remaining superpower whereas 74% preferred if the United States shared problem-solving in the international arena with other countries.

In the same pages, Brzezinski attributed this phenomenon of the unwilling hegemon to hedonism and hesitation to sacrifice the lives of its young men on other shores. He discerned instead a popular fixation on 'mass entertainment and social escapism,' saying: 'The cumulative effect has made it increasingly difficult to mobilize the needed political consensus on behalf of sustained, and also occasionally costly, American leadership abroad."

One might have thought that the wake-up call of the attack on the World Trade Center and President Bush's war on terrorism would have changed this moral laxness in the American public, but in his 2007 writings Brzezinski feels compelled to devote far more attention to the domestic problems limiting America's effectiveness as global leader and the problems appear to be intractable.

In the concluding 30 pages or so of *Second Chance,* he catalogues vast changes in public consciousness and governmental processes of the United States which are needed for the country to lead less badly than during the past three presidencies. Going through his list, it is patently obvious that such change cannot and will not occur. There is no reason to believe that Americans will change their educational system to compensate for disgraceful ignorance of its young people about world geography and history, change the procedures of legislative oversight of foreign policy to limit the pernicious influence of foreign and domestic lobbyists, change from being carefree hedonists into self-sacrificing practitioners of universal patriotic service in the name of world leadership.

The elitist Brzezinski has reached the point where he suffers fools with great difficulty. He tells us in *Conversations* that "our public is woefully uninformed …parochially ignorant." But the sad tale does not end there: "I think Americans are curiously, paradoxically, simultaneously very well-educated and amazingly ignorant. We are a society that lives within itself. We're not interested in the history of other countries."

I have spoken earlier of the youthfulness of Brzezinski's writing style well up to his latest published works. However, there can be no more reliable tip-off to his eighty years than his disparaging remarks on the younger generations of Americans. Here we see his world-weariness exposed.

He cites a *National Geographic* survey showing few Americans entering college could find Great Britain on a map.

Assuming this is the case and changing the *people* is not an option, then the first principles of his strategy for American foreign policy must be reexamined: America must abjure claims to world domination, or 'world leadership' and try to get on better with the curs snapping at its heels in the name of a multipolar world. Is there anything wrong in its becoming, as Dennis Kucinich proposed in his short-lived presidential bid last year, a nation among nations rather than a nation over nations?

Without meaning to be disrespectful, even Dr. Zbigniew Brzezinski the polyglot, the world traveler, the man who shows he is conversant with the issues and personalities around the globe, at times speaks in an ignorant manner about other locales and customs, and it is not always clear whether this is by intent or not. In *Conversations,* he lets down his guard and expresses his gratitude to his adopted country for being so receptive to immigrants like himself. Rather touchingly he sees proof of American exceptionalism in the way someone with a name that is nearly unpronounceable for Anglo-Saxons could be sitting together with a Brent Snowcroft recounting their respective experiences as National Security Advisor to presidents.

America the land of opportunity! Indeed there is much to be proud of. However, it also is true that countries like Argentina, Canada, Australia and New Zealand have been and remain just as much melting pots for immigrants arriving from the world over. And the Old Continent, known for its centuries long population outflows, has also assimilated and promoted talented foreigners and continues to do so in our own times. The improbably named Briton Benjamin Disraeli was the United Kingdom's first Prime Minister of Jewish descent back in the 19th century. In more recent times, in 1992-93, a certain Pierre Bérégovoy served as France's Prime Minister, while the incumbent president of France, Mr Sarkozy is the son of an immigrant from Hungary.

Lapses are less acceptable when they concern Brzezinski's core expertise, Russia. In *Conversations,* he seeks to demonstrate the absence of a level playing field in Russia for foreign businesses, in particular energy concerns by remarking that there is no Texaco gasoline station in Moscow whereas a Lukoil station is situated just around the corner from the building where his interview with David Ignatius is taking place. Why Moscow has no Texaco pumps I cannot say. But I do confirm that British Petroleum and Finnish Neste are among the foreign companies operating gas stations in Moscow today. My point is not to cavil or disparage, but to highlight the epistemological impossibility of any one elite in any one capital running the world and doing a good job of it.

DETERMINISM AND VOLUNTARISM

It is a curious thing that at the beginning of *Second Chance* Brzezinski calls attention to Francis Fukuyama and his seminal work *The End of History* calling it a major contribution to the social acceptance of Neoconservative thinking in the 1990s following the end of the Cold War. He tells us that after 9/11 Neoconservatives found in Fukuyama's explanation of the inevitability of democracy a compelling argument for acting as history's agent, leading to governmental policies which he calls 'dogmatic activism.'

It is still more curious that towards the end of the same book, Brzezinski reiterates the guiding motifs of *End of History* without attribution and speaking on his own behalf. I have in mind his passages on the 'global political awakening' which mark our times and which the United States should take as its North Star when formulating foreign policy. The driving force of this awakening is the quest for human dignity as embodied in freedom, democracy and respect for cultural diversity.

Brzezinski is describing what in another age was called the *Zeitgeist*, or spirit of the times. It is a notion which belongs firmly in the 19th century and may be associated with Idealism. The content of the particular *Zeitgeist* which Brzezinski is promoting happens to be Hegelian Positivism, of which Fukuyama was a popularizer, in the tradition of his teacher's teacher, the French-Russian émigré philosopher Alexandre Kojève-Kozhevnikov. In this tradition, the imperative of self-expression and dignity was taken back to Plato and the concept of thymotic pride of humankind.

It would be no exaggeration to say that Brzezinski himself was very receptive to the notions of Fukuyama and imbibed deeply at the well of Neoconservatism.

Like Brzezinski, Fukuyama eventually turned against the Neocons in the first term of the George W. Bush presidency when the excesses of the unilateralist policies they promoted within the administration became clear and the US proceeded to flaunt international opinion by invading Iraq.

In his 2006 work *After the Neocons*, Fukuyama cites the scholar Ken Jewitt on how after 9/11 the Bush-ites found the Marxian determinism of *The End of History* to be too laissez-faire and instead moved on to what could be called a Leninist foreign policy, meaning identifying where history was headed and accelerating the process by willful intervention.

Looking at the body of Brzezinski's writings from 1997 to 2008, I must conclude that this 'Leninist' feature of the Bush-ite Neoconservatives perfectly describes the working principles of Brzezinski's own foreign policy strategy: to identify the spirit of the times and proactively, consciously accelerate events during the window of opportunity one is granted for transformational purposes. This explains, by the way, his criticism of Bush Sr. for lacking vision and his disdain for the laid-back determinism of Bill Clinton during his first term in office when globalization replaced foreign policy strategy. His biggest disagreement with Bush Jr. was not the intent to transform but the crudeness and incompetence of the planners and implementers.

MORALITY ANYONE?

This brings us to the question of whether Brzezinski the idealist working for the grand cause of human dignity and fighting injustices is also guided by conventional morality. Unfortunately, the answer is a resounding 'no' as we learn under the shrewd questioning of David Ignatius in *Conversations* (pp 109-110).

The specific issue which Ignatius presented is very much in the news today: collateral damage and civilian deaths incurred when U.S. drones based in Afghanistan attack suspected Al-Qaeda leaders across the border in Pakistan and cause civilian casualties. Brzezinski responded in his characteristic hawkish manner, making plain that as far as he was concerned the principal question of whether to go in or not was feasibility of eliminating the enemy:

"It depends on the consequences of their flying. If they engage in strikes which kill a lot of locals in addition to suspected Al-Qaeda, *then it may not be productive.* You may breed more Al-Qaeda members than you destroy. But it's one of those judgments where it's very hard to generalize. If we have really hard-nosed evidence that some senior Al-Qaeda officials are in some area, and we really have a chance to knock 'em off, I suppose we should do it." [emphasis added]

With advisors like this, it is understandable why the United States does not recognize the jurisdiction of the International Criminal Court in The Hague.

Ad hominem

In American academic circles, it was traditionally not considered good form to bring up the national origins and do ethnic profiling when addressing one's debating opponent.. And indeed I would never suggest national characteristics are something carried in the genes. But they are carried in collective memory and shared culture, and in this respect it would be very inappropriate to keep silent about the past which undoubtedly has helped to shape Zbigniew Brzezinski's persona and the contours of political advice he has offered with some consistency over the past 5 decades.

I believe it becomes especially permissible when the subject himself can at times personalize politics and argue from ad hominem principles. In *Conversations,* he tells us about Putin's grandfather and mother as if they were relevant to explain current state policies of the Russian Federation.

I'll cut to the quick: Brzezinski is by predisposition a Polish Romantic, a bearer of Polish *messianism* which he has transposed to his adopted motherland. Moreover, you might say he imbibed his anti-Russian views with maternal milk.

It is commonplace these days to refer to the origins of the Neocon movement in a mostly Jewish milieu of erstwhile Menshevik sympathizers who became fervently anti-Communist, have family origins in the southeast Polish region called Galicia and received their education at CCNY in New York City. The outstanding cases for this phenomenon include the publicists Irving Kristol and Norman Podhoretz.

Why then should we be silent about where key anti-Communist…. and anti-Russian scholars who advised American presidents and senior American statesmen in the 1970s and later came from? These academic personalities include two former Poles, one Polish-Polish and the other Polish-Jewish, who were both holders of Harvard doctoral degrees from roughly the same period: Zbigniew Brzezinski and Richard Pipes, respectively. Brzezinski's curriculum vitae has already been summarized. In the case of Pipes, alongside his decades long career as senior professor of Russian history at Harvard, he served as foreign policy advisor to Senator Henry Jackson of Jackson-Vanik amendment fame and would likely have had a brilliant career in the nation's capital as foreign policy specialist had his sponsor not died prematurely. During the Reagan presidency, he was a member of the National Security Council and served as Director of East European and Soviet Affairs. He established his Neocon credentials as a member of the Committee of the Present Danger as from 1997.

Looking at the background of Brzezinski, the offspring of petty Polish nobility, it is an amusing coincidence to note that the family nest was not just anywhere in Poland but precisely in Galicia, the *Heimat* of our aforementioned Jewish Neocons. While Brzezinski has never sympathized with their strong pro-Israeli convictions and opposes their unilateralism, he clearly shares their belief in American exceptionalism and messianism.

The conviction that among all nations Poland has a mission to save humanity was a well-established feature of its 19th century Romantic movement. The notion that part of this mission was to defend the Catholic faith against the Tatar-Muscovite hordes to the East was written into the national ethos.

It was no accident that Poles provided a large contingent to Napoleon's Grande Armée in its Russian campaign as well as to lesser military actions on behalf of Liberté, Fraternité and Egalité. Pilsudski's war on the Reds was a continuation of a well-remembered national tradition.

For his part, Brzezinski reminds us in *Conversations* of the glorious democratic traditions of Eastern Europe going back to remote history: "Poland had the Magna Carta just after Britain. It had the second constitution in the history of political systems, after the American and before the French."

This same homeland of *Rzeczpospolita Polska* had quixotic procedures like the *liberum veto* which, in a context of struggle for survival amidst acquisitive neighbors in the 18th century assured its early disappearance from the map of Europe.

It is understandable that for public consumption Zbigniew Brzezinski is usually silent about his family background and the national traditions of his ancestors. To be most charitable, when you take the policies on NATO expansion into Ukraine and Georgia, on establishing the anti-missile system in Poland and the Czech Republic, on promotion of the Nabucco and trans-Caspian gas pipeline projects which are in the news today but which Brzezinski has been promoting for more than a decade, you must bear in mind his fundamentally flawed understanding of Russia, where the tendentiousness comes from and why it is so very dangerous for world peace.

REALISM AND REVISIONISM:

HENRY KISSINGER FROM *DIPLOMACY* TO *DOES AMERICA NEED A FOREIGN POLICY?*

PART ONE

Henry Kissinger needs no lengthy introduction. National Security Adviser and then Secretary of State to Presidents Richard Nixon and Gerald Ford, Kissinger was awarded the Nobel Peace Prize in 1973 for bringing the lengthy war in Vietnam to a conclusion. After leaving office following the Republican loss to Jimmy Carter in the 1976 elections, he established a very successful consultancy serving multinational corporations and foreign governments. His private life was followed closely for years by the paparazzi who reported on his romances and socialite habits to a curious general public.

Even in his late 80s, Dr Kissinger remains very much in the public eye. In 2009 he played a key role in preparations for the first summit between Presidents Obama and Medvedev in London on April 1st. His articles on current major issues in international affairs appear frequently in the *New York Times* and are carried in syndicated mainstream media.

Henry Kissinger's public persona was formed in academia, more specifically at Harvard University, where he graduated *summa cum laude* from the College and completed his doctorate in 1954. He directly proceeded to become a member of the faculty in Harvard's Department of Government and Center for International Affairs. His first book on *Nuclear Weapons and Foreign Policy* was published already in 1957 and brought him nationwide attention. A succession of scholarly works followed. From the very start of his academic career, he was invited down to Washington periodically to advise federal agencies on international security issues. He was drawn into the Foreign Relations Council. In the 1960s, he came to the attention of Nelson Rockefeller, whose presidential ambitions he served in the capacity of foreign policy aide. In 1968, he was taken on by Richard Nixon.

Notwithstanding his intense work for the federal government and then his years in business, Kissinger never let go of his intellectual preoccupations. In 1973, he published *A World Restored* based on his doctoral dissertation and dealing with the peace concluding the Napoleonic wars. His weighty tomes of memoirs from his government service in Washington culminated in *Years of Renewal,* published in 1999.

From among his many publications, there are within the post-Cold War period two which may be said to represent Kissinger's response to the new opportunities and risks of the 21st century and we shall examine them here at some length. These are his 835 page scholarly work *Diplomacy* published in 1994 and the facetiously titled *Does America Need a Foreign Policy?* published in 2001 .In a way these two works are highly complementary. The first is 95% backward looking, setting out the historical context for the present day division between American *realists* and *idealists* over how to understand and manage international relations and 5% forward looking, setting out policy recommendations for the present and future. The second book has an inverse relationship, consisting primarily of specific recommendations for American policy towards four major regions of the world and key individual countries within these regions based on principles of *Realpolitik* softened so as to be acceptable to an American readership. Abstract or philosophical observations taken from *Diplomacy* are thrown in as leavening along the way.

Although Henry Kissinger's *Curriculum Vitae* places him at the very center of the American foreign policy Establishment, the two volumes under consideration, particularly *Diplomacy* would, if authored by anyone of lesser prestige and proven gravitas, merit characterization as revisionism. These works are more critical, more revelatory of national weaknesses and misperceptions than one could find in the writings of many nonconformist or irresponsible intellectuals in ivory towers.

Kissinger himself would probably vehemently deny that anything like revisionism was his intention. It emerges time and again as an almost involuntary subtext which, despite his praise in major for the positive contributions of his homeland to peace and justice worldwide over the past century by acting out the national myths, nonetheless carries a minor motif which is derogatory of those same myths and of simplistic good-heartedness. He never lets us forget how peace and justice are often contradictory objectives before foreign policy makers and implementers.

Diplomacy

As you first leaf through the 835 page text of *Diplomacy* plus the Notes, it is to all appearances a textbook on how foreign relations were conducted in Europe and the United States over the course of 300 years with particular attention to the accepted notions of statecraft and the view of mankind these presuppose. The frequent repetition of general conclusions throughout the book suggests that the publishers expected readers would not have the patience to swallow it at one go but would possibly see in it a reference work to be dipped into as needed. Kissinger's dedication of the book to officers of the U.S. Foreign Service adds to this view.

However, nothing could be more erroneous than this initial impression. Upon full reading, it becomes clear that the author had a very insistent message, one which is not so much scholarly as practically oriented, to guide and inform an appreciation of what must change in American thinking and practices to deal with the new international landscape of the post-Cold War world. The book was meant to be very topical in 1994 and it has become even more so today following the experience of two presidencies, Democratic and Republican, in which outworn policies and mentalities proved their inability to deal with the present and future much as Kissinger had reasoned.

Like any classic, *Diplomacy* operates on several different levels and appeals to readers having different interests and objectives. This is a history of statecraft, but one that has been selectively assembled with enormous care by a seasoned educator to serve immediate needs.

In *Diplomacy*, Professor Kissinger delivers what could be masterful lectures to undergraduates, describing events and statesmen in an entertaining manner and ending each segment in small discoveries or paradoxes, drawing parallels between the past and the present that are useful for mnemonic purposes. At the same time, he conducts a graduate class elucidating the big picture, in this case the vindication of realism and a severe rebuke to idealism in the management of international affairs.

Competing Principles

By *realism* is meant the focus on national strategic interests in a world where moral considerations may be a guide to ultimate objectives but the amoral calculus of relative power and feasibility determine day-to-day conduct of international affairs. By *idealism* is meant the values-based management of international affairs serving universalist principles and altruistic commitments.

In the first quarter of the book, Kissinger deals with the formative periods and, in particular, the personalities who contributed significantly to the evolution of the concepts and practices of power-oriented statecraft. This begins in the 17th century, which in the terms of the Peace of Westphalia (1648) established the modern notion of the nation state in sovereign control of its domestic affairs and in the diplomacy of French minister Richelieu practiced *raison d'etat* to guide the defense and expansion of the nation state by all means fair or foul.

We then follow step by step the formulation of the 'balance of power' concept in 18th century England where it meant occasional intervention in Continental power arrangements at turning points to prevent the emergence of hegemonic control by any one power. Next we are led through the golden age of *realism* following the Congress of Vienna in 1815 which ended the Napoleonic Wars, established a Europe-wide status quo based on shared values of conservative dynasts and kept the peace for two generations. We arrive finally at the age of Bismarck and the launch of *Realpolitik,* entailing the judicious use of raw force to achieve national objectives followed by the implementation of a new 'balance of power' model weaving direct ties with all competing powers to prevent hostile blocs from forming among those countries which lost out in the new pecking order.

This survey course in the evolution of what we would today call a geopolitical or geostrategic approach to international affairs drives home several distinct points. Firstly, this concept of diplomacy was built on a specific understanding of human behavior as selfish and competitive, in which the normal condition of relations between states is a clash of interests from which is distilled an ultimate harmony in the form of the 'balance of powers' preventing any one from exercising tyranny over the others. Secondly, this assumes shifting alliances among several states of similar strength to preserve the balance. Thirdly, to succeed best it should be supported by a common sense of legitimacy.

We see that the school of power-oriented diplomacy was developed on European soil. Along with other Enlightenment political concepts, it was well known on American shores in the British colonies where it found exponents among the Founding Fathers of the United States in such outstanding states-men as Alexander Hamilton. However, in Kissinger's view, the overwhelming majority of leaders of the new country, among them Thomas Jefferson, was unsympathetic to the political habits of the Continental Europe under the *ancien régime* as much as to the former colonial master, believing instead in the *exceptionalism* of their young democracy and in the universalist values it represented. They held that, unlike the absolutist monarchies, nations built on democratic principles of popular representation would naturally live in harmony and peace. They warned against entanglements in European affairs and took comfort in the security provided by a vast ocean separating them from the disputes of another world. Thus, during most of the 19th century America pursued a stance of isolationism with respect to the Continent. For-eign policy was limited to implementation of the Monroe Doctrine and keep-ing the Western Hemisphere free of interference by the European powers.

The growing mercantile and industrial power of the new republic and the increasing interdependence of the world powers towards the end of the 19th century brought America willy-nilly face to face with the challenge of form-ing a proper foreign policy of worldwide dimensions. This was first met in the new century by President Theodore Roosevelt, who was a sophisticated practitioner of statecraft in the European tradition.

And this approach was countered by his successor, Woodrow Wilson, who developed the theses of an *idealist* approach to foreign policy which became the bedrock of American thinking for most of the 20th century.

In Kissinger's précis, the key elements of Wilsonianism were ethnic self-determination, collective security instead of military alliances, open rather than secret diplomacy. Wilson's vision was an international order defended by moral consensus rather than force of arms. The League of Nations, con-sisting mostly of democratic states, would be the trustee for peace.

The whipping boy of the Wilsonian idealists was the 'balance of power,' which was held accountable for Europe's tragic military conflicts of the past and, in particular, World War I, which drew America into the Old Continent's suicidal civil war against its will 'to make the world safe for democracy.'

Having established the origins and meaning of the opposing principles of *realism* and *idealism* in the conduct of international affairs, Kissinger devotes about 600 pages to exploring how in practice these concepts shaped the major historical events of modern times: World War I, the Versailles Treaty and its follow-on conventions, World War II and the Cold War

INTERPLAY OF REALISM AND IDEALISM IN THE 20TH CENTURY.

Kissinger's overriding message is that supposedly cynical and amoral *realistic* politics often do good in practice and that moralizing *idealism* has often led to disasters. Kissinger painstakingly argues that the 'balance of power' was not to blame for the general European conflagration which broke out in 1914; to the contrary it was precisely the wearing away of the prerequisites for the balance beginning in the 1890s which removed essential restraints on what became a doomsday machine. He tells us that the explicit rejection of geostrategic considerations to guide the peace settlement after the Great War and their replacement by universalist principles of ethnic self-determination and collective security under the tutelage of Woodrow Wilson made possible the eventual return of Germany to the position of dominance on the Continent which it enjoyed before the war since it no longer faced mighty empires on its eastern frontiers but instead contrived buffer states lacking the means to protect themselves. Meanwhile the draconian but unenforced terms of the peace provided grist for the resurgence of German nationalism and *revanchisme*.

Moreover, Kissinger says it was the demoralization of Western statesmen compounded by their lack of confidence in the unfamiliar new tools of diplomacy imposed by Wilson which set in train the pattern of behavior later called *appeasement* of German demands for rectification of the injustices in the Versailles settlement, leading ineluctably to the outbreak of WWII. Kissinger draws a straight line from the 1922 Treaty of Locarno to the Munich pact of 1938.

Turning to the Cold War, Kissinger takes the sources back to the inability of President Franklin Delano Roosevelt, given his idealist mindset on the conduct of foreign relations, to accept the good advice of his realist Ally, British Prime Minister Winston Churchill, and strike a deal with Stalin over what the map of postwar Europe would look like. The proposal was made by Churchill in 1942 and Kissinger assures us that if pursued at the time it could well have resulted in Stalin's settling for the restoration of the USSR's 1941 borders, meaning a democratic Eastern Europe.

However, during the war FDR rejected the kind of horse trading Churchill had in mind. Like Woodrow Wilson thirty years earlier, the American President believed the war was being fought over grand principles, not for the sake of adjustments to national borders in Europe. His vision of the post-war world was of the victors, the United States, the United Kingdom, Russia and China, constituting Four Policemen to keep the peace worldwide under an international order of collective security. Moreover, Roosevelt and his close advisers had convinced themselves of the trustworthiness of 'Uncle Joe' and refused to be drawn into Churchill's machinations, which they believed were motivated by Britain's selfish interest in preserving its empire.

After the war, Stalin took the matter of European borders into his own hands, furthering the state interests of the USSR without any initial resistance from the American allies. In effect he created buffer states to protect against any possible aggressive threat from Germany in the future. Stalin's meeting with the new American President in Potsdam in July 1945 was a dialogue of the deaf in which Truman attempted in vain to advance FDR's agenda of collective security and avoided geopolitical settlements.

Nonetheless, Kissinger contends that as late as 1946, while the U.S. held an overwhelming strategic advantage over Russia as the only nuclear power, the Americans could quite possibly have reached agreement with Stalin on the *Finlandization* of Eastern Europe if they listened to the urgings of Churchill at that time. Throughout the region this would have meant normal democratic societies with market economies subject only to the condition of their neutrality and the understanding they would not pursue anti-Soviet policies.

Instead, President Truman and his team were already looking in other directions for solutions. By 1947 this led to the adoption of the 'containment policy' drafted by George Kennan. The American administration now turned its back on Moscow as untrustworthy and established the principle that it would wait out regime change in Russia before re-entering substantive negotiations over the post-war settlement. The division of Europe into spheres of influence was well under way, advanced by the Marshall Plan and NATO, America's first ever peacetime defense alliance. A final window of opportunity to reach a better deal with the Soviets over the fate of Germany opened by Stalin's peace initiative in 1952 was allowed to lapse without due response

This takes us approximately half way through the century and half way through Kissinger's text devoted to elucidating the interplay of *realism* and *idealism* in 20th century American foreign policy. His narrative on the Korean War, the Suez Crisis, the Hungarian revolution of 1956, the Berlin Crisis of 1958-63 and the Vietnam War are always insightful and authoritative. He systematically peppers the narrative with side remarks on the geostrategic mindset of Russian, French and other foreign leaders versus the frequently moralizing idealism, appeal to legality and the like practiced by the leading American statesmen involved in the given issues.

Time and again Americans' failure to see conflicts in terms of national interests at odds and their invoking grand and righteous principles when commencing military action hindered the definition of war objectives and so prolonged fighting needlessly. Kissinger tells us that "[t]he Wilsonian approach to foreign policy permitted no distinction to be made among the monsters to be slain." Accordingly poor decisions were taken on where to make a stand against what was (mistakenly) perceived to be a centrally directed worldwide Communist threat. After the grand prize of China was lost to the Maoists without significant American involvement, the Americans engaged 'the enemy' in Korea and then later in Vietnam at great cost and for meager results.

There is a special interest in Kissinger's discussion of the 1970s diplomacy of détente with the Soviet Union which was buttressed by the opening of relations with China in a triangular relationship. After Theodore Roosevelt, Nixon was the unique instance of an American President believing in and practicing traditional European-style geopolitical statecraft. In Nixon's achievements Kissinger is able to show what good professional analysis of national interest can yield when properly executed.

When Kissinger dusts off 'balance of power' politics to show its merits and when he marshals vast material for his exposé of the failures of Wilsonian idealism in practice, these are not an end in themselves. It is his overriding purpose to bring to the reader's attention the relevance of geopolitical strategy and especially 'balance of power' calculations to today's needs.

Kissinger states this plainly in the very first chapter and returns to it in the final chapter of specific recommendations on a U.S. foreign policy country by country. He argues that the recent liberation of Eastern Europe from Communist domination, followed by the collapse of the Soviet Union created conditions markedly different from those which predominated during the forty years of the Cold War, conditions much less amenable to management by an ideologically driven, oversimplified American approach to international affairs.

In the new world order taking shape, power will be more diffuse, he tells us, and 'almost every situation is a special case.' Under these circumstances, American foreign policy will have to be more subtle, attuned to the challenges and opportunities of a multipolar world which resembles more the Europe of the 19th century than the bipolar world of the recent past. And in that new-old world, the practices of balance of power typically spurned by today's American politicians as they have been in much of the past century since Woodrow Wilson can make a very positive contribution.

IS IDEALISM AN UNAVOIDABLE OR IMMUTABLE FEATURE OF AMERICAN FOREIGN POLICY?

As I have noted, Kissinger sees the modern archetypes for American practitioners of *realist* versus *idealist* foreign policy in Presidents Theodore Roosevelt and Woodrow Wilson respectively.

Judging by his characterizations of each, there can be little doubt that Kissinger identifies with Roosevelt, whose mastery of 'balance of power' diplomacy was so complete as to earn him America's first Nobel Prize for Peace in recognition of the way he brought the Russo-Japanese War to a satisfactory conclusion. Kissinger admires Roosevelt's worldly wise sophistication and clearly shares Roosevelt's belief that that America is finally a power like any other which must pursue its national interests on the grand chessboard following the European rules and exercise its power prudently. He matches Theodore Roosevelt with Richard Nixon whom he so closely assisted during his own period in power.

At the same time, Kissinger acknowledges that the great reputation and influence of Wilson on American foreign policy thinking for the century which followed was not accidental. The realist Theodore Roosevelt lacked the skills to persuade the nation to enter World War I after he became convinced that it was in America's national interest to oppose Germany, Wilson ultimately led his isolationist compatriots to war by means of his inspirational message of a crusade to spread universal liberties:

"Roosevelt understood how international politics worked among the nations then conducting world affairs – no American president has had a more acute insight into the operation of the international systems. Yet Wilson grasped the mainsprings of American motivation…that America did not see itself as a nation like any other.."

This insight is emblematic of Kissinger's quandary over the merits and drawbacks of his adopted homeland. He tries mightily to deal with this as an irony, as if the negatives were an unavoidable side of the indispensable positive contributions America brings to the world.

Exactly the same question arises in Kissinger's treatment of Franklin Delano Roosevelt, who, as we saw, Kissinger identifies as an enthusiastic disciple of Wilson. FDR was not indifferent to power relations but spoke of them if at all in what we would now call politically correct language. Otherwise he used guile and skirted the limits of his constitutional powers to pursue his objectives.

Kissinger's appreciation of FDR is at times an exact repetition of what he extolled in Wilson: "Few American presidents have been as sensitive and perspicacious as Franklin Delano Roosevelt was in his grasp of the psychology of the people. Roosevelt understood that only a threat to their security could motivate them to support military preparedness. But to take them into a war, he knew he needed to appeal to their idealism in much the same way that Wilson had."

Here Kissinger's delving into the ironies of history is more than the professional habit of a skilled and popular lecturer. His juxtaposition of Churchill and FDR later in the narrative reminds us of his previous matching of Theodore Roosevelt and Wilson: "Churchill's geopolitical analysis proved far more accurate than Roosevelt's. Yet Roosevelt's reluctance to see the world in geopolitical terms was the reverse side of the same idealism which had propelled America into the war and enabled it to preserve the cause of freedom."

And as our final citation relating to FDR which bears on the same issue and is important for understanding Kissinger's feelings about his adopted homeland, we find the following: "Roosevelt's conception of the postwar world may have been far too optimistic. But in light of American history, this position almost surely represented a necessary stage that America needed to traverse if it hoped to overcome the crisis ahead."

Turning to the Truman Administration, Kissinger remarked on the way brilliant geostrategic innovations such as the Marshall Plan and NATO were presented to the nation and the world at large under the ideological cover of Wilsonian universal principles in an enlarging struggle between good and evil.. In the case of Secretary of State Dean Acheson, a man of great sophistication, Kissinger assumes this was a matter of playing the political game by the rules in force in Washington. Kissinger says nothing of the President himself, but given his relatively modest background, past unfamiliarity with the intricacies of foreign policy and down-to-earth personality, we may assume the intellectual contradictions were not a matter of great concern to him.

Kissinger approves of the subterfuge and possibly self-deception which made it possible to get around the predilections of the American people and much of the political Establishment. Although he explains to us how FDR spent three years educating the public on the need to combat Hitler, he does not ask himself why the final appeal had to be to American idealism rather than self-interest.

Is the American psyche which has evolved in so many ways over the past century of industrialization, urbanization and now globalization truly immutable with respect to the principles which drive foreign policy? Could the one *Realpolitik* president of the second half of the 20th century have done something to change the country's thinking in this domain?

This is a question which Kissinger addresses in *Diplomacy* only superficially and unconvincingly. He devotes substantial narrative to the stunning foreign policy successes of the Nixon Administration. Nixon and Kissinger opened relations with the People's Republic of China and leveraged the relationship to bring the Soviet Union into a relationship of détente which significantly reduced Soviet adventurism, reduced the flash points in Europe and, incidentally, brought the United States out of the Vietnam quagmire in a strategically undiminished posture. Yet, these achievements were, by his admission, to no avail in taming domestic critics of *Realpolitik* or in overturning the American infatuation with Wilsonian idealism

Kissinger rather lamely explains that Nixon simply ran out of time. When the successes were safely in house, the Watergate scandal broke out at the start of his second term and the President's prestige was sapped to the point where he no longer enjoyed the moral leadership to bring about changed perceptions of how to manage foreign policy either in the Establishment or among the broad public.

However, I think this explanation is disingenuous. It was hardly in the personality of Richard Milhous Nixon to educate the public. It was much more in character to use of the levers of power silently to get his way and to circumvent Congressional controls. It is a great pity that Kissinger himself never undertook this educational mission in the past. He seems to have limited his efforts to distancing himself from the domestic misdeeds of the Nixon White House and rebutting the charges of his detractors from the right and left over the alleged moral failings of détente. In this context, the writing of *Diplomacy* may finally be Henry Kissinger's greatest contribution to the cause of re-educating America – if only the public and its representatives can be made to see its relevance for the foreign policy challenges before us.

REVISIONISM

As I have indicated at the start of this essay, Kissinger presents in *Diplomacy* what must be called a revisionist history of diplomatic affairs in the 20th century. This is not the result of original new research or access to hitherto inaccessible archives and primary sources. Nor does Kissinger appear to be saying anything that you could not find in the scholarly tomes of others. The extraordinary element here is *who* is saying this and with what intent.

It is widespread practice for retired high civil servants, not to mention former Secretaries of State to accept university professorships in their retirement, to conduct graduate courses and share their insights into statecraft with the up and coming generation. However, what we have in Kissinger is not some ex-official with a law degree assuming a scholarly pose but a full-blooded scholar taking his own conclusions as well as those of others in the historical profession, reflecting on them with the benefit of his own life experience as formulator and practitioner of foreign policy, and serving this up for the edification of the general public to make a programmatic statement that could shake people in power out of their comfortable and homely truths if they took the time to wade through his vast text.

Kissinger's narrative covers many of the major 20th century international issues and revisionist interpretations crop up in a number of places. I will limit myself here to mention of two separate instances where the conventional wisdom which Kissinger overturns has been preached to the American public by its political class, both Democrats and Republicans alike, for decades, to the detriment of intelligent analysis and pragmatic problem solving today.

The first is the question of *appeasement* of a brutal dictator as the major contributing cause to the Second World War. The second concerns our understanding of how and why the Cold War started, more particularly whether it could have been averted if our political leaders had been cleverer or less blinkered by accepted truths.

The question of moral responsibility for the outbreak of World War II remains hotly debated among present day leaders of Europe as we saw in the commemorative events of September 1, 2009 marking the 70th anniversary of the war's outbreak.

It is a sign of how politicized the past has become when serving today's leaders in Central and Eastern Europe, that Germany, the country which started the war was given a pass by the organizers and media at the September 1st ceremony, while suspended judgment shifted to Russian Prime Minister Putin whose speech was very closely watched..

In an interview with the Polish newspaper *Gazeta Wyborcza* just days before the ceremony, Putin acknowledged the cynical and immoral nature of the Ribbentrop-Molotov pact which many Poles consider a significant factor in the German attack by ensuring no two-front war would follow. In his speech on the 1st, Putin called upon other nations to accept their forebears' own guilt in making the war possible, indeed inevitable.

Putin's remarks were notable for highlighting the complexity of causality and shared guilt of world leaders. In fact he was saying no more than what Kissinger sets out in *Diplomacy*. Yet Putin elicited very negative comment not only from the Polish Right but also from the U.K. tabloids which took umbrage at the hint of British accountability.

No top American officials were present in Gdansk for the commemorative ceremony. The blame game which marred the anniversary is not what American politicians engage in when drawing lessons from World War II to justify current policy decisions.

In American consciousness, *appeasement* occurred when British Prime Minister Neville Chamberlain accepted Hitler's demands on the Sudetenland at Munich in September 1938. The Munich agreement led directly to the partial dismemberment, then the complete conquest of Czechoslovakia. It set in train a belated British and French *démarche*, the drawing of a line in the sand making further Nazi expansion by force a *casus belli,* and this in turn resulted in a declaration of war when the Germans attacked the Polish positions outside of Danzig.

What we see every so often in the speeches of our highest officials is the association of *appeasement* with some character flaw in Chamberlain, a weak-kneed syndrome, so to speak, all of which is said to have resulted in catastrophe. Those who would lead us into the next overseas military adventure liken every tin-pot dictator to the psychopathic Hitler, both intent on and capable of regional if not worldwide domination. And the uniform response to such threat is resolve, sanctions and, *in extremis*, preventive military intervention.

What Kissinger has to say *Diplomacy* is dramatically different:

"Munich has entered our vocabulary as a specific aberration - the penalty of yielding to blackmail. Munich, however, was not a single act but the culmination of an attitude which began in the 1920s and accelerated with each new concession. For over a decade, Germany had been throwing off the restrictions of Versailles one by one...By conceding that the Versailles settlement was iniquitous, the victors eroded the psychological basis for defending it..."

In Kissinger's narrative we find appeasement of German interests took the upper hand in British policies almost as soon as Germany ceased to be a threat to Britain following their takeover of the German merchant fleet as partial reparations and the end of the German navy. War-ravaged France had a rather different understanding of their recent foe's potential threat given Germany's greater population and relatively intact industry, which contrasted with France's war-ravaged industrial zones. However, from the beginning the British were unsympathetic to French calls for a military alliance to ensure Germany stayed in line, seeing in France the greater threat to the status quo.

As if struck by a guilty conscience over the territorial concessions imposed on Germany by Versailles in the creation of Poland and by the incorporation of Sudeten Germans in Czechoslovakia against their will following the denial by the victors of a request to be assigned to German Austria, in the Locarno Treaty of 1922 which was the final phase of the peace settlement, the Western powers guaranteed only Germany's western frontiers while the Eastern borders enjoyed no such general recognition.

Indeed, in the Weimar Republic of Chancellor Stresemann a policy of superficial 'fulfillment' of the conditions of Versailles enabled the Germans to largely evade the war reparations and to challenge convincingly the disarmament of their country.

Driving home his core message in this book, Kissinger lays the ultimate blame for appeasement on the efforts of European statesmen to implement the principles of Wilsonian idealism in the Versailles Treaty and its related conventions down to Locarno in 1922 amidst general disillusionment with traditional European diplomacy. At the same time, Kissinger ends this lesson in the manner of the professor relishing paradoxes, telling us that this self-same Wilsonian idealism is what ultimately pushed Britain towards implacable opposition to Hitler and to a more vigorous fight than *Realpolitik* would ever have given rise to once the dictator's violation of its moral criteria was proven beyond doubt.

HENRY KISSINGER

FROM *DIPLOMACY* TO *DOES AMERICA NEED A FOREIGN POLICY?*

PART TWO

THE MISSED OPPORTUNITY TO AVERT THE COLD WAR

One of the most remarkable instances of revisionism in Henry Kissinger's *Diplomacy* is his treatment of Franklin Delano Roosevelt and the origins of the Cold War. At the time of his writing in 1994, the mood in the United States was celebratory, nay triumphalist. Notwithstanding forty years of 'containment' of Communism pursued unfailingly by a succession of American presidential administrations, for many Americans it was the morally sound, uncompromising spirit of Reaganism which brought about the abrupt collapse of the Soviet Union and its 'evil empire,' ending the Cold War. And here Kissinger is telling us with great authority and painstaking detail that the Cold War itself need not have come about if only FDR had listened to Churchill starting in 1942 and sat down with Stalin to agree on the post-war settlement in terms of 'balance of power' analysis. Indeed, Kissinger believes that as late as 1946 a deal could have been cut resulting in a neutral but free Central Europe enjoying market economies and democratic political structures. What was needed was for America to open its eyes and ears to the opportunities its military advantages afforded and engage Stalin in the kind of interests-based exchange his geostrategic analysis expected. Instead, after a brief and unsuccessful attempt to deal with the Russians within the terms of collective security set down by FDR, the new U.S. Administration of Harry Truman turned its back on all negotiations with the Russians to better rally its allies in Western Europe, thereby locking in place the spheres of influence on either side of the 'Iron Curtain' while it awaited regime change in Moscow.

Kissinger is saying, in effect, that the victory over Soviet Communism which Americans were toasting in the early 1990s thanks to their nation's standing true to its idealism merely overturned colossal problems created by that self-same idealism practiced by Reagan's predecessors in the White House four decades earlier.

Surely the boldness of Kissinger's revisionism on this issue arises from something closer to his heart than dispassionate historical research. Kissinger is defending his own record when he undercuts the hero worship of Reagan, since admirers of the policies of the 40th President were often explicitly critical of the détente approach to the USSR which was emblematic of the Nixon-Kissinger foreign policy. In this view, which was honed to perfection by the Neoconservatives, détente promoted accommodation with evil and so perpetuated it when the task should have been to vanquish evil.

Kissinger deals with this threat to his place in history and takes his revisionism one step further in his chapter on the end of the Cold War.

I have already cited in Part One of this essay Kissinger's identification of Reagan as an idealist in the tradition of Wilson and FDR. And while he insists that Reagan was his own man with fixed and consistent views who was not merely the communicator of messages prepared by his speechwriters, Kissinger does not hesitate to remind us that this President had 'the shallowest academic background.'

When he was in office, it was often said of Reagan by both his followers and his detractors that the man was *lucky* - and you don't argue with luck. Kissinger picks up this characterization and fleshes it out to explain why the collapse of the Soviet empire happened on Reagan's watch.

It was fundamentally a question of timing. Reagan's confrontational policies could have worked at the very beginning of the Cold War, achieving a settlement with Stalin that averted the division of Europe in the manner proposed at the time by Churchill. On the other hand, if Reagan had come to power in the middle of the Cold War, his words and deeds would have only provoked a dangerous and unproductive clash with Moscow while straining relations within the North Atlantic Alliance. In that period of a still dynamic and aggressive Soviet leadership, Nixon's policies of détente were both appropriate and effective.

By arriving in Washington when he did and implementing policies of military build-up and rhetorical pressure on a Soviet regime which had already become fragile, Reagan administered a push which hastened the demise of Soviet Communism. Whether these policies were based on intuition or analysis is academic.

For the Neoconservatives in the early 1990s, the apparent success of actively opposing the evil of Communism reinforced their missionary zeal to advance democracy and human rights in those parts of the world still living under tyranny so as to realize the dream of Jefferson, a world of democracies living in peace and the natural state of harmony.

Starting from his very different interpretation of the contribution of American idealist ideology to seeing off Soviet Communism, as well as from his different evaluation of the international landscape of the emerging post-Cold War world, Kissinger issued his programmatic statement:

"...the Reagan foreign policy was more in the nature of a brilliant sunset than of the dawn of a new era. The Cold War had been almost made to order to American preconceptions. There had been a dominant ideological challenge rendering universal maxims, however oversimplified, applicable to most of the world's problems. And there had been a clear and present military threat, and its source had been unambiguous...In the post-Cold War world, there is no overriding ideological challenge or ...single geostrategic confrontation. Almost every situation is a special case."

This is the message which guided Kissinger's writing of the very last chapter in *Diplomacy* in which he sets out his specific recommendations for American foreign policy around the world.

THE NEW WORLD ORDER RECONSIDERED

Assuming that professional readers would restrict their perusal of *Diplomacy* to the final chapter in which he moved from history to his analysis of the present state of international relations and offered advice on future policy, Kissinger spent the first few pages restating his lessons from the 800 preceding pages.

As might be expected, he argued the case for geopolitical analysis to inform policy formulation. He called for differentiating between challenges and prioritizing diplomatic efforts on issues of critical national interest while husbanding resources and avoiding making blanket commitments. The only strategic threat facing the United States would be domination of either Europe or Asia by a single power.

Though a superpower militarily, America would have to accept that it was finally a nation like the others. This was not a sign of national decline but merely the reestablishment of the situation prevailing through most of its history.

He tells us that America should stop trying to remake the world in its own image, but that its foreign policy must nonetheless reflect its core values so as to resonate with the public. It should attempt to forge the broadest possible moral consensus around the world. Here Kissinger makes his peace with his adopted homeland and tries to put behind him the lingering charges of being cynical and amoral.

In the *tour d'horizon* of countries and regions which follows, Kissinger applies the discerning, case by case approach. He pauses to reflect on the various challenges in relations with Russia, the European Allies, Central Europe, China and Japan, and the Western Hemisphere. He stresses the need to pay attention to history, geography and all the local specifics rather than broad-brush application of universal maxims.

Compared with the policies of the last Republican Administration of George Bush, Sr. and the current Democratic Administration of Bill Clinton, Kissinger offers few immediate changes of course. The most notable perhaps is his criticism of Clinton over NATO enlargement. As Kissinger reminds his readers, NATO is after all a military alliance and this must not be confused with an instrument of collective security which the recently created Partnership for Peace tended to do by bringing into NATO deliberations the views of not only the former Soviet satellite states of Central and Eastern Europe but also successor states of the Former Soviet Union. Kissinger urges that Hungary, the Czech Republic, Slovakia and Poland be fully integrated into Atlantic institutions as well as into the European Union. He also urges that NATO be reorganized to deal with 'out of area' threats.

The period 1993-1994 was a critical moment in US-Russian relations. In his 1993 visit to Warsaw, Boris Yeltsin withdrew his objections to Poland joining

NATO and in turn the Clinton Administration was weighing the possibility of extending full membership in the Alliance to Russia. It has to be said that at this juncture Henry Kissinger expressed his strong objections and played a significant role in the defeat of Russia's candidacy.

We can get a fairly good idea of Kissinger's reasoning in the passages relating to American policy on Russia generally in the last chapter of *Diplomacy*. His remarks here are completely in line with what he said about Russia and its imperial expansion in the chapters on 19th century European diplomatic history.

A *realistic* approach to Russia meant America had to look at the respective foreign policy interests and national traditions, and to pay less attention to domestic Russian politics and the personalities of its leaders. George Bush, Sr. had viewed Russia through the prism of facilitating relations with Mikhail Gorbachev, the man first tipped by Margaret Thatcher as someone you could do business with. Clinton was similarly building his Russian policy on the 'democrat' Yeltsin.

From Kissinger's standpoint, an appropriate policy towards Russia had to take into account the country's long tradition of expansionism, which he believed continued to be evidenced by Russian military bases in the former Soviet republics and interventionism in their 'near abroad.'

And as if to drive a stake through the heart of unnecessary chumminess with Moscow, Kissinger reminded his readers that Russia had always stood apart from the Western world. It had no democratic traditions or familiarity with modern market economics.. In his words, it did not partake of the Reformation, the Enlightenment, the Age of Discovery.

Indeed, Kissinger's thinking about Russian history is so clear one might imagine he knows what he is talking about. That is an issue I will return to in a moment in my remarks about the methodology of his scholarship, when I also take up his understanding of history itself.

.The book ends with an appeal for the United States to apply 'balance of power' policies to its overall foreign policy in a manner that he believes will be both an improvement on the received practices and acceptable to his skeptical compatriots: maintaining open lines of communication and close relations with as many nations as possible through overlapping alliance systems in the manner of the grand master of *Realpolitik*, Otto von Bismarck.

METHODOLOGY

Diplomacy is not a work of new scholarship. A large part of the material on the history of diplomacy in the 17th – 19th centuries was surely taken from his lectures going back to the 1960s and, in turn, was anchored in his own dissertation research in the 1950s. The Notes point to classics in the field of European history, mostly published well before Kissinger's graduate studies. For the second half of the 20th century he draws on presidential papers and other documents published by the U.S. Government Printing Office, on his own private papers and recollections and on some unpublished writings of associates, as well as later monographs.

As critics of Kissinger's *Diplomacy* pointed out, he belongs to the 'great man' school of history, very conservative and very traditional. Given that diplomacy is almost everywhere even today the domain of the executive branch of government with little or no legislative supervision, the 'great man' approach is, by itself, not necessarily wrong-headed or currently inappropriate.

There has to be something truly dramatic going on in the body politic for foreign policy to generate so much heat that people go out onto the streets and bring down a regime. This happened in living memory when Lyndon Johnson resigned in the face of massive civil disturbances over the conduct of the Vietnam War. It is telling that in this unique situation Kissinger saw fit in *Diplomacy* to criticize Johnson for not resisting the popular tide and continuing to pressure Hanoi by massive offensive weaponry while the transition of power to a successor was going on.

Kissinger's conservatism as an historian has another dimension which commentators seem to have ignored totally. This is his adherence to the school of historical fact as kiln-fired bricks from which one can build a strong structure of interpretational certitude. This confidence in history as science is misplaced. There are many professionals today who walk more humbly with their God and acknowledge that their craft is an art, no more. If this is so, Kissinger's confidence in the safe footing of realism for formulation of foreign policy has to be questioned.

I would not begin to pass judgment on the quality of Kissinger's treatment of the vast swathes of world history he presents in *Diplomacy*. It is generally my practice to 'stick to my knitting,' which means Russian history. Though

Russia is not central to this particular book in the same way as it was central to Kissinger's government service in the 1970s, neither is it insignificant.

Kissinger's academic focus before he left the university for Washington was on European diplomacy in the 19th century. In the event, Russia was one of the three decisive players in the first half of the century (Holy Alliance) and one of the 5 or 6 decisive players in the second half of the century. Kissinger's inability to use Russian language materials was an undeniable disadvantage. In *Diplomacy* he shows us that he compounded the problem by relying on very dated 19th century classics of Russian history like Vasili Kliuchevsky.

Kliuchevsky is unquestionably a good starting point for students of Russian history. He was the father of the historiography that came down to Kissinger in the person of Michael Karpovich, the founder of Russian studies at Harvard who taught while Kissinger was a student and faculty member. But his comparative understanding of Russia's own *manifest destiny* of borders moving out across the Eurasian land mass was, shall we say, limited and by today's standards, reading him has mainly curiosity value. To put the issue in terms which will be closer to an American reader, it is as if Kissinger were using de Toqueville as the key source for writing about contemporary America.

Among the main 20th century works on Russia cited in Kissinger are those by his comrade in *realism*, George Kennan. Without question, George Kennan has a generally high reputation in Washington, where his 1946 'Mr.X' article in *Foreign Affairs* magazine setting out the theory of containment will always get a round of applause even if his shift in the 1970s to favor détente is graciously overlooked. Yet, it has to be said that he came to his scholarship only after a diplomatic career of variable success and he brought with him considerable intellectual baggage from his life experience. Kennan's choice of sources and interpretation of Russia is tendentious in ways that Kissinger is unable to judge; and this is why it is unsatisfactory that Kissinger does not bring in other sources.

Kissinger's argument in *Diplomacy* for the separateness of Russian history may be no more than the conventional wisdom of his times. His remark on page 140 that "Paradox was Russia's most distinguished feature' is a variation on Churchill's 1939 witticism about 'a riddle wrapped in an enigma.' But then Churchill was not a serious scholar and Kissinger is assumed to be one. The notion of separateness is in fact misleading if not fallacious.

Indeed, there was no Reformation in Russia, meaning no church-state conflict expressed in political treatises against absolutism. But to say that Russia missed the Enlightenment is simply ignorant. As for missing the Age of Discovery, Kissinger seems to forget about Russian naval adventurers in the northern seas, the discoverer of the Bering Strait, the colonizers of Alaska.

It is true that Tsarist Russia rightfully never enjoyed a reputation for practicing democracy, as Kissinger claims. But it had proto-democratic institutions of local self-administration going back to the 1860s (zemstvos). Parliamentary institutions of the variety Kissinger describes in the Germany of Bismarck came into existence under Nicholas II following the Revolution of 1905 and endured right down to the end of the regime.

Kissinger makes far too much of the seemingly unique Russian autocracy as it bears on his own specialty of diplomacy. He tells us that the Tsar's power was such in the 18th century that foreign alignments could be changed in a moment by imperial whim. I would ask firstly whether the same could not be said of the Habsburg Empire under Maria Theresa or Joseph I. And I ask secondly why Kissinger is overlooking the activity of cabals with the support if not direction of foreign embassies. The question surely surrounds foreign policy changes during the successive reins of Peter I's immediate female successors. It recurs in the pressures on the Russian court to adopt one or another position with respect to Napoleonic France and the murder of Emperor Paul I whose diplomatic initiatives seem to have gotten in the way.

But I will not cavil. The larger issue and the one bearing on Kissinger's prescriptions for a policy vis-à-vis Russia after the Cold War, as I already mentioned, is 'imperial expansionism.' Kissinger presents this as the defining national tradition. Reading this I must ask to what major world power, including the United States, such a tendency to fill all available space does not apply? National variations of imperialism were practiced by most of Europe and America in the 19th century just as they exist today with less colorful plumage. It is surprising to see Kissinger, the ultimate realist, find anything untoward in Russia's national egoism.

If we may approach the same issue from another angle, one could make the argument that for 250 years Russia was among the key world powers. It emerged on this stage in the second half of the 18th century and never left it. Therefore, how can one expect that the break-up of the Soviet Union and the shaking loose of its appendages after 1992 would change the determination of this nation to be a major world power once again. Even in its pre-imperial borders, the Russian Federation is more than 10% of the Earth's land surface with vast natural resources. Anyone who thinks it possible to compel such a nation to settle for the ranking of, say, a medium sized European state is ignoring history and geography.

It is regrettable to see Kissinger indulge in tired mystification of Russia when talking about Russia's 19th century nationalist movement for which he draws on the publicist Mikhail Katkov, Fyodor Dostoevsky and other sources which have literary merit but are less than scientific.

It is only by such smoke and mirrors that he can arrive at generalizations like the following which he would otherwise scorn as unduly psychological and irrelevant to foreign relations if, for example, someone served them up as a description of Germany:

"The paradox of Russian history lies in the continuing ambivalence between messianic drive and a pervasive sense of insecurity. In its ultimate aberration, this ambivalence generated a fear that, unless the empire expanded, it would implode."

It is rather sad to consider that one of the country's great scholar-statesmen of the 20th century was persuaded by mystical tripe when formulating and implementing the nation's policies towards its nuclear adversary. This puts in question the validity of attention to history and local specifics which Kissinger says are distinguishing features of *realism* versus *idealism* with its universalist over-simplifications.

DIPLOMACY IN THE BOOK REVIEWS

The outsized persona of Henry Kissinger, his intellectual brilliance, his challenge to academic scholars and people of action alike, ensured that the publication of *Diplomacy* would not pass without notice, nor would the work end up on the overstock tables of discount booksellers.

Soon after its publication, on March 28, 1994, *The New York Times* issued a review of *Diplomacy* by its staff literary critic Michiko Kakutani ('Books of the Times: A Policy Maker on the Subject He Knows Best"). The generally favorable commentary discerned very well that the author had several objectives at work, not merely to provide a reference work on statecraft. She chose to emphasize the way in which Kissinger was justifying his policies when in office and she finds these chapters more enlightening, because they provide more insight into his strategic thinking and are less burdened with detail, than his couple of massive volumes of memoirs devoted to the same period. She also aptly matches points made in *Diplomacy* over the period of Kissinger's government service with accusations and negative marks directed against him by his political detractors in the already very substantial literature of the day.

This particular review is noteworthy because it demonstrates magnificently that one does not have to be a foreign affairs specialist to pick through Kissinger's vast text and understand what he is about. Kakutani's formal education consisted of a B.A. in English literature from Yale University (1976). But then again, her hard work and intellectual prowess are out of the ordinary. In 1998 she was awarded the Pulitzer Prize for Criticism.

Perhaps the most piquant scandal surrounding the appearance of *Diplomacy* was touched off by Kissinger's former colleague at the Harvard Department of History and the Kennedy School of Government, a leading specialist on the uses of history for decision making, Professor Ernest R. May. Kissinger had crossed swords with May during the Vietnam War era in a behind closed doors spat in Washington over conduct of the war. Their 1994 exchange of courtesies took place in full public view in the pages of *The New York Times*.

The opening shot was May's three-page review of *Diplomacy* entitled "The 'Great Man' Theory of Foreign Policy," published in the *Times* on April 3, 1994. His critique was at once penetrating and picayune, respectful and vengeful. May's most dismissive comments were delivered right in the opening paragraph, when he called it "a book of maxims disguised as a history of statecraft. The maxims are often splendid. The history is not."

As May picked up, *Diplomacy* is most interesting for what it says about Kissinger himself and his world view, and this is not an inconsiderable attraction give the author's status as one of a handful of Secretaries of State who personally shaped foreign policy. In this regard, our first insight is Kissinger's reverence for power. Second, his 'great man' approach to history rather than looking at wider trends or the economic drivers. Third, without his identifying it as such, May points to the cynicism in many of Kissinger's characterizations, to what he identifies as Kissinger's contemptuous treatment of moralizing statesmen like Britain's 19th Prime Minister William Gladstone. He points to Kissinger's unconcealed attraction to the *sang- froid* and analytic skills of tyrants like Stalin

In all fairness, May also highlighted Kissinger's seeming appreciation of Wilson and Reagan for their ability to tap into the wellspring of American motivation to realize their policies whereas Kissinger concedes that realists like Theodore Roosevelt and Richard Nixon left the public unsatisfied emotionally and thus fell short in their objectives. Professor May saw in this and in Kissinger's occasional favorable mention of values as a necessary component of policy as an offsetting positive to the book. As noted above, I doubt Kissinger meant these seeming bouquets to *idealists* in earnest; they more likely reveal purely intellectual enjoyment of life's ironies.

It is interesting that May saw in *Diplomacy* parts having 'the mind-provoking quality of great teaching." By this he meant the author's ability to move back and forth between past and present to reveal unseen, even at first glance improbable likenesses that can provide practical direction to policy issues.

However, after distributing the flowers, Professor May concluded his essay with the judgment that Kissinger had written shoddy history, that he didn't get his facts straight telling us "'Diplomacy' makes the types of mistakes for which students fail to get pass degrees in history."

May faults Kissinger's survey for giving a spotty account of the history of diplomacy, for focusing on a relatively few major personalities and periods while ignoring whole epochs. Finally, he closed the review with a parting insult: "As a history, Mr. Kissinger's 'Diplomacy' is amateurish."

While this kind of personal, acrimonious attack may be commonplace in faculty dining rooms, it must have made titillating reading in *The New York Times*. Kissinger's response came in a letter published in the paper three weeks later, on April 24th. He answered directly the alleged factual errors, acquitting himself well. He moved the dispute to its broader philosophical level of his own insistent realism vs May's moralizing. He refuted the innuendo that he never met a dictator he did not like. And he dismissed as 'silly' the notion that his work was amateurish.

On May 1, 1994 *The New York Times* gave Ernest May the last word. He claimed Kissinger was ignoring the lavish praise he had given the book as a source of wisdom for generations to come even as he denied its quality as a history. And he elaborated on this very point in a way which has great relevance to the way the book has been generally received since:

"Mr. Kissinger's scholarly credentials and public stature give his name on the title page the quality of a Good Housekeeping Seal of Approval. Thousands of readers may think 'Diplomacy' an authoritative history of statecraft since the 17th century. Many may never look at another. That will be their loss, for the book does not take pains to reconstruct the past as the past rather than as a source of parables for the present."

In the autumn of 1994, *Orbis,* the journal of world affairs of the University of Pennsylvania, published a lengthy review of *Diplomacy* by its editor, Walter A. McDougall, Professor of History and Alloy-Ansin Professor of International Relations.

This excellent article is basically a review of reviews. McDougall describes briefly and very effectively the comments of some of the best minds in the profession, including May's critique in the *Times* with pertinent facts on relations of the two former Harvard colleagues, a very thought-provoking review by Simon Schama's in *The New Yorker* and contributions by Robert Tucker in *The National Interest*, Gordon Craig in *The New York Review of Books*, Michael Howard in *Foreign Affairs*, Peter Grier in *The Christian Science Monitor* and Robert Divine in *The Philadelphia Enquirer*. With few exceptions, the reviewers did not coddle Kissinger. McDougall himself points to some questionable interpretations throughout the work, though he finds chapters that are insightful, even superb (World War I from origins through peace-making). In the end McDougall gives *Diplomacy* high marks as a history:

"…Diplomacy is like an oriental carpet, as interesting for its flaws as its brilliant patterns. For it tells us much not only about the past but about history as a craft, about Kissinger himself, and (through our reactions to it) about ourselves. You can't ask much more of a history book."

McDougall directs particular attention to the question of Kissinger the foreign-born, the 'European' among us with his *Realpolitik* versus idealist native-born Americans, an issue raised by Robert Divine and several of the other reviewers. In McDougall's opinion the dichotomy between European power politics and American universalism is false. First, because Americans have never fully lived up to the ideals and second, because the ideals themselves were inspired by Europeans. We are urged not to confuse the rhetoric of American foreign policy with the substance based on national interest. In fact, such a compromise is what Kissinger himself is offering in *Diplomacy*, McDougall concludes.

McDougall also takes up the various opinions of reviewers about Kissinger's treatment of the Vietnam War. The most insightful comes from Divine, who sees a heresy in Kissinger's analysis which explains why he remains a stranger in American hearts: "First Kissinger indicts the 'idealistic' cold war liberals for the misapprehensions and hubris that got us into Vietnam, then he blames the 'idealistic' Vietnam protesters for contributing to the agony rather than a resolution, then he castigates the whole country for cracking up when it needed to pull together." Says Divine, this is not the verdict Kissinger's compatriots will be thankful for.

McDougall concludes his article by telling us that perhaps everyone has got it wrong. After all, the Founding Fathers received from Europe a doctrine of human imperfectability which led them to put separation of powers, checks and balances into the Constitution. Thus, says McDougall: "What we now think of as hard-boiled 'realism' is not some import carried to America by the likes of Hans Morgenthau or Henry Kissinger. It was fundamental to the classical wisdom on which the country was founded....Could it be, therefore, that Kissinger truly reflects the philosophical sobriety of our nation's founders? That Kissinger is more American than Wilson?"

In 2010 it is not possible to speak of the impact of a work like *Diplomacy* without taking into account the reviews on the sites of major book retailers, our modern day *vox populi*. The site of Amazon.com presently posts 89 customer reviews which give a fairly consistent impression of who is reading the master work and to what effect. The impression is that May's prediction of how the book would eventually be used was prescient.

It is sadly apparent that in their attempts to describe the experience of reading *Diplomacy* most of its lay reviewers are clutching at straws. Their comprehension of what Kissinger is trying to do is very superficial however much they like the narrative The author has so overwhelmed his amateur readership with his erudition that most are breathless and...happy that this outsider, this thinker in the European fashion, is 'on our side.'

Most reviewers in amazon.com view the book as a detailed history of the art of diplomacy written in a polished style which is enjoyable to read. One reader summed this up with memorable directness: "What surprised me was the quality and beauty of Mr. Kissinger's prose. This book is heavy on content, but not to the exclusion of the finer points of literature."

The amazon.com readers found in *Diplomacy* much fascinating information about how statesmen went about their business during major events of the past. To quote one enthusiast whose review was cited as being 'very helpful' by 75 out of 83 visitors to the site: "Important stuff, well articulated." Another calls it "easily the best single volume on diplomacy that I've ever read." Another glowingly satisfied reader came away with this remarkable conclusion from reading Kissinger: "....it is astounding how the errors and travails of one generation of diplomats set up the conditions for war or peace for the next. Indeed, one can trace back the antecedents of the cold war to the events in the Concert of Europe."

Of course a polarizing figure like Kissinger could not avoid receiving some brickbats, such as one caustic reader who commented: "This is a wonderful book. I especially love his winning descriptions on the William of Orange. Brilliant stuff. Too bad Kissenger is a liar and a war criminal. How can you reconcile the blood upon his hands and his obvious erudition, his wit, his intelligence? God knows."

But even those politically unsympathetic to Kissinger's politics seem to have been caught out: "As much as I despise the policies and actions of Henry Kissinger, I must confess that I found this book to be a very well thought out look at the major historical events of the past century..."

A small minority of readers of *Diplomacy*, including the one voted 'most helpful' in Amazon's poll of visitors to the site, appreciated the dominant theme of the swings in U.S. policy between *Wilsonian idealism* and *Realpolitik*. Yet it is not always clear that the substance of these concepts penetrated reader's minds and their occasional attempts to summarize the distinctions often show confusion.

Only one of the reviews spotted how Kissinger marshaled history to inform decisions which modern day statesmen face each day. It would appear future educators of American practitioners of 'Realpolitik' and 'balance of power' have their work cut out for them.

Henry Kissinger

from *Diplomacy* to *Does America Need a Foreign Policy?*

Part Three

Does America Need a Foreign Policy?

This book was written in 2001 before the September 11th attack on the World Trade Center and followed the American tradition of seasoned experts in the field of foreign policy giving advice to the new Prince either prior to the presidential election or soon after the new Administration is put in place.

In his campaign for the presidency, George W. Bush suggested that he favored constraining foreign policy more narrowly to the defense of America's geopolitical interests. He and his supporters were especially critical of the many humanitarian interventions of the Clinton Administration. Accordingly it was reasonable to expect that the new Washington team would be receptive to pragmatic policy recommendations from the grand master of *Realpolitik*.

Why the title?

The facetious title arose from Kissinger's positioning of the book as a critique of the foreign policy of the Clinton Administration, which professionals on both sides of the aisle in American politics faulted at the time for the President's apparent belief globalization could substitute for a foreign policy in the post-Cold War world when there was no longer a global enemy to confront. In a way, Clinton's domestic priorities ("It's the economy, stupid!") carried over into his treatment of international affairs.

Kissinger chose to deal with Bill Clinton's eight years in office as one seamless period, though there were significant policy differences from the first term, when Warren Christopher was Secretary of State and brought an inbasket-outbasket approach to the job, and the second term, when that post was filled by Madeleine Albright, who clearly had an agenda of foreign policy objectives to achieve during her tenure, whatever the President's personal enthusiasms. Her agenda, of course, was rather close to that of her one-time mentor and boss, Zbigniew Brzezinski.

Kissinger sees in Bill Clinton and his close foreign policy advisers an ideological predisposition towards *idealism* and an antipathy to foreign policy strategy. The roots were generational. In the person of the President, Kissinger was dealing with precisely the generation of Vietnam War protesters who had so complicated his efforts to end the war with U.S. honor intact, as he told us at length in *Diplomacy*. The self-righteous idealism of those protesters had turned against Washington. They condemned the war policy of Lyndon Johnson and then of Richard Nixon and Kissinger on grounds that America had shown itself to be unworthy of its high ideals. Thus they called upon the country to lower its profile in the world.

In *Does America Need a Foreign Policy?* Henry Kissinger continues to educate the general public on the two opposing overarching concepts of foreign policy which have dominated thinking in America for the past 100 years, *idealism* and *realism*. He also stops to consider several sub-schools which have moved to center stage since the fall of Communism. One dates back to the middle of the 19th century (*Jacksonian isolationism*) and the other is of more recent coinage, *Neoconservatism* dating from the 1970s.

After dispatching the competing notions, Kissinger proceeds to concentrate on his recommended choice, a foreign policy built on *realism*. This means formulating policy to best defend America's national interests. It means calculating carefully respective power relationships vis-à-vis other state actors and the feasibility of implementing your preferred objectives. This, in turn, assumes that policy makers have at their command an in-depth knowledge of the specifics of each given country and region, in contrast to Wilsonian *idealism,* where the U.S. stretches a one-size-fits-all policy across the globe in the mistaken belief that people everywhere have the same interests and that any conflicts which may arise are just due to misunderstandings.

We have already seen in Part Two of this essay how Kissinger's command of Russian history failed to meet his own requirement of good country expertise essential to the success of a realist foreign policy. In our examination of his 2001 book, we will come back to this very question because it bears on the much more detailed policy recommendations he issues here and on why, in the end, his recommendations country by country are often not so different from those delivered by his intellectual opponents, the idealists.

Though Kissinger deploys in his 2001 work many of the lessons about the workings of international relations which he set out previously in *Diplomacy,* here they are just connective glue between very detailed advice for Washington to follow.

The problem with writing a book which has so direct and immediate an objective is that it very quickly becomes dated, whereas his historical interpretations and theoretical musings in *Diplomacy* are and will long remain a classic. Also by the very specificity of the author's recommendations he exposes himself to ridicule if he gets any of his facts wrong. Given the vast scope of his enterprise, it was inevitable this would happen in at least a couple of instances.

Indeed, it is much easier to say what foreign policy should not be – dogmatic and ideologically driven – than to say what *realism* dictates. One man's strategy is another's tactics. And as Kissinger himself argued in his treatment of Napoleon III in *Diplomacy*, a winning analysis of relative power requires great acumen. He might have added that a winning policy also requires a good measure of luck.

KISSINGER'S GROUPING OF NATIONS TO GUIDE FORMULATION OF FOREIGN POLICY

For purposes of policy formulation, Kissinger divides the world into four international systems. These groupings are defined by the political and economic structures operating within the specified countries and by the kind of interstate-relations they practice among themselves. Each region requires its own approach from American policy-makers:

1) *The United States, Western Europe and the Western hemisphere.* Here we find democratic nations with market economies living peacefully with one another. The principles of *Wilsonian idealism* apply.

This section of the book is probably the most focused on the question of how the end of the Cold War has changed the international landscape and the issues currently facing US foreign policy. Why? Because the North Atlantic Alliance was the bedrock of US foreign policy and for a number of reasons that partnership has now experienced greater difficulty than heretofore.

In Western Europe, the collapse of the Soviet threat deprived the relationship with the U.S. of a unifying principle. Meanwhile, the European Union proceeded with its expansion and consolidation. These processes led to a bureaucratization of its relations with America and major fissures appeared in the North Atlantic alliance. Kissinger devotes considerable attention to the European military force and its relationship to NATO, missile defense systems and to expansion of free trade pacts.

As for the Western hemisphere, Kissinger takes us by the hand through foreign policy options. He relates at some length the history, the current political context and individual statesmen of Brazil, Argentina and Mexico. However, the central issue he sees for American policy in the region is economic. He credits the North American Free Trade Agreement negotiated by George Bush, Sr. and ratified early in the Clinton presidency with driving significant progress in relations with Mexico and other participating states. He faults Clinton for not doing more. Specifically, the United States should seek accommodation with Mercosur where possible and expand free trade at every opportunity. He spends less time on areas like Colombia with intractable problems of the drugs cartels and guerrilla warfare.

2) *The great powers of Asia*: India, China, Japan, Russia, Korea, Southeast Asia. They treat one another as strategic rivals. War among them is not inconceivable, though not imminent. Their approach to foreign relations is the traditional 'balance of power' as practiced in the 19th century. Kissinger explicitly rules out the applicability of Wilsonian principles to managing relations with countries in the region given the near absence of democracies there.

The American objective in Asia should be to ensure that no one nation or bloc emerges to dominate the region, particularly an adversarial one. It must be recalled that this is a homely truth shared by nearly all American foreign policy specialists, whether they place themselves in the *realist* camp or otherwise.

Kissinger's overriding advice in this situation is for America to follow the centuries-long tradition of the British with respect to the European Continent and seek to maintain equilibrium by throwing its weight to the weaker powers against the strongest. At the same time, the U.S. should seek to maintain good relations and open lines of communication with all the nations of the region.

Here Kissinger makes one obvious misstep which bears on his overall prioritization of relationships. This arises from his expectation that the Japanese economy will remain number one in Asia for at least 25 years to come. In fact, as we now know, just nine years after his writing, 2010 is likely to be the year when China overtakes Japan as the leading Asian economy and number two in the world after the United States. It is not a very impressive demonstration of this consultant's predictive powers to have been so very wrong.

Having set out the conceptual framework, Kissinger plunges into details of political history and current trends in the major countries of the region, particularly Japan and the PRC, to a lesser degree with Korea, also India.

He identifies the very timely question of whether the United States should try to prevent China's emergence as a major power. Kissinger argues that it should not: to do so would only expose the U.S. to isolation in the world. He tells us unequivocally and as a general rule that America should not try to play the world's policeman and prevent other nations from growing.

In a prescient concluding remark which bears directly on the entire US foreign posture though it flows from his remarks specifically on the Chinese situation, Kissinger advises: "It would exhaust America's resources…if permanent interventions and crusades became the defining characteristics of American foreign policy…"

Kissinger's analysis of relations with India similarly prompts him to pronounce some remarkable conclusions about non-proliferation which have special relevance today when Barack Obama has made the nuclear issue one of the defining priorities of his presidency: "The United States must do its utmost to prevent the spread of nuclear weapons technology. But once proliferation has taken place, it should not tilt against windmills." He urges his compatriots to exercise discernment between countries representing no threat to American interests or world peace and those countries intent on upsetting the balance of power.

3) *The Middle East*. Kissinger likens the inter-state relations in this region to those in Europe before the Peace of Westphalia (1648), when the warring parties held irreconcilable positions on religion and ideology.

He goes through the history of Israeli-Palestinian negotiations and devotes particular attention to the failure of the peace talks held under the aegis of Bill Clinton. It is Kissinger's view that the time is not yet ripe for a final solution to the regional dispute since both sides continue to cherish hopes of victory of their cause. The best approach will be to seek an interim settlement and coexistence for the foreseeable future.

Kissinger next gives us an overview of the complexities of the Gulf, once again telling us that the analytical terms of Wilsonianism are inapplicable since there are no democracies in the region. He concentrates attention on the problem of the two major regional powers which are hostile to the U.S. today, Iraq and Iran.

In this 2001 discussion of Iraq, it is notable that Kissinger is criticizing the decision of George Bush, Sr. not to take military action during the First Gulf War to its logical conclusion, instead stopping the advance on Baghdad after the Iraqi invaders were ousted from Kuwait. In Kissinger's view it had been possible to oust Saddam Hussein if only the war had been prosecuted for another week, attacking directly the elite guards who were the mainstay of his regime, and letting the Iraqi Army do the job of removing him.

Considering what followed two years later, it bears mention that in his 2001 book the consummate *realist* Kissinger was very sympathetic to regime change, a policy later blamed on the *idealist* Neoconservatives in the George W. Bush Administration. In the Afterword, without citing any sources, Kissinger fully accepted the idea that there was a threat from Saddam's ongoing manufacture of weapons of mass destruction and its nuclear program. His recommendations on how to carry out regime change are there in black and white – a military attack on Iraq must be quick and have a clear plan for post war political structure replacing Saddam.

4) *Africa*. Here we have a continent with no unifying principles, perpetual ethnic conflict and civil wars.

Kissinger tells us how and why the artificial borders left behind by its colonial past have resulted in festering ethnic conflicts. These are exacerbated by parliamentary institutions in which there are permanent majorities and minorities which they do not moderate. All of this provides the breeding ground for endless civil wars and coups.

He emphasizes that the United States has few security interests in sub-Saharan Africa, that in the post-Cold War world no outside country is in a position to dominate the continent, and so there is no strategic justification to consider a new policy on Africa.

For all of these reasons, Kissinger urges America to avoid taking sides in civil wars and to exercise great restraint in leading humanitarian interventions, all of which potentially raise accusations of neocolonialism. Instead African security issues should be left to African nations. The United Nations, NGOs and international institutions should be given the lead in development and other dealings with the region.

SEPARATE ISSUES: RUSSIA

As a general rule, I believe that to the extent possible we all should try to work within areas of our own core expertise. For this reason, I propose to look closely at only one country from among the dozens which Kissinger treats in magisterial fashion in the book under review. That country is Russia.

Kissinger's remarks on Russia start badly. He tells us "Russia has always been sui generis – especially when compared with its European neighbors." His highlighting the 'mystical' Russian Orthodox Church and autocracy suggests a trite approach to this complex nation.

Indeed, Kissinger pursues an unhelpful line of analysis, telling us that "… creeping expansionism has been the recurring theme of Russian history" in which over the course of centuries it pursued a relentless outward thrust threatening all its neighbors. Are we getting here facts or only interpretation? Kissinger is stressing uniqueness and ignoring the insistent parallels with the history of other countries. It would be helpful, for example, if he gave some thought to comparing or contrasting Russia's territorial advance across the Asian steppes and American 'manifest destiny'.

Kissinger rightfully faults American policy to Russia for excessive personalization of relations at the expense of sober reflections on respective interests and institutions to drive and implement any rapprochement.

But then he falls prey to personalization himself. He characterizes the recently installed Russian President Vladimir Putin as a KGB operative whose secret police background presupposed a strong national commitment: "It leads to a foreign policy comparable to that during the tsarist centuries, grounding popular support in a sense of Russian mission and seeking to dominate neighbors where they cannot be subjugated."

If this argumentation, this jumping to conclusions, were delivered by anyone other than Henry Kissinger, one might dismiss it offhandedly. What we have here is the soft underbelly of *Realpolitik*: realism can be only as useful as the expertise and judgment of its practitioner.

At the same time, Kissinger's bark is more fearsome than his bite. In his specific remarks on how America should conduct its foreign policy towards Russia which follow, he urges continued readiness to assist the country with its transition to democracy and free markets, moderation and attentiveness to Russia's voice in international forums.

One example of this moderation is his comment on prospective NATO expansion to the Baltic States, which Kissinger believed in 2001 would be provocative, saying it would put NATO forces within 30 miles of St Petersburg, one of Russia's largest population centers: "Advancing the NATO integrated command this close to key centers of Russia might mortgage the possibilities of relating Russia to the emerging world order as a constructive member." Yet at the end of the same book, in the postscript written in 2002, Kissinger seems to have forgotten that issue. As we know, in 2004 Estonia duly entered NATO.

It is curious that in this book Kissinger was unable to offer any serious incentives for Russia to behave nobly. He derided even the watered down affiliation of Russia with NATO in the NATO-Russia Council. He believes it gave the Russians too much say and was 'not the wisest solution.' Finally, he drops all pretence at diplomatic niceties, telling his readers that: "NATO is basically a military alliance, part of whose purpose is the protection of Europe against a reimperializing Russia...To couple NATO expansion with even partial Russian membership in NATO was, in a sense, merging two contradictory courses of action....[A]s Russia becomes a de facto NATO member, NATO ceases to be an alliance, or becomes a vague collective security instrument."

It is surprising that in the Afterword, written in 2002, Kissinger changed his view of Vladimir Putin, comparing him now to tsarist Chancellor Alexander Gorchakov who for the 25 years following the Crimean War worked to restore the nation's position in international affairs, and largely succeeded. Gorchakov was one of the brightest figures among Russian imperial officials in the second half of the 19th century. He enjoys great prestige in the country today.

For Putin, this likeness is most flattering. But then Kissinger otherwise misjudges Putin's character and interests. He clearly misinterprets why Putin was so generous in his support to George Bush after the terrorist attacks of 9/11. At the time, Russia allowed the U.S. to set up military bases in its backyard, Central Asia, for the sake of logistical support to the war effort in Afghanistan. Kissinger believes that Islamic fundamentalism was a 'dominant concern' of Russia given the threat along its southern border, and sees Putin's gestures in this light. I think Kissinger misses the Russian President's calculations. Putin likely hoped that these concessions would help bring in the promises of full acceptance in the West held out to Russia early in the Yeltsin years, including NATO membership, but then forgotten in Clinton's second term.

THE SOVEREIGN NATION-STATE AND GLOBAL INTERVENTIONISM

Putting aside the details of country and regional policies to be pursued, we may say that there is a grander intellectual issue which draws this book together, namely Kissinger's examination of the multifarious assaults these past several decades, most often US-led, on what is, for realists, the fundamental building block of international order, the sovereign nation-state. As Kissinger never tires of informing us, this notion which underlay the Treaty of Westphalia (1648) ending the Thirty Years War in Central Europe was the corner stone of international relations well into the 20th century. The follow-on principle of the 'balance of power' was intended to ensure that no one nation became dominant.

What we are witnessing is insistent challenges to the notion of non-interference in the domestic affairs of other nation-states and its replacement by humanitarian intervention and universal jurisdiction. Meanwhile the nation-states themselves are exposed to contradictory centrifugal and centripetal forces: either breaking-down in ethnic conflict, as we have seen in the former Yugoslavia and in Central Asia or merging into larger regional groupings such as the European Union which dilutes sovereignty.

The issue of noninterference in the domestic affairs of nation-states is not merely the hobby-horse of Kissinger and the small community of realists in the American foreign policy Establishment. As Kissinger himself points out, the assault on the sovereign national state in the name of human rights and universalist principles is denounced by the developing world, as well as by certain other world powers, first and foremost Russia and China, as a device whereby the United States and fellow industrialized nations exercise their worldwide hegemony.

American Domestic Politics and Foreign Affairs

As in his earlier work *Diplomacy*, Kissinger carefully explains what he considers to be the fundamental fault line in American thinking on foreign relations, that between realists and idealists.

In this book Kissinger takes his study of Wilsonianism forward into the 1980s and 1990s.. He points out how these very principles were drivers behind Western policy in the Balkans – namely the interventions in Bosnia and Kosovo under U.S. leadership. These had nothing to do with strategic interest and were all about satisfying domestic political pressures to alleviate human suffering in areas highlighted by the media.

This new 'ethical foreign policy' was, as Kissinger demonstrates, applied selectively rather than universally and so lost its legitimacy. He insists that management of foreign policy has to accept what is feasible and so parts company with moral principles on a day to day basis. Kissinger is arguing for focus, for an end to mission creep of humanitarian interventions, to a definition of US vital interests, strategic as well as moral.

Kissinger singles out the Kosovo policy of NATO and dismemberment of a state, Serbia, which had full diplomatic relations, telling us this was a move into new and dangerous grounds where NATO is no longer just a defensive alliance, as it has insisted to the Russians, but acted to make war.

"Whatever one's view of the obsolescence of the doctrine of national sovereignty, the combination of flagrant disregard of it by an alliance of democracies and its truculent diplomacy amounted to a departure from the very international norms on which those democracies had insisted throughout the Cold War. As a consequence, a glaring gap opened up between the claims of the various allied leaders extolling their new ethical foreign policy and the reaction of most of the rest of the world."

Today, in 2010, Russian Foreign Minister Sergei Lavrov would hardly describe the situation surrounding NATO action in Kosovo differently.

Universal Jurisdiction

Kissinger devotes a long section to the latest assault on national sovereignty – the concept of universal jurisdiction, both in the form of trials by national justice pursuing violations of international conventions and in the form of the International Criminal Court in The Hague.

He argues this replaces tyranny of governments with potential tyranny of judges, that it interferes with possibilities for national reconciliation such as occurred in South Africa and before that in post-Franco Spain, and does not put in place due process. Universal jurisdiction easily becomes political warfare, Kissinger insists.

This particular issue from the book was set out separately by Kissinger in a *Foreign Affairs* article (July/August 2001) entitled "The Pitfalls of Universal Jurisdiction.' As such it was rebutted in the following issue of the magazine by Kenneth Roth, Executive Director of Human Rights Watch ("The Case for Universal Jurisdiction").

While Roth scores many points against Kissinger, the issues moving them are asymmetrical and Kissinger's placing this issue within the overall context of erosion of the nation state with all its associated protections for citizenry remains standing when all the dust settles.

Striking a Balance

More than in any of his previous writings, in *Does America Need a Foreign Policy?* Kissinger presents himself as the reformed realist who wants to strike a balance. He tells us: "Excessive 'realism' produces stagnation; excessive 'idealism' leads to crusades and eventual disillusionment." One may be allowed to be skeptical about his sincerity, although the book ends with some observations and sage advice which suggest mellowness.

In this book Kissinger makes mention in passing of the notion of an American empire and he returns to it at the very end of the book delivering a couple of thoughts which would by themselves justify several more chapters:

"No matter how selfless America perceives its aims, an explicit insistence on predominance would gradually unite the world against the United States and force it into impositions that would eventually leave it isolated and drained."

With that thought Kissinger clearly set out his direct challenges to the Neoconservative enthusiasm sweeping the nation at the time of his writing. And he added a further comment no less pithy than President Eisenhower's Farewell Address warning against the military-industrial complex:

"The road to empire leads to domestic decay because, in time the claims of omnipotence erode domestic restraints…A deliberate quest for hegemony is the surest way to destroy the values that made the United States great."

REVIEWS

In 2001, professionals were not indifferent to Kissinger's latest opus. Foreign affairs consultant to the *New York Times,* multiple Pulitzer Prize winning journalist Thomas Friedman wrote a highly perceptive review just after the book was released entitled "How to Run the World in Seven Chapters" (*NYT,* June 17, 2001). Friedman is the rare case of a reviewer who called attention to the methodology of Kissinger's realist approach to foreign policy, namely the master's stress on immutable, 'geological' features of national behavior which must be comprehended to arrive at proper policy.

Noting that Kissinger's latest work repeated many topics he had covered amply in previous writings, he asks for whom the book was intended and goes on to answer that question without hesitation: "In many ways it has an audience of one: President George W. Bush." Friedman likened the book to *The Prince* by Machiavelli.

Friedman takes his time calling out contradictions in this book: "While ceaselessly scorning the Clinton administration for its woolly-headed approach to international relations, he says virtually nothing about some of the more lunatic, ideologically driven positions of his Republican colleagues." Friedman explains this reticence by Kissinger's fear of bringing down the ire of the Right on his head.

More to the point, he sees inconsistencies in Kissinger's advocacy of NATO expansion and of the Bush plan for a high-technology missile defense shield, given that both policies are ideological and very divisive, at odds with his general call for moderation.

Coming from the world of journalism, Friedman does not surprise when he faults Kissinger for a weak chapter on globalization and for not dealing with how modern communications are shaping the behavior of nations in our day.

Friedman tells us that he believes Kissinger's detractors when they characterize him as a "cynical, mean and ...nasty bureaucratic infighter and player of the game of nations." And yet he sees much merit in the master's writings, including the latest:

"Everything that makes Kissinger the most reviled, and most interesting, statesman of his generation is on display here: the Machiavellian Kissinger that liberal internationalists love to hate, the coolly incisive Kissinger that balance-of-power realists love to love and the statesman-historian that students of diplomacy have to read."

The New York Times literary critic Richard Bernstein had fewer column inches at his disposal for "Books of the Times; A Realist's Reflections on Foreign Policy," June 22, 2001. He went straight to Kissinger's more interesting policy recommendations about accommodating a rising China, the future of NATO and the warnings against humanitarian interventions.

Bernstein perceptively notes that when he stops generalizing and focuses on specific policy issues, what Kissinger sets out as realist policy is often not very different from what the Clinton administration ultimately did, for example its backing down on human rights in China.

He concludes: "'Does America Need a Foreign Policy?' is cogent because it is informed by a consistent vision, one in which morality is measured not by purity of intentions but by the nature of results. President George W. Bush and his advisers would do well to read this book."

Writing in the small circulation weekly newspaper *The New York Observer* read by Manhattan's socialites, James P. Rubin captured the essence of Kissinger's new work correctly in the title of his review: "Dr. Kissinger Makes War on Clinton's Foreign Policy," June 17, 2001.

Rubin explains how Kissinger has cleverly positioned himself as a centrist in this book, criticizing those on the left, the 'mushy Wilsonians' who turn foreign policy into 'social work,' and those on the right, who see the solution to all the world's ills in the exercise of American hegemony. But this only shows how Kissinger misreads his own homeland. According to Rubin, the real divide in the nation is between activist Republicans and Democrats and minimalist Republicans and Democrats.

Rubin expresses his surprise that Kissinger is promoting a blend of realism and idealism in the policies he recommends for the various regional groupings: a policy 'in which our ideals are pursued with care and due regard for the history, culture and complexity of the regions of the world.'

Like Friedman, Rubin thinks Kissinger misses factors changing the nature of international relations in our day: "The realities of democracy and the Information Age mean that unelected diplomats can no longer decide the fate of the world by drawing maps and making treaty commitments over dinner in European castles."

In this comment, we see how journalists, by their narcissism and enthusiasm for what is deemed to be new, can overlook the general disconnect between democracy and the day to day management of foreign policy in the Western world, not to mention the less progressive nation-states. One need only consider the polls on military intervention in Iraq conducted among the Spanish or Italian populations to be persuaded that it was a long wait before the participation of their troops in the 'coalition of the willing' came up for a vote in the respective national elections, and still longer for their votes to take effect in changed policies. In Britain, popular fury over Tony Blair's decision to throw in his lot with Bush in the face of some of the largest anti-war demonstrations ever held in London prior to the invasion has only recently been given some tepid consolation through the public proceedings of the Chilcot inquiry.

Finally, it is important to consider a 'dissident' voice which appeared in a journal of the highly influential Johns Hopkins School of Advanced International Studies: John-Paul Ferguson, "Our Own Private Pinochet: Prosecuting Henry Kissinger," *SAIS Review*, vol. XXII, no. 1 (Winter-Spring 2002).

Ferguson reviewed the latest Kissinger work together with a book by Christopher Hitchens, *The Trial of Henry Kissinger*, which came out earlier in the year and argued for Kissinger's being called before a war crimes tribunal for a variety of offenses dating from his government service.

Ferguson recognizes that Kissinger did not respond directly to Hitchens's work in his new book but says it determined the 'tenor' of *Does America Need a Foreign Policy?*

That may be a doubtful proposition, except for Kissinger's chapter on universal jurisdiction and the ICC which, like the chapter on globalization, is not really integrated into the main body of his book.

However the case may be, the juxtaposition of books by Kissinger and Hitchens provides Ferguson with the opportunity to set out the bill of charges against Kissinger and to argue that while they may not constitute an indictment in court terms, they are sufficient to justify a proper judicial inquest against Kissinger.

Moreover, an indictment of Kissinger would ultimately be a death blow to his cause of *Realpolitik*, with which his career was inextricably linked. Ferguson concludes:

"..*The Trial of Henry Kissinger* undoes all of the work laid down in *Does America Need a Foreign Policy?* The great project that has consumed the second half of Henry Kissinger's life – making us all forget the first half – stands in danger of being publicly and thoroughly wrecked."

These issues were also featured in the review of Kissinger's book carried by a mainstream British newspaper read by the chattering classes: Nick Cohen, "Evasive manoeuvres," *The Observer*, 9 September, 2001.

As we now know, the threats to Henry Kissinger's reputation and peace of mind dissipated without consequence. The dogs howled and the caravan moved on.

Joseph S. Nye, Jr and Smart Power

In her programmatic speech to the Council of Foreign Relations on July 15, 2009, Secretary of State Hillary Clinton found a key inspiration for the foreign policy concept of the Obama administration in the writings of Harvard Professor Joseph S. Nye.

The central issue in Nye's work for the past decade or so has been 'soft power,' the power of attraction and co-optation in international relations. Nye revisited and refined the concept in several books before arriving at a formula for combining soft power with traditional 'hard power' of military and economic coercion to arrive at 'smart power" as the optimal way to deal with a world which divides between democracies, where cooperation and mutual influence are the rule, and the remaining half of the world where force or the threat of force is often the only way to resolve differences. This balanced approach to foreign policy is set out at length in his book entitled *Soft Power: The means to success in world politics* (New York: 2004).

Going back to her maiden speech to State Department staff following her confirmation by the Senate, Hilary Clinton had spoken of 'smart power' as her guiding spirit. And in her magisterial presentation in July she devoted considerable time to explaining concretely how 'smart power' would shape the architecture and inform the behavior of US foreign policy, thereby setting the preconditions for achieving its policy objectives.

Nye's obvious success in reaching his intended audience of top American policy makers places him among the leading thinkers who have shaped the debate on foreign policy since the end of the Cold War and justifies the careful attention to his 2004 book which I will attempt in the analytical essay which follows.

A Gentleman and a Scholar

Joseph S. Nye's career in many ways embodies the finest principles of Harvard University, where he has occupied a number of different positions and now is a senior professor. Nye has alternated periods of scholarship with university administration and high level public service in the nation's capital. He is a former dean of the prestigious Kennedy School of Government. In Washington he served as Chairman of the National Intelligence Council and was Assistant Secretary of Defense in the Clinton Administration.

Nye's 2004 book *Soft Power* is all about symbolism, advertising and public relations. In this sense, it is fair to consider for a moment the portrait of the author which we find at the very start of the book. This black and white photograph presents Nye in a dark suit, his chin resting on his left hand. He is staring off into the distance, with a glint in his right eye. The pose projects introspection and deep thoughts on the great issues of state.

It is also obvious that we are looking at someone in his late 60s or 70s. This is clearly a writer who brings great personal experience to bear on his scholarship, weighs his words carefully and conveys *gravitas*.

At the same time we note that Joseph Nye belongs to the relatively younger cadres of the Democratic Party brain trust in foreign policy. For reasons that we have explored elsewhere, namely the exclusive occupation of the foreign policy stage for the past 20 years by young and rambunctious neoconservatives and their followers, a whole generation of 'senior' thinkers in their 40s and 50s is missing on the left of center in American politics.

THE UNWILLING PARTISAN FIGHTER

Let us say right away that the period when Nye wrote this book was a time of high partisanship in American political life. It was slightly more than a year after the US invasion of Iraq, when a brief domestic debate over the advisability of pursuing a military intervention without the legitimacy of a UN Security Council resolution was cut short by the *blitzkrieg* overthrow of the regime in Baghdad and the subsequent lock-step conformism of American society, including its institutions of higher learning, in support of 'our boys' serving valiantly in wartime.

In these conditions, Nye tried his level best to present a neutral, scholarly persona. The text has the feel of the passive voice or third person as the author sets out the views of his chosen sources without ever appearing to side with them He treated the then raging neoconservatives with kid gloves.

He was deferential to the pamphleteer Robert Kagan, referring in a complimentary fashion to his popular book *Of Paradise and Power* with its justifications for a warlike America versus pacifist Europe. His differences of opinion with Charles Krauthammer, the widely read neoconservative columnist in *The Washington Post,* are couched in the most respectful terms. Moreover, Nye's critical words with respect to the Bush administration are reserved only for the second-tier players like Rumsfeld and Cheney, whom he faults for arrogance and unilateralism which undermined US 'soft power.' As for the president, Nye only extends bouquets as he praises George W. Bush repeatedly for launching his HIV/AIDS programs abroad and for supporting increased development assistance though the Millennium Challenge initiative, both of which meet his conditions for creating the public good that enhances soft power.

This attempt at being accommodating and loyal does not seem to have earned for Nye any reciprocal respect from the other side of the aisle. It is a commonplace of the political science establishment that 'one hand washes the other,' by which I mean that the big names from all political persuasions tend to come out with recommendations on behalf of one another's latest contribution to the debate whether they agree with the argumentation of the author or not. Curiously this is not the case with Nye's *Soft Power.* Instead what we have is glowing tributes coming strictly from the stars in the Democratic Party firmament. On the front cover of the paperback edition which I bought, Madeleine Albright delivers the following encomium: "As brilliant as it is timely, Professor Nye's book is must reading for anyone who cares about the success of America and the world." And a very complimentary remark from Zbigniew Brezizinski graces the back cover: "An important and incisive conceptual contribution to a deeper understanding of world politics and to a wiser foreign policy by one of America's foremost scholars of international politics."

In fact, from the time when he first proposed it, Nye ran into opposition to his concept of 'soft power' that ranged from skepticism to outright dismissive treatment. In the Preface to his book, Nye himself calls attention to the remark by Defense Secretary Rumsfeld that he did not know what was meant by 'soft power.' And one does not have to be a neoconservative to give short shrift to the concept. In his recent bestselling book *Power Rules,* middle-of-the-road *realist* foreign policy analyst. Leslie Gelb writes that hard military power is the currency of international relations, and condescendingly calls 'soft power' just foreplay. Gelb somewhat maliciously traces the

shifts and turns in Nye's thinking over the years from single-minded attention to soft power to a more nuanced appreciation of the balance between
the forces of attraction and coercion in management of international relations.

Unlike Gelb and other skeptics, in the critique below I will not question the
notion of 'soft power' in terms of its efficacy or recommended weighting in
a nation's foreign policy. Instead I intend to direct attention to the methodology of Nye's research. The point will be to see just what level of scholarship
we have before us, what kind of critical faculty is at work and the degree
of scholarly seriousness, namely how this compares with the photographic
and biographical portraits of the author offered by the publisher.

Secondly I will spend some time exploring the mindset that gave rise to
the concept of soft power. The central notion of soft power/smart power is
embedded in a broader view of the world in general, the threats and opportunities facing the United States, the priorities for foreign policy. These have
to be flushed out to better understand what the adoption of 'smart power'
in the Clinton formulation means for American foreign policy generally.

THE THESIS

Though the notion of soft power can be summed up in one sentence, Nye
offers an expanded explanation which comprises his entire first chapter and
takes 32 pages. It makes you wonder what is left for the remaining 115 pages
plus 27 pages of notes. However, Nye is a seasoned writer and the pace of his
exposition is masterful.

In chapter two, he sets out the sources of America's powers of attraction to
others around the world, which include the particulars of the world's largest economy, its massive immigrant inflows, the large contingent of foreign
students at American institutions of higher learning, the numbers of Nobel
Prize laureates and scholarly articles published, etc. A particular strength is
found in America's popular culture, ranging from the Hollywood movies,
entertainment and informational programming of television and the media
generally.

Nye also directs our attention to the negatives which reduce the country's
attractiveness. These exist in domestic politics, where the country's values

are tested against its actions. We are told that the absence of gun control legislation or the practice of capital punishment alienate people in the prosperous democratic countries which otherwise are friendly to the US. Then there are the negatives in U.S. foreign policy, most recently connected with U.S. unilateralism and its invasion of Iraq without cover of UN legitimacy, the scandal of detentions in Guantanamo and the abuses revealed in the Abu Ghraib prison, all of which tarnish the American commitment to respecting human rights.

In chapter three, Nye tells us about the soft power resources of other countries and regions of the world. By his account Europe is America's closest competitor in attracting the admiration and envy of others. European art, literature, music, design, fashion, and cuisine are said to be global cultural magnets, while the Old Continent is now also a thriving economic center with the world's largest domestic market, generous social safety nets and regulated labor markets. Its advanced democracies promote progressive policies in such areas as climate change, the rights of homosexuals and the other issues which elicit positive appraisal from younger people in rich countries around the world. At the same time, Europe is known as a peaceful oasis in a troubled world. Its foreign policy generates public goods through relatively generous development aid, cutting-edge policies to combat global climate change, support for human rights treaties, defense of international law and significant contributions of peace keeping troops. Europeans are said to invest more in public diplomacy, to support international institutions better and to attract large numbers of foreigners to its institutions of higher learning.

Nye believes that Europe's soft power resources can either work against or in combination with American soft power depending on how America behaves towards Europe, how multilateral or unilateral the U.S. is in its foreign policy.

Otherwise Nye places East Asia in third place in terms of soft power resources. He sees Japan, with the world's second largest economy and renown for its consumer electronics and entertainment industry, as the leader in the region. Meanwhile China is the rising power, with its dynamic economy and expanding participation in world institutions.

Chapter 4 on 'Wielding Soft Power' is the key transition chapter in the book, taking us from an inventory of soft power resources to the processes by which the U.S. administration can convert these resources into foreign policy tools. Most of the resources Nye has catalogued are generated by society at large and are outside the direct control of governments in democratic countries. That is the case with the economy, high and low culture, social life. However, the government has the ability to market and promote these resources abroad through its management of information and communications policy. This means broadcasting facilities such as the Voice of America and specialized stations serving particular foreign audiences. It can also finance activities which generate soft power, such as international development aid, sponsoring cultural and artistic exchanges, assistance to higher education exchanges, people to people programs of all sorts. The military can also play a role through its own programs of officer exchanges and joint training with the forces of friendly nations, as well as through 'weaponization' of reporters – embedding journalists with forward military units. Finally, the government can encourage non-state actors such as foundations and educational institutions to do more in the international arena.

Nye decries the curtailment of U.S. government budgets for public diplomacy in the 1990s: "With the end of the Cold War, Americans were more interested in budget savings than in investments in soft power." During this period the staff of the United States Information Agency was nearly cut in half from peak levels of the past and the USIA itself disappeared as a separate entity in 1999, with its remaining operations folded into the State Department. Meanwhile U.S. cultural centers and libraries abroad were closed. All of this happened at the very time when the worldwide 'information revolution' put a premium on the structured management of communications to a world flooded by facts and deprived of editorial guidance. Concludes Nye: "Only after September 2001 did Americans rediscover the importance of investing in the instruments of soft power, and even then inadequately..."

Having told us how soft power can be harnessed, in the final chapter Nye provides specific recommendations on what should be done now. He calls for doubling the federal budget allocations to public diplomacy, including the state directed broadcasting media. Its profile should be raised by making it directly accountable to the White House. Visa problems introduced in the aftermath of 9/11 should be revised with a view to removing unnecessary obstacles inhibiting educational and other exchanges with other countries.

In terms of domestic politics, Nye urges review of policies on gun control, gas guzzling vehicles and agricultural subsidies for the sake of improving the country's image abroad by bringing it into line with worldwide values.

In foreign policy, he calls for a turn away from unilateralism to greater cooperative efforts through the international institutions.

NYE'S METHODOLOGICAL FAILINGS

At the level of his argumentation, Nye is logical, consistent and persuasive. The problems with his work lie elsewhere: in his selection of sources and his apparent failure to exercise any critical faculty with respect to those sources.

Soft Power is a compilation rather than a work of original research. The extensive Notes at the end of the book show that the periodical press accounts for the lion's share of his sources. Here we find articles from the *New York Times, Newsweek, Economist, Financial Times, Atlantic Monthly, Boston Globe* and the *Washington Post*.

The Notes lend a scholarly form to the work, but this is deceptive since they serve only the purpose of attribution. There is almost no comment by the author in these Notes setting out his critical evaluation of one or another source. It would be appropriate to be told how he weighted these varied publications, considering that some are presenting the writing of individual journalists, others were prepared by teams of reporters, and still others, such as the *Economist* or *Newsweek*, are blends of reporting and editorial commentary without identified authors.

Similarly, Nye only occasionally tells the reader about the political affiliations of individual authors whom he cites, including Robert Kagan, Thomas Friedman, Michael Ignatieff, Fareed Zakaria, John Ikenberry and Andrew Bacevich. It would be an understatement to say that these authors represent a wide and mutually contradictory spectrum of views.

I freely admit that scholarship in the area of current international affairs is more essay-like and subjective than driven by hard science. Nonetheless, either you accept Neoconservative concepts or you accept realist or idealist concepts, but you DO NOT take all of these on board at the same time as Nye does.

For all of these reasons, I would characterize the level of scholarship in *Soft Power* as exemplifying the 'honey bee' approach to research. Nye is gathering nectar from all flowers, whether roses or stink weeds.

A believer in the 'Information Revolution'

Nye's methodology becomes all the more problematic given that he is letting his media sources talk about… *themselves*. It quickly becomes evident that this senior statesman is enthralled by the 'information revolution' and the media representatives who hype its supposedly revolutionary effect on our world which marks a discontinuity justifying new approaches to international relations. What Nye fails to consider is the media's capacity for self-delusion and /or unjustified self-congratulation.

If I may be allowed to argue by analogy, it is one thing to let CNN tell us that it reports the news accurately and comprehensively; it is something else to allow CNN to take credit for making the news.

In the same way, where it serves his purposes Nye serves up to the reader as objective truth or as a relevant 'admission' what is merely an exaggerated claim made by the opposition for purposes of propaganda. To put it in other words, he is blind to the tendentiousness of his sources. I have in mind concretely Nye's repeating to us the words of Iranian mullahs to the effect that Western television broadcasts are subverting traditional values. He also quotes journalists on how U.S. soft power, namely movies and pop culture, have 'corrupted' minds abroad.

Although the reasons for the collapse of the Soviet Union are and will long remain a highly contentious issue among serious historians, the superficiality of the following resume by Nye is fairly stunning: "The Cold War was won by a mixture of hard and soft power. Hard power created the stand-off of military containment, but soft power eroded the Soviet system from within."

The war on terror and clash of civilizations as the defining context for smart power

The problem with Professor Nye's failure to exercise critical judgment and detachment from his sources does not end there. It extends to his description of the context in international relations which raises soft power to an importance of the first order, namely the war on terror.

Nye argues that technological and social changes have made terrorism more lethal and difficult to manage in our new century than at any previous time in history. Our ever more sophisticated advanced democratic societies are increasingly vulnerable to attack at the same time that weapons of mass destruction are increasingly smaller, cheaper and more readily available to non-state actors.

As he warns us, "it is now all too easy to envisage extremist groups and individuals killing millions without the instruments of governments."

According to Nye, the only way to respond effectively is close cooperation with other states to share intelligence and implement financial controls, working with civilian forces to deprive extremists of support and refuge. All of this requires powers of attraction and is not achievable by Diktat.

I submit that the utility of having friendly and cooperative relations with other states is self-evident and has no need of such proof *in extremis*. This type of fear-mongering over terrorist threats finds an excellent reproof in Zbigniew Brzezinski's most recent book, *America and the World*. Brzezinski reminds us that during his tenure as National Security Advisor to President Carter the nation's leaders were always mindful of the possibility that half the population could be destroyed in 6 hours of nuclear exchange, yet the government proceeded calmly about its business and did not stoke fears among the population.

Another argument which Nye adduces in favor of paying more attention to soft power also suffers from lack of perspective and *sang froid*: this is the special case he makes for the Middle East. To all appearances, Nye has given his blessing to the Bush administration's transformational mission in the region, turning from propping up authoritarian governments towards regime change. The difference is that Nye believes this transformational role can be better performed by building libraries and information centers, translating more books into Arabic and promoting visiting fellowships instead of by moving in tanks. It never occurs to him that the best policy might possibly be not to play God by proactively developing 'a richer and more open civil society in Middle Eastern countries,' just to let go and allow local forces to sort out their relations without U.S. help.

THE MORAL DIMENSION

The subjects which have interested Joseph Nye professionally over the years include nuclear war and ethics. He coauthored one of his books in this area with fellow Harvard professor and fighter against nuclear proliferation Graham Allison. Moreover, as we have seen in this essay, Nye is an *idealist* in the strict sense of the word, i.e., a believer in ideas changing the world. Accordingly it is fair to ask whether he is also a moralist today? Judging by the argumentation he produces in *Soft Power* the answer is: decidedly 'no.'

One example pertains to covert government support for cultural organizations to promote the image of the U.S. abroad. Nye tells us that CIA funding in such cases can be very "counterproductive" since leaks are inevitable in a democratic society and the revelations of such support have a negative impact on soft power. The notion that such covert funding might be unethical and corrosive to academic, cultural and artistic freedom in a pluralistic society seems not to trouble Nye. All that counts is efficacy.

Similarly, his discussion of the question of legitimacy in launching the Iraq war comes up in the book only in the context of how costly Bush's decision to ignore the UN was for American soft power. Indeed Nye trespasses conventional morality in his characterization of the prosecution of the Iraq war in general: "It is still too soon to tell whether the hard-power gains from the war in Iraq will in the long run exceed the soft-power losses, or how permanent the latter will turn out to be, *but the war provided a fascinating case study* of the interaction of the two types of power." [emphasis added]

Form and substance

In what looks like a rare moment of candor, Nye acknowledges that: 'even the best advertising cannot sell an unpopular product, and…policies that appear narrowly self-serving or are arrogantly presented are likely to consume rather than produce soft power… A communications strategy cannot work if it cuts against the grain of policy. Actions speak louder than words, and public diplomacy that appears to be mere window dressing for the projection of hard power is unlikely to succeed."

Yet, Nye himself does not go beyond questions of technique in the management of foreign policy. He does not for a moment raise or question the ultimate objectives and priorities of American diplomacy. The conclusive proof of his self-imposed limitation of vision is provided by the author himself:

"The place where the government can do the most in the near term to recover the recent American loss of soft power is by adjusting the style and substance of our foreign policy. Obviously there are times when foreign policies serve fundamental American interests and cannot and should not be changed. But tactics can often be adjusted without giving up basic interests. Style may be the easiest part."

This message has clearly shaped the conduct of the Obama administration in its first months. It remains to be seen if and when some reexamination of fundamental American interests will lead to changes of substance in the months and years to come.

IMPLICATIONS FOR THE OBAMA FOREIGN POLICY

The first take-away from our examination of Joseph Nye's latest work on soft/smart power is that the concepts he is promoting rest on shaky legs. His generalizations are superficial and he is overly influenced by media personalities claiming historical discontinuities in what turns out to be a wholly self-serving manner.

The second lesson is that his recommendations operate largely at the tactical level, dealing by his own admission more in the packaging than in the substance of foreign policy. Nye is a public relations man. We can only hope that not all members of the foreign policy and security team in the new administration allow themselves to be seduced by 'spin.'

Can Common Sense fix what is wrong with American foreign policy?

Leslie Gelb, *Power Rules*

Judging by his long, distinguished and varied career in the American foreign policy Establishment, Leslie Gelb might be thought to be one of the *doyens* of his field. He held a number of high level positions in the State Department including the rank of Assistant Secretary of State. He won the Distinguished Service Award from the Pentagon and the Distinguished Honor Award from State. He later became a national security correspondent, editor and columnist for the *New York Times*. And still later, beginning in 1993, he served as President of the Council on Foreign Relations, publishers of *Foreign Affairs* magazine, the most widely read and listened-to public deliberators on the foreign policy issues in United States. Since 2005 he has been its President Emeritus.

And yet this insider, this permanent invitee to the most exclusive foreign policy events in Washington for decades, appears before us as an *outsider*, a member of the bipartisan *realist* school of foreign policy which has been on the outs for the past 30 years as a rival coalition of bipartisan *ideologically driven* thinkers and practitioners took over the management of foreign affairs in the nation's capital and, acting in the name of spreading democracy, fighting ethnic cleansing, defending human rights and upholding our values steered the ship of state onto the rocks. Like his fellow directors of the Nixon Center, until very recently Mr Gelb was whistling in the dark.

However, beginning in 2009, Gelb was once again very much in the public eye as he traveled the lecture circuit promoting his newly published master work bearing the typically witty *double entendre* title "Power Rules."

The book itself equates Common Sense with a non-ideological approach. Foreign policy must be grounded in a carefully crafted strategy. Once this is put in place, it is the author's firm belief that "common sense can rescue American foreign policy" from the failures of the past 20 years.

It is my purpose in this short essay to explain why, however desirable common, pragmatic problem-solving may be compared to the kind of ideological self-indulgence we had under both the Bill Clinton and George W. Bush administrations, it is by itself not enough to turn American foreign policy from its ongoing pursuit of overblown objectives which may threaten world peace. Instead what is needed is a thorough reexamination of the first principles of foreign policy.

That is something you will scarcely see in the book under review. Instead, from page one Gelb is off to the races with his 'power rules.' Only midway through his treatise does he take a brief detour to tick off his recommended list of 7 goals for foreign policy. They are so self-evident in the circles he travels in that he does not bother to defend them or to consider any possible alternative objectives. What we have here is a senior thinker who descends from Mount Sinai with the law graven on tablets of stone. He allocates to the whole purpose of foreign policy one page in a three hundred page book. Though *en passant*, Gelb dismisses the view of his one-time boss Cyrus Vance that "policy is baloney" – finally he falls into a correlative trap of arguing the need for proper mechanics and ignoring the intellectual exercise of vetting the objectives, aside from the meager test of feasibility. This is precisely what was wrong with the Democratic critique of Bush's Iraq policy in the 2004 electoral campaign: it was all about how and nothing about why.

Gelb's book has some very endearing refrains. He argues in favor of *military power*, meaning the psychological bargaining tool resulting from objective superiority in men and materiel to wage war, the record of successful military interventions and the clear determination to use that force in future as needed. Such power is the currency of international relations, he tells us, alongside economic power and diplomatic power. He contrasts it with the 'Just Do It!' exercise of brutal military force beloved by American Conservatives and Neo-conservatives to solve most of the world's problems. Armed intervention is something he insists must be put to one side and used as the very last resort, when the psychology of carrots and sticks fails to change the behavior of adversaries in the desired way. Wars are to be avoided because of the high cost, dangers and unforeseeable outcomes of armed conflict. He also contrasts military power to so-called "soft power," such as many American Liberals and Moderates have proposed as a kinder, smarter alternative. For Gelb, soft power is just 'foreplay,' the stage-setter and not genuine power in itself.

Another positive refrain is the need for cooperation in foreign policy initiatives. He eschews unilateralism. America is the indispensable super power which can take the lead and succeed in solving the world's problems when it is joined by... indispensable partners. These partners will mostly be drawn from among the 8 second tier countries – China, Japan, India, Russia, the UK, France, Germany and Brazil - whom Gelb calls the 'managing directors' of the global realm –though other countries from the lower tiers of the pecking order may also be drawn in for support. This is not to be confused with multilateralism for its own sake as promoted by the European Union's foreign policy team. For Gelb, the United Nations and other international organizations which cannot be American dominated and controlled serve a purely decorative function on the world stage. He is completely untroubled by the issue of legitimacy of power.

There are also several especially endearing chapters in this book. Chapter 6 on Intelligence and Power is both likeable and very useful. Gelb puts intelligence back in its box and explains where it can reasonably contribute to the formulation and implementation of foreign policy. As the director of the project which produced what became known as *The Pentagon Papers*, Gelb knows through and through what he is talking about.

Chapter 7 on U.S. Domestic Politics and Power is also very helpful in showing how the public free-for-all that ostensibly shapes U.S. foreign policy actually operates. Regrettably, the bottom line is that in practice there are no effective checks and balances, and the U.S. President can do pretty much whatever he likes in foreign policy, enjoying all the latitude of a medieval potentate.

And here is the explanation of the book's very concept. Gelb assumes the role of a modern day Machiavelli and his treatise is an updated version of *The Prince*. The sly, sophisticated and witty author has seen a great deal of the personalities and issues involved in U.S. foreign policy in his decades-long career. His intent is to distil from this varied and high-level experience a set of rules to guide the newly elected President as he sets out on his way.

Without meaning it, this nominally secondary and didactic work is absolutely fascinating as a *primary source*. It reveals both the strengths and, more importantly, the blind spots, the failures in the way the makers of U.S. foreign policy approach their task.

Let's look for a moment at his 7 ultimate goals of US foreign policy. The first two have been Mother and Apple Pie ever since 9/11: "contain and diminish the threat from international terrorists" and "prevent the spread of weapons of mass destruction." I would argue that they are derivative issues which sprang to life and persist only because of the breakdown of the international order that came with the collapse of the Soviet Union and the end of the Cold War. In that bipolar world of well controlled client states belonging in one or another camp, terrorism and nuclear proliferation were not the hot issues. They did not have a life of their own, nor are they likely to remain genuine threats if and when a new and sustainable multipolar world order with regional dominant powers comes into place.

Position four, "promote freer trade and investments" is more the sphere of interest of a Secretary of Commerce and Secretary of the Treasury than of a State Department. Position five, "reduce dependence on foreign oil and gas" is by definition a domestic policy matter, hardly a goal around which to mobilize the Pentagon or the diplomatic corps. The same is true of point 6, "protect against global environment and health threats." Point 7, "promote the rule of law, democratic institutions and respect for human rights" coming from a 'realist' is just a pillow on his backside to defend against the charges of cynical disregard for these same values that hounded Nixon and Kissinger, the authors of American *Realpolitik*.

All of which leaves us with one very genuine goal of American foreign policy these past several decades: "prevent any state or group of states from organizing the power and resources of Europe and Asia against the United States."

In another place in the book, Gelb deals with the same issue in a more revealing and less appealing way: "Today, American power derives in good measure from the United States' being the ultimate regional balancer throughout the world – in Asia against China, in the Middle East against Iran, and in Europe against Russia."

And there you have it: the key problem with American foreign policy which Gelb identifies and then moves on as if nothing happened.

We hear a lot about the *Pax Americana,* which is rolled out by its backers as the proud successor to the *Pax Britannica* of the 19th century. From the perspective of the Continent, the foreign policy of 'balance of power' enabling British rule gave us the epithet 'perfidious Albion.' And so the United States is now called upon to be perfidious and the very source of instability in the world which it then feels authorized to address as the indispensable power.

However, timing is everything. The British concept of 'balance of power' was exercised at tipping points to right an equilibrium going askew. Today's balancing acts enumerated by Gelb are pre-emptive. They are being set up well in advance of any emergence of regional hegemons and they have the effect of creating, not dissipating tensions with potential for conflict. Drawing power from inciting or exacerbating regional instability means undermining the security of others to further one's own interests.. It is destructive and ultimately unsustainable.

Having brought out this flaw in the approach of a strategist who is attempting valiantly to do battle with a host of wrongs in the U.S. foreign policy Establishment, it is not my intention to churlishly criticize Leslie Gelb at every turn. Moreover, my own expertise is in Russian affairs and I am cautious questioning his analyses or recommendations in a great number of other issues he cites in this book. However, Gelb is also something of a specialist on Russian matters having been responsible in the State Department for strategic arms limitations negotiations with the Soviet Union for a good part of his government service.

From this perspective, it is depressing to see a major authority speak in such trivial, superficial manner about the Russian Federation today, repeating the facile generalizations that you could pick up in five minutes of listening to CNN. His explanation of the collapse of share prices on the Russian stock exchanges in the fall of 2008 and the sharp devaluation of the ruble in terms of market punishment for the invasion of Georgia is shameful in its omission of the broader context of generalized collapse of world commodity prices and emerging market equities in the same time frame, nor does it take in the anti-Russian hysteria whipped up by Washington at the time. His brief remarks on how the Russians artificially created an issue of secessionist provinces in August 2008 so as to punish Georgia for its pro-American policies reveal a woeful ignorance of the history of the region and its civil wars going back to the break-up of the Soviet Union.

Given the disarmingly honest insights Gelb shares with his readers elsewhere in the book, I am left to conclude that his primitive observations in areas like his Russian analysis come from a...closed mind. Like so many of his compatriots, and especially those of a certain age and experience who have seen it all, he has closed his ears to new facts that might challenge his comfortable old generalizations.

My point in mentioning this kind of analytical sloppiness on the part of one of America's best known and respected foreign policy strategists is not to diminish the man, but to demonstrate the impossibility of knowing objectively what one would need to know to rule the world in the way that the American foreign policy Establishment still assumes is its right and the expectation of other nations.

Albion once ruled the waves. And that was a relatively easy thing to do. Ruling over peoples today is less easy. It requires intelligence, extraordinary knowledge of every society on earth. And Gelb himself in his chapter on intelligence makes it patently clear what kinds of problems arise in the intelligence community. The situation there is even worse than he suggests since he does not take into account the changes in intelligence which followed 9/11 – namely the massive outsourcing of intelligence gathering and analysis to private contractors, with perhaps two-thirds of the US's $46 billion budget for intelligence services in 2007 going to external service providers who feed literally from the hand of the Executive Branch with no Congressional oversight. This ensures even greater skewing of information and recommendations to tell the boss what he wants to hear.

Atypically for an American writer reaching out to the broad public, Gelb ends his book on a somber, almost dispirited note. The failure of American foreign policy over the past two decades has clearly paralleled a loss of moral fiber in the nation's elites, a rot from within. Reversing this decay requires such vast change that its likelihood is highly uncertain.

What is at issue? It is clear from Gelb's words that the elites are not performing their function as defenders of pluralism. Everywhere careerism is triumphing over civic courage. Leaders do little more than pander to popular expectations of chest-thumping patriotism.

Gelb shares with us his dismay over the truculent partisanship in Washington which trashes any policy advisor who would suggest compromise or the taking into account of the interests of others, even stalwart allies, when formulating policy. Who else is speaking up against this?

Stanley Hoffmann and Heroic Idealism:

from *World Disorders* to *Chaos and Violence* in the company of *Gulliver Unbound*

Part One

Stanley Hoffmann has a number of points in common with our other great American thinkers on international affairs in the post-Cold War period, but there are still more points where he is in a class by himself.

The first shared point is his institutional affiliation. Hoffmann belongs to the group of nine out of the ten writers in our survey whose career is linked to Harvard University. At the age of 81, Hoffmann has spent more than 50 years there as professor. Yet, unlike Fukuyama, Huntington, Nye, Gelb, Brzezinski, Kissinger, and Kagan, Hoffmann did not himself take a degree at the university. Nor was he a resident Fellow, like Chomsky. Rather he received his entire education in France before coming to America as a young man. He graduated from the Institut d'Etudes Politiques de Paris, or 'Sciences Po' as it is familiarly called by the French elites

Vienna-born, French trained Stanley Hoffmann belongs to the same generation of talented Europeans including Henry Kissinger and Zbigniew Brzezinski who arrived on American shores in the wake of the Nazi assault on the Old Continent. We have seen how the notion of 'foreignness' dogged the public image of Henry Kissinger, due in part to his accented English which betrays his German-speaking childhood but due more fundamentally to his *Realpolitik* intellectual persuasion which many Americans, rightly or wrongly, have considered to be an alien concept imported from Europe and incompatible with the popular faith in idealism. We have seen Zbigniew Brzezinski's self-consciousness about his unpronounceable name and foreign origins. However, among these arrivals who made very successful careers in their adopted country, Hoffmann is, without a doubt, the least typically American in terms of self-awareness and lifestyle choices. This is so even though his position as exponent of idealism and advocate for the moral dimension in managing international affairs would if taken by itself make him 'American as apple pie.'

By lifestyle choices, I mean firstly his staying clear of government service. Hoffmann chose not to follow Harvard and other Ivy League colleagues down to Washington for prestigious assignments advising the President and Congress on national security issues. Partly this follows from his stated belief that the role of the scholar is to advance human knowledge, not to counsel policy makers. Partly it is the logical consequence of his candid understanding of his profession as essentially philosophy and rhetoric rather than hard science with predictive value such as Washington policy-makers demand.

Hoffmann explicitly rejects futurology or mathematical modeling of international relations on epistemological grounds. He tells us that 'the search for general laws remains futile.' There are substantial imponderables surrounding human behavior, such as unshared objectives and values, all of which find expression in the exercise of free will that defies prediction. He issues a piquant rejoinder to his *confrères*, pointing to their uniform inability to foresee the collapse of the Soviet Union due to their misreading of Gorbachev and under-appreciation of the role of individual personalities in the causal chain [*World Disorders*, Chapter 1.]

In Hoffmann's view, the purpose of political philosophy is to present a clear vision of the present, to take into account as many of the factors driving events as possible. Then these insights may inform our efforts to implement what is both feasible and morally correct.

Hoffmann very comfortably wears the robes of a philosopher. He is at one with the thinking of the *Ur*-liberal Kant and he moves effortlessly back and forth in his writings between the grand masters of centuries gone by. and modern essayists whom he particularly respects and frequently cites, such as Judith Shklar.

It has to be said that Hoffmann is the only author in our survey who goes back to first principles. In *Chaos and Violence*, he tells us "The questions for American statecraft are, Leading for what? And with whom?" In their volumes running into hundreds of pages, none of our other thinkers poses such a challenge and then attempts to answer it.

While he declines to be a gray eminence advising princes, Hoffmann is the embodiment of the 'man of letters' in the European tradition, striving to *enlighten* the thinking public outside the campus. He has for years been a regular contributor to intellectual journals including *The New York Review of Books*, where his articles go from fairly straightforward book reviews to general commentary on current affairs in the journalistic genre. These more accessible writings constitute a significant part of the essay collections we will review below.

By his own admission, Hoffmann's experience of America has been limited geographically to New England and he has maintained close professional and personal ties with colleagues and friends in France. He is the only writer in our stable who publishes some of his works in his native tongue (French) before translating them into English.

Hoffmann is a towering intellect who has substantially shaped American political discourse even if his name and works are not widely known or popular in the general public. Indeed despite catchy titles and the often appealing chapter headings of his books, they make difficult reading because of the ponderous writing style of the author and a certain lack of discipline which a good editor could but evidently does not take in hand.

Hoffmann gives us page length paragraphs consisting of paragraph-length sentences which contain too many qualifications and side thoughts. Many of these subordinate ideas could be taken out as separate sentences for the sake of greater clarity and not to distract us from the dominant flow of ideas. It is a genuine pity that Hoffmann's compositional style is frequently impenetrable and will put off the unmotivated reader who is not yet aware of the rich ore to be mined in his works.

Hoffmann emerges from his writings as a very honest man, though not especially 'democratic.' There is a bit of the French *hauteur* here. He can be dismissive of opponents at times, and it is rare for him to counter the arguments of others directly and point for point. He does not reason with his reader so much as reason with himself and allow us to be witnesses.

In the two part analysis which follows, we will look at three of Stanley Hoffmann's books from the 1990s and the first decade of the new millennium. Two of them are collections of articles having a certain thematic unity. One is a more personal piece entitled *Gulliver Unbound* which was prompted by the American invasion of Iraq in March, 2003 and the strain this placed on Hoffmann's split identity as both French and American while his two motherlands were pitted against each other in a diplomatic *furore*.

World Disorders. Troubled Peace in the Post-Cold War Era (1998)

This collection of essays which were written over the preceding ten years has material addressed to different audiences – both very specialized and general readers – and it deals with a great many issues, including some which have no longer existed for a good long time and look unacceptably dated, such as relations with the Soviet Union. It is a pity that a strong-willed publisher did not persuade Professor Hoffmann to tighten the focus and to throw out those materials which probably had a readership of a couple of hundred persons worldwide when they were still fresh and now do not add to the author's reputation for perspicacity. However, the general reader will find that in this book Hoffmann also answers directly and with characteristic brilliance the issues which interest us, namely what has changed in the post-Cold War international landscape, what new challenges the United States faces and how they may be approached.

In *World Disorders*, Hoffmann gives us a highly detailed critique of the main currents of thinking about international affairs, realism and idealism, together with their updated continuations, neo-realism and neo-idealism. His consistent message is that these currents are all too limited in where they direct attention; they miss too many causal factors and so cannot stand alone as a guide to understanding and shaping the world in all its complexities. Involuntarily he proves the very same point when he deploys his own hybrid analytical apparatus.

It becomes clear very quickly that Stanley Hoffmann's intellectual predilections and political convictions prepared him admirably to interpret here one of the key policies which defined the presidency of Bill Clinton: humanitarian intervention in failing states to stop ethnic cleansing, genocide and other egregious violations of human rights. Hoffmann's contributions to our understanding of why this issue arose at this point in history, in the post-Cold War world, and what interests were in play are far more sophisticated and helpful than the cursory mention humanitarian intervention receives in the writings of nearly all the other major

thinkers in our survey. This is so because Hoffmann is interested primarily in international relations above and below the classic state-to-state
relations of hard power that provide the grist for our other thinkers. He
believes we are living in a post-Westphalian world, where state sovereignty is constrained from above by globalization, transnational private
transactions and pooling of sovereignty in new combinations such as the
European Union, while at the same time it is undermined from below by
newly emergent nationalism, calls for self-determination from among
peoples long kept in place by Communist regimes that have now disappeared. The '90s were indeed a period of cascading disintegration of multiethnic states into ever smaller groups bound by ethnic identity, often
creating in the process conditions of chaos which demanded outside
intervention.

His intellectual predilections and political convictions also led Hoffmann
to devote comparatively little attention in the 1990s to the way the Clinton
Administration handled relations with other great powers and in particular
to the redefinition of the NATO mission and its expansion into the former
Warsaw Pact countries, which was another defining feature of the years
when many of these essays were written. And yet we may say that it was
precisely America's solutions to the security architecture of post-Cold War
Europe and its ambivalent handling of China which preordained the major
powers pulling in different directions by the end of the 1990s and so frustrated the search for peace with justice that was and is central to Hoffmann's
theoretical writings.

Hoffmann's analysis of the weak points of the competing schools of
thought in international relations makes very stimulating reading precisely
because of the author's combination of incisiveness and moderation. Notwithstanding an attention-getting blurb of a review on the back cover of
this book, Hoffmann rarely 'skewers' his debating opponents.

This does not mean he is kind to fellow theoreticians. Turning to the new,
post-Cold War paradigms advanced by Francis Fukuyama and Samuel Huntington he tells us why they are either premature (the former) or lead us into
a *cul de sac* (the latter). Indeed he calls the 'end of history' spelled out by
Fukuyama 'a silly notion based on a series of mistaken assumptions' and
Huntington's 'clash of civilizations' as 'no more than an arresting idea,' which

is indeed pernicious insofar as it suggests an inevitability of conflict among countries belonging to different, and ill-defined civilizations.

Hoffmann's description of Henry Kissinger and Zbigniew Brzezinski as 'people who made a heady discovery of American power....and reveled in it' (Chapter 4) was certainly no compliment.

And generally, Hoffmann exposes the American foreign policy Establishment as being disoriented, out of touch not merely with the world as it is but lagging behind the American public in adapting to new times because it is mired in 'old modes of thinking'.

In this book, Hoffmann blames his peers for having become ensconced in the comfortable ideas of American predominance. He argues that the power to command and control needs to be supplemented by greater power to persuade. Hoffmann was in the 1990s already at one with Joseph Nye's notion of soft power.

Besides the failure of realism to factor in the many influences shaping international affairs above and below sovereign states, Hoffmann points to the inability of realists themselves to arrive at common analytical findings and policy recommendations on major issues of traditional power politics such as the prosecution the Vietnam War: if the leading theoreticians of the realist school were themselves at loggerheads, then clearly there was a problem with their tool kit.

Yet, the liberal idealist Hoffmann was not being partisan when he took on the realists. In this book he goes on to highlight the contradictions between and among the various principles which make up the basis of liberal internationalism tracing its roots back to Woodrow Wilson: national self-determination, human rights, state sovereignty, and democracy. He argues for differentiated weighting of these principles and, in particular, for a more cautious approach to self-determination.. Hoffmann believes the optimal solution for minorities is extensive autonomy, while secession and the further break-up of nation-states may be considered only as a last resort.

And Hoffmann does not spare the holy cow of the idealistic school, the notion that democratic countries live peaceably with one another, whereas other regimes foment war to gain greater control over their domestic population. This is no more than an unproven hypothesis, he tells us.

As for neo-realism and neo-idealism, he explains why they are 'anemic' and why their pseudo-scientific equations are no more than 'scholasticism.'

Turning from criticism of the various competing schools of thought, including his own liberal internationalism, to the positive recommendations on how to proceed, Hoffmann describes the new post-Cold War challenges and threats in terms that are, in the end, not so very different from those used by all of his peers in the Establishment. A subheading to his chapter on the New World says it all very succinctly: 'No End of Conflicts.'

This New World, Hoffmann insists, will not resemble any world of the past. Yes, it will be multipolar, but with rankings of states varying along the different vectors or, as he calls them 'different currencies of power.' Whatever the superficial resemblances to the 19th century world system may be, the post-Cold War world has its own specific features shaped by a number of unique new elements. One is the way the global economy and private actors such as multinational corporations or global investors remove traditional instruments of control from national governments. Another is the proliferation of intrastate conflicts resulting from competing nationalisms.

This is a world where the domestic weaknesses of the United States – 'growing debt, poor infrastructures, obsession of business with short-term profit, low savings, lack of leadership, popular resistance to taxation' – have caught up with it and limit its ability to provide the leadership it has long reserved for itself. We now have a world where the moderating role of the superpowers is greatly diminished.

It must be acknowledged that in expressing this view of the limits of American resources for ruling the world at the very time in the 1990s when the foreign policy Establishment, including its 'realist' wing, was caught up in triumphalism following the downfall of Communism speaks in favor of Hoffmann's *sang-froid*.

However, in specific policy areas Hoffmann's predisposition to distrust American projection of force abroad can leave him wrong-footed: I have in mind his warnings against armed intervention in 1991 to repel Saddam Hussein's seizure of Kuwait. The inclusion in *World Disorders* of this seven-year-old commentary on then current events is an ironic proof of the author's overriding point: political philosophers are uncertain guides for men of state.

Hoffmann has a full load of recommendations on how to achieve what he calls a 'more balanced order' among the powers. In several of the chapters he tells us that the U.S. should encourage the Western Europeans in their efforts at setting a new common identity and even to build their own defense organization. He proposes to draw Japan into greater participation in international organizations. He says the U.S. should share responsibility and authority more with both Japan and Europe in the international financial organizations.

In one chapter Hoffmann raises the prospect that Russia (the Soviet Union) and China might join the others in forming a 'central steering group' for the world (page 120). However, he does not seem to expect his advice on sharing power and responsibility to be followed. His remarks relating to humanitarian interventions assume no changes that would lead to greater cooperation and consensus among the global board of directors.

Hoffmann spells out small steps which he believes are achievable and would lead to a more peaceful and orderly world. True to his beliefs as a liberal internationalist, he calls for strengthening the peace-making powers of the United Nations by providing it with fighting forces. He seeks definition under international treaty of the ground rules for humanitarian interventions in response to domestic violence within nation states.

In *World Disorders*, Hoffmann devotes a chapter entitled 'In Defense of Mother Teresa' to the proposition of 'morality in foreign policy.' This is a direct response to the criticisms directed against Bill Clinton's military interventions in the Balkans and elsewhere on behalf of humanitarian values which opponents said turned foreign policy 'into a branch of social work.' Hoffmann tells us that values and interests need not be in contradiction. He claims that morality *is* in the national interest for down-to-earth, pragmatic reasons given the interconnectedness of societies and economies today, given the need for a stable international environment in which states do not disintegrate and refugees do not turn up at the door, tipping neighboring states into turmoil.

In other chapters, Hoffmann discusses at great length the theoretical pros and cons of intervention, the modalities of intervention and he gives us a score card, largely negative, of recent specific instances of intervention, whether unilateral or multilateral, in the affairs of nation states to redress chaos, violence, human rights abuses. Nonetheless, failures and all, he insists

that it is a moral obligation not to reconcile ourselves with evil and to continue to seek solutions by doing. Hoffmann freely accepts the burdens and
the grief of Sisyphus as being the lot of man.

Resurgent nationalism was surely the factor in the global order which Fukuyama least expected when he predicted the 'end of history.' It was the driver
of disorder and conflict in the 1990s and it is a subject which Hoffmann
examines closely under the magnifying glass in several chapters of this book.

Nationalism, he tells us, is a secular ideology that has proven much hardier
than anyone expected. Its reemergence in particularly malevolent forms in
the 1990s has disproved the hypothesis that ideologically driven conflict was
buried with the Soviet Union. Hoffmann differentiates among the 'brands' of
nationalisms but finds that all are potentially dangerous to the world order
even if some do provide material and spiritual goods for peoples, underpinning their sense of identity and self-worth.

This book also contains an interesting chapter on 'Nation and Nationalism in America Today.' Hoffmann deals here with some of the same issues
surrounding the American national identity which was one of the key
preoccupations of his fellow faculty member in Harvard's Department
of Government Sam Huntington and on which Huntington published
controversial articles in roughly the same time period as Hoffmann's
essays.

Hoffmann places Huntington's writings on the dangers posed to American
identity by the influx of Latinos from South of the Border among the 'mul-
titude of jeremiads' which U.S. culture periodically throws up. He expresses
his faith in the ability of American pluralism to integrate the latest arrivals as
it has done with past waves of immigrants and he sings the praises of American multiculturalism. What storm clouds hover on the nation's horizon come
not from shifting ethnic balances in the population but from institutional
failures created by present elites. "A political system entirely dominated by
money, where fund-raising and rewarding the funders eclipse the concern
for issues, is obviously a threat to the liberal democratic ideal so important
for American distinctiveness and self-image."

We find here a very illuminating comparison of the notions of national identity of the two leading countries which promote throughout the world what
they claim as universalistic values based on their own historical experience

and 'exceptionalism' – France and the United States. The distinctions in perspective inform his rather indulgent view of what American behavior on the international stage is really all about: "Foreigners will believe that American policy is purely self-serving even when it isn't; and Americans will believe they are serving the world even when they are mainly serving themselves."

The concluding chapter to *World Disorders* is the only one not to have been pulled out of Hoffmann's desk drawer of prior publications. It constitutes a draft for a new book on ethics and international relations and, though heavy going, it contains some nuggets of insight and boldly drawn 'normative outlines' that deserve mention.

Going back to first principles of political philosophy, Hoffmann reminds us that inherent rights belong only to individuals, not to groups or nations or states; that when states trample on the rights of individuals they lose their legitimacy and the Westphalian principle of nonintervention in domestic affairs is forfeited.

Here he also takes on directly the newly aired counter-attack from China and other states resentful of Western lectures about human rights and imposition of sanctions for their violation. Defending human rights is not a new form of imperialism, Hoffmann insists. These values are shared by many non-Western societies.

Hoffmann fleshes out here his notion of a limited right to self-determination, saying that a nation created by secession deserves international recognition only if it has respected human rights and allows international monitoring. He proposes measures not merely to safeguard the rights of minorities claiming oppression but also to protect nation-states against the 'excessive demands and intransigence' of minorities.

In this same chapter we have proof that in his most recent writings Hoffmann was in the vanguard of thinkers coming to grips with the newly arising issues of international relations: immigration and asylum; and environmental 'rights' of future generations. .

STANLEY HOFFMANN AND HEROIC IDEALISM:

GULLIVER UNBOUND

PART TWO

The idea of writing *L'Amérique vraiement impériale? (Is America Really Imperial?)* was put to Stanley Hoffmann by one of his former students and it was realized in the form of transcribed responses to questions posed by another of his former students, the historian Frédéric Bozo, who is a Professor at the University of Sorbonne. A year later an English language edition appeared under the title *Gulliver Unbound,* which for those with long memories, alludes to one of Hoffmann's early works, *Gulliver's Troubles,* published back in 1968. The English edition had a couple of new chapters written in 2004 by Stanley Hoffmann on his own and bringing the material on Iraq up to date.

The impulse for this work was to elucidate for interested readers on both sides of the Atlantic how it was that America and France found themselves in a sharp diplomatic row in 2002- 2003 over America's armed intervention in Iraq to remove Saddam Hussein. French efforts in the UN Security Council effectively stymied a resolution sought by the Americans to provide diplomatic cover for their planned invasion. The result was outrage and a loud anti-French campaign across America which put those with dual French-American sympathies like Hoffmann in a soul-searching position.

Accordingly, the first order of business in this book was to examine the positions of then French President Chirac and his Minister of Foreign Affairs Dominique de Villepin, the positions of President George Bush and his close advisers and to highlight where the sides misread each other's intentions and so exacerbated the underlying differences in national mentalities and interests to the point where tempers flared out of control on the American side while the French dug in their heels and stood their ground before the world hegemon.

Hoffmann makes it fairly clear that the American administration was acting in bad faith: they were 'cunning,' willfully deceptive and manipulative towards their allies. For their part, the French did not say all they meant, expecting the Americans to read between the lines and to do what they felt they must without compromising their friends in the eyes of the Muslim world and turning a great power game into a clash of civilizations.

However, *Gulliver Unbound* goes on from there to explore the nature of the American Empire under George W. Bush as its French title indicates. And the opening question he grapples with is typically the priority concern of every Parisian intellectual: is the imperial behavior we are witnessing in present-day America just more of the same, a line of continuity, or something genuinely new, a 'rupture,' as the French put it.

On the one hand, Hoffmann tells us we see in the policies of the Bush administration the legacy 'exceptionalism' that can be traced back to Woodrow Wilson. On the other hand, the break with the past is considerably more important than continuity: what Hoffmann calls the 'directed multilateralism' of Bush Sr. and Clinton was replaced under Bush Jr. by a 'triumphant unilateralism.' After September 11th this became a very new kind of exceptionalism based solely on projection of military strength. It was formalized by the National Security Strategy of the United States of September 2002 which *inter alia* brought in the doctrine of preventive action and identified the threat from rogue states trying to acquire weapons of mass destruction.

From this point on, *Gulliver Unbound* meanders this way and that. Hoffmann is behaving rather like a Lilliput, describing an ankle, then an elbow, then an ear but not giving us a comprehensive portrait of Gulliver, not providing an integrated explanation of what he clearly believes is a frightening authoritarian political climate developing in the imperial America of George W. Bush.

In what follows, I will string together Hoffmann's passing remarks on what should be the pillars of American pluralism and, using his own words, draw the missing picture of Gulliver.

He tells us there is a new 'cult of force' afoot in the United States. Meanwhile rule of law is being eroded as evidenced by Guantanamo and the Patriot Act. The war on terror is being used by the Executive as 'a lever in order to mobilize opinion, smother political controversies and seduce both idealists and realists.'

Who is to blame for this dire situation? Hoffmann is very cautious about laying responsibility at the door of the Oval Office, though his words about George W. Bush are none too kind. In his view, the President exploited the events of September 11th to obtain 'a lever usable to increase his own and America's might, and his and his partisans' grip on the nation.' He calls the President 'more than a little devious and often vindictive' saying he 'doesn't hesitate to lie, either in domestic or in foreign policy.' But he also reminds us that when he came into office the President had no experience in foreign policy and was 'malleable.'

In effect, Hoffmann lays responsibility for the new and dangerous direction of American political life on the Neoconservatives, a small but determined group who were formerly 'embedded in the think tanks' and now are advisers to Vice President Cheney, the decisive figure behind much of the change in U.S. government policies since 9/11. Neocons also figure among the Pentagon civilian team headed by Paul Wolfowitz. These are people who are contemptuous of public opinion and who are admirers of the former emblems of rule by force: the Roman Empire and the British Empire. They deeply dislike international organizations, international law, in a word, any constraints on the free exercise of American might.

Of course, it would be nice to know how Neocons succeeded in moving out of think tanks and into the corridors of power. But Hoffmann is not drilling down very deep in this book; rather he is building a little platform for making his own policy recommendations to counteract the dismaying current.

He tells us that the chauvinism emanating from the Neocons is supported by popular media like Fox television, whom Hoffmann singles out for its 'epic vulgarity.' Mainstream news providers like CNN and the Washington Post have fallen into line with what he calls 'a saddening conformity.' During the post-9/11 period, and particularly in the run-up to the invasion, the media supplied analyses which Hoffmann describes as 'often simplistic, often ignorant of the outside world, but also chauvinistic or delirious with naïve idealism.' The press was not alone in its subservience to government policies: even academic circles showed what Hoffmann calls 'extraordinary weakness.' And a grass-roots movement providing resonance for the issues delineated by Neocons has emerged in the 'significant and growing force of far-right Christians.'

The Neoconservatives' domination of political space was facilitated, according to Hoffmann, by the way September 11th primed the public for a hard line and firm leadership to redress wounded patriotism. On key issues, the Democrats now behaved in a 'cowardly' manner. Congress buckled under to the Executive on the Patriot Act and much else.

In *Gulliver Unbound*, Hoffmann takes up the question of the Bush Administration's changing justifications for its 2003 invasion of Iraq, beginning with the supposed threat of Weapons of Mass Destruction in the months leading up to the start of hostilities and ending, post facto, in expressions of humanitarian concern: America had removed a vicious dictator who murdered countless of his own citizens. He talks about whether intelligence reports supporting the worst case scenario of Saddam's WMD may have been directed from the Executive or tried too hard to please the Executive. He exposes the falseness of the argument for armed intervention on humanitarian grounds given past U.S. failure to react to Saddam's excesses, including his bloody repression of Kurds and Shiite uprisings following the First Gulf War. He reminds us of the glaring abuses of American forces on the ground in Iraq since the start of the occupation including the Abu Ghraib affair. It all looks quite bleak.

The darkest passages of *Gulliver Unbound* come in the final chapter, 'The Dangers of Empire,' which was written by Hoffmann alone before the book went to print in English. Here he remarks that the thinkers guiding the Democratic opposition to Bush like Brzezinski are themselves still caught up in 'a grandiose view of America's power and vision.' Meanwhile the country is 'sliding from an imperfect liberal democracy towards a kind of populist authoritarianism.' He characterizes the supporters of George W. Bush as 'radical, utopian and imperialist abroad, reactionary and antiliberal within.'

In his catalogue of the nation's domestic ills and nasty behavior abroad, Hoffmann begins to sound here like America's most widely known dissident, Noam Chomsky. In a manner similar to Chomsky's books, he switches from gloom and doom to an upbeat final few lines, telling readers that 'This too will not last forever.' He professes to believe there are enough opponents of the reactionary movement in America to eventually prevail: '...the imperial temptation is strong, but it is not inevitable or irreversible.'

Unlike the dissidents, Stanley Hoffmann is not suggesting there is a systemic or institutional failure behind America's current problems. And if he is cautious in pointing his finger at individuals who are to blame, I think it is not for lack of courage. Rather, he seems persuaded that you are more likely to win at chess by concentration and deliberate continuation of play than by overturning the chessboard. He uses *Gulliver Unbound* to deliver a set of instructions on how to get America out of the 'trap' that Iraq has become, whereby continued U.S. military presence there only feeds the insurgency and recruits for terrorism. The list of things to do just happens to be a cut-to-size version of Hoffmann's general views on how he would like American domestic and foreign policies to develop.

Hoffmann tells us the first thing to do is to get US combat troops out of Iraq within six months of the election of a new assembly which forms a new government. Sovereignty is then returned to the Iraqis who will decide what kind of assistance they need from the international community. Meanwhile, the United States would scrap its plans for military bases and curtail its over-blown diplomatic presence.

The next thing to do if we are to return to 'reality, to good sense and to morality' is for the United States to pursue policies in the Middle East which reduce rather than enhance the appeal of terrorism. This means working together with the U.N., the EU and Russia to end the Israeli occupation of Palestinian territory and to bring about a viable Palestinian state.

One interesting new element in Hoffmann's thinking which appears in *Gulliver Unbound* is his attempt to respond creatively to the unacceptable logic of the Neoconservatives, and finally of the Bush Administration, that America must reserve for itself the right to act unilaterally and intervene militarily abroad when the UN Security Council proves unable to act, as happened in the run-up to the 2003 invasion of Iraq.

Hoffmann suggests that in such cases, a motion on military intervention should be sent for review to a new institution: 'an association of democratic nations including members of NATO and democracies of Asia, Africa and Latin America such as India, South Africa, Chile, Australia and New Zealand.'

The idea of a Community of Democracies had been promoted by liberal hawks in the Clinton Administration as an instrument for promoting democratic governance. Secretary of State Madeleine Albright and Polish Foreign Minister Bronislaw Geremek convened the first such gathering in Warsaw in 2000, and the Warsaw Declaration stipulated as an operating principle that members might constitute a democratic caucus within existing international organizations. In 2004, at about the time Hoffmann's English edition of *Gulliver Unbound*, such a caucus was launched within the United Nations General Assembly. However, the Community of Democracies was rather lax in its admissions criteria and included 'democratizing' and well as genuinely democratic members.

Hoffmann's version of this idea differs from the Albright initiative by setting strict criteria of democracy for membership and by concentrating on the task of ruling on whether any given tyrannical regime should be overthrown, by force if necessary. With respect to mission if not membership rules, Hoffmann was thinking along lines not very dissimilar from his ideological foes, the Neocons though he claimed that such an institution would merely fill a lacuna in the UN Charter. Apart from removing from the Republican Right one important justification for unilateralism, his idea would put on a sounder and less arbitrary footing the whole notion of humanitarian interventions which Hoffmann basically favors.

* * *

Chaos and Violence. What Globalization, Failed States, and Terrorism Mean for U.S. Foreign Policy (2006)

Given the long lines of continuity of Stanley Hoffmann's thinking, it should come as no surprise that this new collection of essays which appeared in periodicals over the preceding six years carries forward many of the central theoretical concerns that he discussed in his 1998 book *World Disorders,* such as humanitarian interventions, defense of human rights and the improvement of world governance. And yet there are new perspectives here which arose from his shock at the muscular and, at times, brutal direction of U.S. foreign policy after 9/11. There is no mistaking that Hoffmann is also more down to earth. There are no Festschrifts in this collection.

Some of the best material in this book comes at the very start, in the introductory chapter entitled "The State of the World and the State of the Discipline." Here Hoffmann expresses his several disappointments which have summoned the creative response this book represents:

"...I am struck by the consensus of the American establishment on the virtues of unipolarity and of American hegemony."

And, equally telling:

"The discipline of international relations remains an American social science, meaning the perennial search for certainty...desire for greater rigor, predictive power, and modelization. This leads to a frequently slanted view of the world."

In keeping with these unpleasant realizations, in this book Hoffmann indulges less in pontification and engages more in argumentation. He resumes his long running critique of realism, idealism and their many off-shoots. But he is no longer dismissive of other prophets.

Here we see for the first time that he is taking seriously two of the paradigms which emerged from the early post-Cold War thinking on international relations, Fukuyama (*The End of History*) and Huntington (*Clash of Civilizations*). We no longer hear about 'silly notions.' And yet his remarks on the inadequacies of these works are, it should be noted, concentrated on the end results rather than methodological failures.

It is interesting to note that in one of the later essays, a review article he published in *The New York Review of Books*, Hoffmann speaks in complimentary terms of Fukuyama's *America at the Crossroads*, picking the raisins out of the cake: namely Fukuyama's newly formulated 'multi-multilateralism' and 'realistic Wilsonianism.' At the same time Hoffmann remains silent about those aspects of Fukuyama's thinking which suggest he never moved very far from his Neoconservative roots.

Hoffmann also devotes attention in some of these essays to writings on international relations by non-scholars which had gained great currency among the general public. In particular, he chooses to deal with the theories of Thomas Friedman, a *New York Times* journalist and political commentator who rode to worldwide fame on the back of his several books on globalization, beginning with *The Lexus and the Olive Tree* (1999). Hoffmann also felt obliged to respond to the Neoconservative foreign policy strategist Robert Kagan's ideas on Europe and America in *Paradise and Power*. Hoffmann draws on his own unusual cross-cultural experience to deal with the issue exploited by Kagan: why Americans and Europeans see world challenges differently. Here Hoffmann occupies a far more balanced and informed position not merely than a publicist like Kagan but than his more heavy weight peers Kissinger and Brzezinski writing on the same subject.

Hoffmann turns his attention to 'other imperialists with a good conscience' in the Neoconservative camp: Charles Krauthammer and William Kristol. And he pulls at the line of fellow-thinkers among the 'friends of Israel' such as Paul Wolfowitz and Richard Perle. In a word, Hoffmann has descended from the ivory tower and is engaging the street fighters on their turf.

Several chapters identify the major issue emerging from the end of the Cold War that shaped the international scene ever since and is the direct result of America's emergence as the sole remaining superpower: the hubris of the entire U.S. foreign policy Establishment and its susceptibility to the dangerous illusion that the U.S. can act as the world Leviathan and put an end to interstate strife. This updating of the Hobbesian vision is beloved by American realists and liberals alike. In many of the essays in this book Hoffmann returns to this illusion and its consequences, including a marked worldwide rise in anti-Americanism: "Other states do not want American governance of the world. Without a thorough rejection of this new doctrine and a return to a policy of leadership without dictation, the state of world governance can only get worse."

As the sole superpower, America was no longer in need of alliances, no longer constrained to be nice to allies so as to highlight its difference from its Cold War adversary. And so America had come to focus on its own capabilities rather than ideals. It was looking after its own national interest 'pure and simple.'

Instead of American hegemony, Hoffmann tells us once again that what the world needs is stronger institutions, both at the global level and at regional levels. He calls for endowing the United Nations with military forces sufficient to carry out peace-making as well as peace-keeping missions, for vastly augmenting the financial resources at its disposal.

Hoffmann holds up to his analytical scalpel his ideological opponents in the Bush Administration. He tells us about Dick Cheney's 1992 draft Defense Planning Guidance which a decade later became the *The National Security Strategy of the United States* (2002), i.e., the official justification for preemptive war that we know as the Bush doctrine. He tells us about the way President George W. Bush and his team brandished the fear of terrorism to control the political space and roll back civil liberties.

At the same time, in this book Hoffmann exposes the inconsistencies in foreign policy practiced by the Administration of Bill Clinton, which spoke in internationalist terms but, in the person of Secretary of State Madeleine Albright, either imposed outcomes in international conflicts which hardly were supported by consensus or purely and simply acted unilaterally. He highlights the kind of 'bossism' whereby in the Clinton years the United States used international agencies as if they were internal bodies of the American government. Albright's grating words about America, 'the indispensable nation' were cover for often brutal action, as he catalogues.

Hoffmann's brickbats for the Democrats extend into the new millennium when, in the opposition, they responded in what he characterizes as cowardly fashion to the Bush Administration's lies and distortions surrounding the invasion and occupation of Iraq. He explains why pusillanimity cost John Kerry the election in 2004. The party 'seemed anxious not to upset voters…. who did not want to hear about the limits on American power."

Throughout, Hoffmann keeps a matter-of-fact tone when talking about the new imperial America, its blind hubris and its acts of aggression. He has once again positioned himself in space otherwise occupied by dissidents. Though he despairs over the elites, he remains optimistic about the American people who, he insists, have no stomach for the imperial adventure.

The very last essay in this book gives us a succinct and updated set of recommendations for a better world. There are few surprises in Hoffmann's latest 'to-do' list. A settlement of the Palestinian-Israeli conflict is at the very top, with Hoffmann yet again calling for the United States to adopt a balanced position. As in *Gulliver Unbound* he is again urging U.S. withdrawal from Iraq under a fixed timetable.

Here Hoffmann is fairly specific about what a policy of demilitarization of U.S. policy would mean. He is calling for a 50% cutback in the defense budget with re-allocation of the resources to look after the poor, provide health care and improved education, and step up funding of state building abroad through international agencies.

Hoffmann recognizes that these and the additional items on his recommended list 'may appear utopian." But he insists they would make the world safer and would not work against America's basic interests. The country he wants America to be will be primus inter pares. Full stop.

G. John Ikenberry,
Liberal Internationalism
of the Next Generation:

Liberal Order & Imperial Ambition (2005)

It may seem to some readers to be a stretch too far when I list Princeton University Professor G. John Ikenberry among the leading post-Cold War American thinkers on international relations. To be sure, his is not a household name and his books on the theory of IR are written for fellow scholars rather than undergraduates, not to mention the general public.

And yet there are strong reasons for his presence on our list. Within the American foreign policy establishment and the broader circle of those who regularly follow world affairs, Ikenberry's writings appear before them every two months or so. The 160,000 subscribers of *Foreign Affairs* magazine know Ikenberry as one of the ten 'in-house' book reviewers whose responsibility is for the 'Political and Legal' genre.

Ikenberry is also an occasional contributor of articles to *American Interest* magazine published by (former) Neoconservative theoretician Francis Fukuyama which aims to inform the non-specialist public. His name appears on the magazine's masthead as a member of the Editorial Board. For reasons we shall explore below it is not in the least surprising that he would find common cause with Fukuyama. But then again Ikenberry is on the Editorial Board of a half dozen other periodicals read by the foreign policy establishment.

As was the case with Stanley Hoffmann, I would put the emphasis on 'influential' more than on 'widely read' in justifying Ikenberry's place among our great thinkers. His position as leading theoretician is inextricably associated with an issue which has been at the forefront of attention both in the profession and in the broad public ever since the collapse of the Soviet Union: namely the nature and staying power of American hegemony.

Hegemony has been Ikenberry's abiding interest going back to his earliest scholarly articles in the 1980s. However, at that time, like other academics, he was responding to the widely expected loss of hegemony. After all, the hegemonic position in military force which the U.S. came into as the main victor of WWII was built upon the world's largest . economy by far, with economic might which soared above the war-ravaged landscape of its erstwhile competitors in Europe and the Far East. With the restoration of peacetime economies among both the vanquished and the allied nations over the course of several decades, the relative world economic standing of the U.S. had significantly declined by the late 1980s, placing the question of the new world order on the agenda of political scientists led by exponents of the realist school, for whom a rise or fall in these measurable indicators determines the configuration of international relations. Ikenberry emerged at this time as a contrarian, arguing that the hegemony would be more durable than many supposed because of the way it was institutionalized.

In the early 1990s, doubt about the staying power of American world leadership found another leg to stand on. Many scholars anticipated the system of American-dominated military alliances and economic institutions would unravel now that the common cause of resisting world Communism had disappeared. Once again Ikenberry gathered persuasive arguments why this would not be the case, telling us that the free world had developed not merely as a counterweight to Russia's empire of unfree but had all along found its own justification in shared benefits of liberal democracy and participative decision-making of the security alliances.

In the mid-1990s, generalized euphoria in the American foreign policy establishment put paid to all doubts over the longevity of American domination of the global landscape. The collapse of the Soviet Union upset all previous calculations of the world pecking order. Talk about a Pax Americana and the 'indispensable nation' signaled the revival of imperialism as a respectable ordering of international relations after a half-century of ignominy.

The rise of a new age economy built on advanced telecommunications and the internet enhanced both the reality and the perception of American dynamism. Ikenberry quickly picked up the new questions relating to America's unipolar moment and its fast accelerating advance on the Rest of the World in measurable military force, technological prowess and relative economic buoyancy, not to mention its role of worldwide arbiter of popular culture.

At the very end of the '90s, Ikenberry explained to those at home and abroad who were worried by the emergence of the new Leviathan why America's liberal-democratic, open-markets and rule-based hegemony served the world's interests nearly as much as it did U.S. interests. And in the new millennium, when the Bush administration opted for reckless unilateralism in its first term, Ikenberry rose to the occasion, boldly reminding all who would listen why restraint and strengthening rather than overturning existing alliances was the better way to serve American security.

In this way, Ikenberry has been in the thick of the debates over U.S. foreign policy for a couple of decades and his theories on *structural liberalism* as the best way forward in international relations have been built upon incrementally to form an imposing body of scholarship.

In many respects, G. John Ikenberry may be said to be a younger version of Stanley Hoffmann, from whom he is separated by one generation. Both are the intellectual's intellectual, with a high level of abstraction in their thinking. Ultimately their contributions have directional bearing on public policy rather than providing solutions to specific issues arising in one country or another.

Unlike Hoffmann, Ikenberry appears to have had no principled reasons for avoiding government service. Indeed, his official CV informs us that in the period April 2004 – January 2005 he was a member of an Advisory Group in the Department of State. Earlier still, in 1991-92, he served with the Policy Planning Staff at State.

Throughout his career, he has been mobile and visible in the profession. Ikenberry has had an association with leading think tanks including the Carnegie Endowment for International Peace, The Brookings Institution and the German Marshall Fund-USA.

He did not stay planted at one institution of higher learning. He completed his graduate studies at the University of Chicago, then taught at Princeton, the University of Pennsylvania and Georgetown University before returning to Princeton. Given his views, there would seem to be something inevitable about his staying definitively at the Woodrow Wilson School.

Like Hoffmann, Ikenberry's declared political philosophy is eclectic but finally is not far removed from Wilsonian idealism. And this is what brings him at times to within a hair's breadth of some of the basic tenets of the Neoconservative movement, who have drawn their water from the same well.

I have in mind here Ikenberry's unfailing belief that regimes matter. Democratic states can more easily live in peace with one another than autocratic states. He tells us that: "Democracies are particularly capable of making constitutional commitments to each other..." that "Because policy-making in democracies tends to be decentralized and open, the character of commitments can be more clearly determined and there are opportunities to lobby policy-makers in other democracies.. Democracies do not just sign agreements; they create political processes that reduce uncertainty and build confidence in mutual commitments."

These and similar remarks in defense of American hegemony as being tame, reliable and in everyone's interest appear repeatedly in the pages of the work we are about to examine. They sound nice when proclaimed ex cathedra but are, in the end, just unproven opinion, as his fellow liberal Stanley Hoffmann would be the first to say. However, they may explain the warm praise for Ikenberry in the blurb from Francis Fukuyama on the dust jacket.

In a rough way one could describe both Hoffmann and Ikenberry as believers in international institutions as bringing order in global relations out of the famous Hobbesian chaos. However, Hoffmann puts the emphasis on global institutions with universal scope such as the United Nations, which he wants to see equipped with the resources for peace making as well as peace keeping. By contrast, Ikenberry is interested primarily in the international institutions within the liberal West. As we will see, his 'structural liberalism' is a description of the American hegemony, not of the world at large. The problem he does not seem to deal with is what happens when legitimacy for American projection of force abroad is granted by some or even all of America's security allies in Europe and the Far East but is repudiated by other world powers who cannot be dismissed as irrelevant, such as the BRIC countries.

Resuming our delineation of differences between the two giants of modern liberalism in our stable of thinkers, Ikenberry is more generous to the realist school than Stanley Hoffmann. He sees America's post-WWII foreign policy as having had two constant and leading components - containment of the Soviet Union, which was an expression of realism; and the construction of a liberal democratic order, which is very much in the Wilsonian tradition.

He gives the realists some credit for seeing off Communism, though ultimately in his view the Soviet Union collapsed due mainly to contradictions within the system and not to outside factors. Back in 1992, when the US foreign policy establishment was already intoxicated with triumphalism, he co-authored an essay in *Foreign Affairs* with Daniel Deudney ("Who Won the Cold War?") which took issue directly with the claims of the neo-conservatives that it was the ideological purity and hard line policies of their hero, Ronald Reagan, that had brought down Communism. No, said Ikenberry, to the extent that U.S. policy may have been a contributor, it was not a hard line but precisely a soft line which may have done the trick. Reagan's contribution was his anti-nuclearism which Neocons prefer to forget, his cutting slack for Gorbachev which made it possible for the Kremlin to undertake the reforms which ultimately brought down the whole structure.

Set against the senior statesmen and philosophers who populate our list of great thinkers, Ikenberry is one of the youngest. He is a mature scholar in the prime of his career who shares some of the habits of his peer group. First among these is what I would call a 'team' approach to the métier, something akin to what goes on in a think tank.

For much of his career, he has co-authored. In the late 1980s, his first partner was Charles Kupchan, a realist school political scientist who eventually found his home in Georgetown University. From the early 1990s to today, Ikenberry has collaborated repeatedly with Daniel Deudney, now at Johns Hopkins University, who stands outside the classical division of realists and idealists.

Besides jointly written analytical essays, Ikenberry's bibliography also lists many books where he figures as editor. I mention these features of his work because they make it somewhat difficult to select a volume that is uniquely Ikenberry's own. The 2005 opus *Liberal Order & Imperial Ambition* which we are about to analyze comes as close as any, though even here we find two co-authored chapters.

Finally, I wish to make a brief comment on Ikenberry's writing style, which is perhaps his biggest difference with Hoffmann. Ikenberry is a masterful presenter. He frames his essays extremely well. He sets up the questions to be addressed, is logical and thorough in his treatment and then produces a resume at the end which drives home his points. He follows the classic formula of: here is what I am going to tell you, here is what I am telling you, and in conclusion, this is what I just told you. Qualifications and amplifications go into footnotes, thereby providing the reader with a text that is easy to digest. Moreover, the footnotes lead the reader to relevant additional readings and do not merely catalogue where specific facts or ideas have been picked up.

In terms of methodology, Ikenberry frequently alternates between two kinds of argumentation to set out his case: deductive reasoning and the introduction of historical cases (inductive).

* * *

Liberal Order & Imperial Ambition is a collection of Ikenberry's previously published articles going back 15 years. This is a dangerous thing to do in a field which is classified by booksellers as "Current Affairs." Like journalism, the material is susceptible to fast obsolescence.

Ikenberry provides us with a substantive introductory chapter which weaves his material together very nicely. In fact, you might think there is no reason to go beyond the introduction, since he telescopes all punches here. Indeed, in one short paragraph at the end of this introduction he seemingly says it all:

"These essays seek to show that America achieved something extraordinarily special in 60 years since the end of WWII – the creation of an international order more durable and complex than realist theory can explain and more successful than neo-conservatives can appreciate. American power and liberal order are tied together and rely on each other."

However, it would be pity if the reader closed the book at this point, because he would miss all the tactical shifts Ikenberry made over time to respond to the changing terms of the scholarly debate. The reader would also miss the chinks in Ikenberry's armor which come out in his detailed argumentation.

Overall the articles presented in this collection appear in chronological order, though there are a few exceptions, some backtracking to accommodate the structure of his 2005 argumentation. They appear without any updating and so are of uneven quality when taken separately, given that circumstances have moved on.

The tasks which Ikenberry set for himself in these articles/chapters are exciting from the word 'go.' His Chapter 1 on 'Rethinking the Origins of American

Hegemony' takes on directly the question which inevitably arises among students of the American empire: was it something a country predisposed to isolationism stumbled upon or was it the logical culmination of a process going back to 19th century Manifest Destiny thinking and gunboat diplomacy (as argued by Boston University Professor Andrew Bacevich, for example). Ikenberry sets out and solves the question slightly differently, drilling down to the period just after WWII when the American-dominated world order took its recognizable features of today. The concrete historical record shows that:

"the U.S. got both less than it wanted and more than it bargained for in the early postwar period. The U.S. was clearly hegemonic and used its economic and military position to construct a postwar order. But that order was not really of its own making."

Ikenberry demonstrates that Europe sought a tangible U.S. commitment to its defense in the recognition that the Continent was too weak economically and militarily to proceed on its own as the East-West confrontation arose. The result, he tells us, is that "U.S. hegemony in Europe was largely an empire by invitation."

The second chapter, on "Socialization and Hegemonic Power,' co-authored with Charles Kupchan, seeks to explain what might be called the 'buy-in' of secondary powers to American rule. In exchange for mutually accepted restraint by the hegemon, the others acquiesce in its dominance. This reduces for the hegemon the 'transaction costs' of exercising its will by providing legitimacy and obviating the need for coercion. Meanwhile the others benefit from tangible and predictable public goods. Ikenberry is accounting here for the 'bandwagon' effect which overturns behavior patterns (balance of power) predicted by the realist school

In the third chapter, co-authored with Deudney, Ikenberry sets out his theory of 'structural liberalism' which he claims captures better the unique properties of the American dominated world order which both the realist and idealist schools miss, causing them to underestimate its long term prospects.

Several of his five elements of 'structural liberalism' are persuasive and easy to accept. That is surely the case with 'security co-binding,' by which Ikenberry means that in the liberal world order institutions lock in reciprocal restraint on all the members, making power balancing unnecessary. The prime example, he tells us, is NATO.

Another point, 'penetrated hegemony' might also be reasonable, if one doesn't look too closely. Here Ikenberry has in mind that the 'transparency, diffusion of power into many hands and the multiple points of access to policy-making' in America, all of which allows the country's European and Japanese allies to share in decision-making, forge a consensus however asymmetrical the power of the participants. This feature enhances the resiliency and stability of the system. My caveat here is that from time to time, American decision making is far less transparent and open to outside pressures of friends than Ikenberry would have us believe. The entire unilateralist adventure of George W. Bush revealed how easy it can be for the Executive to run roughshod over domestic opposition in a supine Congress and reduce those who hope to temper U.S. policy from within to the status of 'poodles.'

However, another element of Ikenberry's 'structural liberalism' – what he calls 'civic identity' - is simply wrong, without any qualification on when and under which U.S. administration.

Here is his flat and unproven assertion:

"An essential component of the Western political order is a widespread civic identity that is distinct from national, ethnic and religious identities. This is consensus around a set of norms and principles, most importantly political democracy, constitutional government, individual rights, private property-based economic systems and toleration of diversity."

The idea that the Constitution is the glue binding American national identity is common currency among a goodly number of the country's political scientists. But as Stanley Hoffmann told us, this is the distinguishing, almost unique feature of the *American* identity. It is curious that Ikenberry was not listening.

Apart from a thin stratum of politicians having regular intercourse with American interlocutors, it would be hard to find many Europeans, for example, thinking about themselves firstly or even lastly as participants in liberal democracies with market economies. Language, religion and ethnicity never were displaced as the markers of personal consciousness on the Continent even as the European Economic Community became the European Union. Moreover, a rising tide of national passions swept into Western Europe from the East after the fall of the Berlin Wall in general as new states emerged, rewrote the past, invented anthems and other trappings of nationhood.

Scenes of the brutal wars on the territory of ex-Yugoslavia filled the evening news for more than six years reminding the citizens in Europe's heartland a few hundred kilometers away about the emotive power of the new nationalisms. Another wave of anti-cosmopolitan feeling swept across Europe in the new millennium as thinking about the Muslim immigrants in their midst hardened after 9/11.

This particular blindness to nationalism in Ikenberry's argumentation is symptomatic of his focus on the way Americans think and his failure to consider that others living in friendly countries, not to mention our adversaries, might have mental processes that operate quite differently. For a political scientist who has long-time professional interests in Japan and China, as Ikenberry does, it is hard to understand this manifestation of what I must characterize as America-centrism.

Now that I have let drop the accusation of provincialism, I have to mention another instance where Ikenberry projects his reading of the American political system onto other countries without any proof and, finally, wrongly. He speaks of transparency and political openness in 'democratic countries' as the reason why such countries can bond so well and live in peace. But this is just wishful thinking if applied to much of Western Europe. If he were to stand forth in any public square in Europe and assert that the voting public exercises oversight and control of foreign policy, Ikenberry would be met only by derisive laughter. On the few occasions when the political elites put their concoctions to a referendum, as happened in France and the Netherlands when the European Constitution was put to a vote, the results have been fairly uniform rejection of what is being done at the highest levels without any public say.

Chapter 4 on "Constitutional Politics in International Relations" explains at length how the post WWII agreements on new institutions and architecture for international relations between the United States and its friends and allies resemble the kind of constitutional settlement which is made within states from time to time after some grave crisis: the newly powerful freely submit to restraints at the outset in order to lock in acceptance of their dominant position on the assumption that over time their relative power advantage will erode. The result is predictability in relations and an absence of arbitrariness that is to everyone's advantage. Ikenberry tells us that such settlements typically come about on the international stage following great wars. This is what happened after 1648, 1815, Versailles and WWII.

Chapter 5 takes on directly the question of whether the American hegemony is also an empire. Ikenberry insists that it is not, that the new world order is not coercive in the manner of empires from the past. Instead America is embedded in a system which is bigger than itself and in which there is distributed power even if it is dominant. What has developed under American encouragement is a 'democratic-capitalist empire' with shared values of the participants.

Because the American unipolar order has deep foundations, it will not be replaced anytime soon. There will be no return to the traditional multipolar world of great power politics, Ikenberry insists.

In chapter 6, "The Myth of Post-Cold War Chaos," written in 1996, Ikenberry says that the end of the Cold War bipolarity has left standing the liberal international order which the U.S. was otherwise building ever since the end of WWII.

In his view, the main legacy coming out of the War was not containment and the Truman Doctrine but the Atlantic Charter pronounced by Roosevelt and Churchill in 1941, then the post war arrangements determined at Bretton Woods (IMF, World Bank, the new world economic order) and at Dumbarton Oaks (United Nations and security structure).

In Chapter 7, "Getting Hegemony Right," Ikenberry is busy defending American hegemony against those who are becoming nervous over the widening gulf between American military might and the capabilities of the rest of the world. He assures his reader that the U.S. has what he calls 'an unusual capacity to coopt and reassure,' so that the hegemonic order will despite all, remain stable.

In Chapter 8, 'American Grand Strategy in the Age of Terror,' written in 2002, Ikenberry finds himself defending America's rule-based hegemony against the brazen unilateralists of the Bush White House. He is whistling in the dark when he ends the chapter with a hopeful note: "overall, the events of September 11 do not seem to signal the unraveling of the old international order. The Bush administration is launching its war on terrorism from a foundation of stable and cooperative relations built over many decades."

That wishful optimism did not last long. Chapter 9, "America's Imperial Ambition," originally published in *Foreign Affairs* later in 2002 went head to head against the underlying principles of the Bush foreign policy as expressed in the 2002 National Security Strategy report. Ikenberry pulls no punches and explains why this 'neo-imperialist approach' is unsustainable and will work against American security and interests.

But he does not stop here. He links the new policies with the Neoconservative movement which inspired them and points an accusatory finger in particular at Robert Kagan. Compared to our other thinkers, Ikenberry is notable precisely for taking the Neocons very seriously and for setting out why and how their policies are wreaking great damage to American prestige and power worldwide. He calls the Neocon principles 'a profoundly flawed vision of order built on false assumptions, failed policies, misread history and misguided notions of power' and he marshals 9 reasons why this 'new fundamentalism' cannot serve as a successful foreign policy.

The very last chapter in this book is the most theoretical and yet it addresses a very topical issue: is the unilateralism and turn away from rule of law under Bush an aberration or will it have lasting consequences. Whereas other thinkers like Chomsky or Hoffmann said they expected 'this too to pass,' they gave few if any solid reasons why the excesses of the Bush years would be transitory. Here Ikenberry tells us exactly why we should not despair of the neo-imperialist behavior of the Bush administration, why it is not overturning 50 years of foreign policy even if it so wishes because there are counter-constraints which it also recognizes. I leave the last word to him:

"The dominant power position of the united States creates opportunities to go it alone, but the pressures and incentives that shape decisions about multilateral cooperation are quite varied and crosscutting. The sources of multilateralism still exist and continue to shape and restrain the Bush administration, unilateral inclinations notwithstanding."

Robert Kagan and The History Wars:

A review of *The Return of History*
and the *End of Dreams*
plus a bit more

When I opened the Amazon UK mailing packet and began leafing through Robert Kagan's 2008 tome, *The Return of History*, I was reminded of a scene a couple of years ago in the lobby of the New York City Opera at Lincoln Center in New York. It was a few minutes before curtain time and a hundred or more of us were slowly moving towards the stairs leading up into the theater. We were typical devotees of that staid institution, for the most part in our 60s, 70s and still older. A portly ticket inspector several stairs above us called out in a stentorian voice: "Ladies and gentlemen, you are going to enjoy tonight's performance. It's very short!"

Mr Kagan's latest but surely not his last contribution to the Neoconservative literature is just 105 small-format pages of text plus 10 pages of notes and a one page description of the typeset style from Adobe Corporation. It is about 40% shorter than his best selling political tract of 2003 which we will talk briefly about at the end of this essay. Clearly Kagan is moving in the right direction!

Robert Kagan's *The Return of History* carries to a new plateau what I would call 'the history wars' which began in 1993 with the publication of Francis Fukuyama's *End of History*, a seminal work of futurology.

It seems that every several years our futurologists find a new world order and without any sense of irony, much less embarrassment, refute their recent predecessors' reading of history's trajectory based on the latest current events.

Back in 1993 Francis Fukuyama explained to us why democracy was triumphing worldwide. Though he reached back in time to the overthrow of dictatorships and installation of democracy in South Europe, Latin America and East Asia from the 1970s onward to show a steady expansion of the democratic roster of nations, the cataclysmic events which gave relevance and immediacy to Fukuyama's thinking were the fall of communism in Eastern Europe in 1989 followed by the collapse of the Soviet Union a couple of years later. These were the coordinates by which the trajectory of history could now be plotted. They indicated the entire world was headed in the same direction towards a peaceful future of capitalist economies and liberal democracy.

In 1997, based on outbreaks of ethnic and religious violence in the Balkans, the Caucasus and elsewhere globally over the preceding 5 years, Sam Huntington revealed to us that no, history had not ended, the ideological divide of the Cold War was being replaced by civilizational divides, fault lines crisscrossing the globe. For his paradigm of civilizations, he drew on Spengler and Toynbee. In Huntington's best-selling tome, far from being triumphant, the West was shown to be already in a nearly century-long retreat that could be orderly and sustained over a long transition period if handled well, or fraught with danger and accelerated if Europe and America did not act in concert to defend their interests.

Now Kagan is telling us to forget this exotic notion of a clash of civilizations, which is passé in any case. The new hemline, the new vision of the future is based on developments which appeared at the very end of the 1990s and beginning of the new millennium as a result of expanding world trade, which brought with it not just the prosperity forecast by positivists but also a heightened assertiveness of its main new beneficiaries. What we have now is old fashioned, 19th century great power rivalry among ambitious nation-states of China, Japan, Russia, India and Iran; the revival of the centuries long divide between liberal democracies and autocratic governments as represented by the anti-NATO coalition of Shanghai Cooperation Organization countries forged by Russia and China; and an overlay of anti-modern, anti-democratic Islamic radicalism.

"As these three struggles combine and collide," Kagan maintains, "the promise of a new era of international convergence fades. We have entered an age of divergence….History has returned, and the democracies must come together to shape it, or others will shape it for them."

Specifically, Kagan uses this potentially violent new world to justify the continuance of American global hegemony, which, with all its flaws, he believes to be more noble and better accepted by the nations of the world generally than any alternative solution to managing international relations. And there is no reason to suppose that this world dominance can be shaken if we keep our resolve.

This tightly argued little volume has provoked lively discussion in the world of professional foreign policy analysts in the United States. Shortly after the book came out, *Foreign Affairs* magazine broke with its normal practice of entrusting reviews to its regular coterie of general-purpose critics who have three or four column inches at their disposal, just enough for a respectable dust jacket blurb. Instead they gave the floor to Boston University Professor of International Relations Andrew Bacevich, a well-known opponent of the 'benevolent global American hegemony' which Kagan promotes in his writings.

Bacevich rose to the challenge and his five page review essay entitled "Present at the Re-Creation. A Neoconservative Moves On," (*FA*, July/August 2008) does what few commentators ever take the time to do: a logic check on Kagan's latest book, both in terms of its relationship to his earlier writings and in terms of its internal consistency of argumentation. The result is, in effect, a finding of intellectual dishonesty which, if correct, makes most other remarks about Kagan superfluous.

Bacevich begins by calling attention to Kagan's sins of omission. He reminds us about the intellectual journey which Kagan traveled before writing *The Return of History* yet which he scarcely mentions in the book at hand.

Kagan amuses himself and readers of *The Return of History* at the expense of those thinkers in the 1990s whose silly ideas or 'dreams' generated in the heady days following the collapse of communism have been disproven by later events. These include the notions of the end of ideological conflict, of cultures intermingling, of nation-states growing together and of increasingly free commerce and communications.

But Kagan remains silent about the ideas which took center stage in American political life in the new millennium for which he and fellow Neoconservative thinkers were fully responsible, ideas which provided intellectual cover for the disastrous invasion of Iraq and the global war on terrorism.

These "fin-de-siècle illusions' of the Neoconservatives, as Bacevich aptly terms them, included misplaced trust in American ascendancy worldwide, in its ability to transform the world in its image and spread democracy at the end of a gun. Bacevich reminds us that in the year 2000 (*Present Dangers*) Robert Kagan and William Kristol had called for regime change in Baghdad and Belgrade, Pyongyang and Beijing.

Bacevich's point would be even more decisive to our appraisal of Kagan if he had juxtaposed Kagan's behavior with his former comrades in arms. To wit, why has another founding futurologist in the Neoconservative movement, Francis Fukuyama, taken stock, acknowledged the tragic mistakes into which his earlier political positions led the nation, while Kagan, has skipped nimbly on and presents his current analysis of the international landscape and road map going forward without any consideration of where his previous recommendations have brought us? To quote Bacevich:

"Now, instead of reflecting, forthrightly and with humility, on all that has gone awry since March 2003, the chief foreign policy theorist of the neoconservative movement has chosen to put the war in his rearview mirror. While American soldiers remain stuck in Iraq, Kagan is moving on to other things"

In 2003 Kagan had described the situation in Iraq as a 'historical pivot.' In his 2008 survey of challenges the United States faces in the world he scarcely devotes a line to Iraq and downplays the Islamist threat generally, while emphasizing instead the problem of old-fashioned great power conflicts:

Bacevich's second line of attack on Kagan relates to his flip-flops between *idealism* and *realism* within the pages of this short book. We have to back up a bit and be reminded that previously Kagan always spoke slightingly of geopolitics as something obsolete. For him the end of the Cold War was proof that America's universal values of freedom, not selfish national interest, were the defining feature of the modern age.

Now, says Bacevich, in *The Return of History* we get 'Robert the Realist' who is telling us that 'the collapse of communism was not transformation but merely a pause in the endless competition of nations and peoples.' Kagan has begun putting 'universal values' in quotation marks to distance himself from the notion.

As Bacevich further points out, Kagan pays tribute in this book to the founding fathers of the 20th century American school of realism, Reinhold Niebuhr and Hans Morgenthau, while he formulates analysis of present day international challenges in terms they would readily recognize. I would add that lurking in the background of this book is a more recent contributor to American *Realpolitik*, Henry Kissinger, whose *Diplomacy* Kagan clearly mined for ideas relating to the golden age of balance of power in the first half of the 19th century and especially to the Holy Alliance of autocratic dynasts, including Russia's Alexander I and Nicholas I, whose shared conservative values made this diplomatic framework operate so well in their day.

The flagrant contradiction which Bacevich identifies in Kagan's overall acceptance of realism and great power politics in *The Return of History* is the United States. American *exceptionalism*, the belief in the nation's inherent goodness and unique altruism, which is one of the articles of faith of Neoconservatism, is set out clinically here. Speaking as if from the sidelines with what might be taken for scholarly detachment, Kagan tells us that American self-righteousness and sense of universal mission to spread democracy comes with assertiveness in international affairs. But in the end he approves of this behavior and says it is all to the good, that in the present world configuration the United States remains indispensable, the 'keystone to the arch.'

"Here," says Bacevich, "Kagan the recent convert to realism gives way to Kagan the unrepentant neoconservative, who refuses to acknowledge that the United States' traditional foreign policy of expansionism has long been counterproductive."

At this point, Bacevich launches into his own view that since the 1960s, American exceptionalism and expansionism have turned from being an engine of national prosperity into a drain on national resources. For the full argumentation, I refer the reader to his *American Empire* and *The Limits of Power*.

* * *

Whereas Andrew Bacevich held Kagan to account for intellectual dishonesty, other political science professionals took a less personal, more conventional approach to *The Return of History* and focused on separate ideas set out in the book for their own merit. However, given Kagan's high profile as foreign policy thinker of the Neoconservatives, his politics were never entirely off the table.

Kagan's 2008 survey of the international arena called prime attention to the challenge posed by the 'autocratic' powers, Russia and China. This idea landed on fertile ground within the United States, where Cold War mentalities have never gone away.

The Return of History especially urged the creation of a league of democracies to confront the resurgence of those autocratic states which, it was alleged, would roil the surface of international relations for decades to come. To be sure, the notion of such a league has numerous parents. However, as adviser in foreign policy matters to Republican Presidential candidate John McCain, Robert Kagan gave it nationwide currency. The 'league of democracies' was trotted out onto the campaign trail in the summer of 2008. This new resonance of the concept subsequently justified many Round Tables and scholarly articles in the American academic community, so that the idea took on its own life even after the election.

In March 2009 the New York based Carnegie Council published position papers on the 'League of Democracies' in its journal *Ethics & International Affairs* (Volume 23.1, Spring 2009) available online at its site www.cceia.org

For its part, the January-February 2009 issue of *Foreign Affairs* magazine returned to the ideas set out in Kagan's *Return of History* via an article jointly written by professors Daniel Duedney of Johns Hopkins University and G. John Ikenberry, of Princeton University, entitled "The Myth of the Autocratic Revival." This heavy-weight answer to Kagan's theses was followed on February 11, 2009 by presentations from these same political scientists plus Dmitri Simes, President of The Nixon Center, the patent-holders on current American *realism*. The event was organized by the New America Foundation and broadcast as streaming video on www.washingtonnote.com.

In his analysis of Kagan's 'autocratic revival' at the New American Foundation event in February 2009, Dmitri Simes said this proposition showed an 'emotional propensity to look for enemies' which was ill-founded with respect to Russia and China since neither was a threat to the vital interests of the U.S.

On the question of the supposed division between autocrats and liberal states, Ikenberry maintained that the autocratic revival cited by Kagan is 'exaggerated and largely mistaken.' He believes that in the long run both the Russians and the Chinese will come to adopt liberal state habits. In this sense, he vindicates the positivist sentiments of Fukuyama.

With respect to great power rivalry, Deudney points to fundamental differences between the international scene today and that which prevailed in the 19th century, making a repetition impossible and pursuit of the policies of that time unthinkable. Duedney insists that today's international institutions of governance create interdependencies wholly unlike what existed in the 19th century. Second, there has been a basic shift in the economy of violence. In the 19th century, war made economic sense. Since the advent of nuclear weapons in the mid 20th century, all out war between the world's major powers has to be ruled out because of its destructiveness. Lastly, the anti-colonial movement of the post-WWII period changed the psychology of peoples around the world and the dissemination of cheap and effective weapons like the Kalashnikov has made 19th century gunboat diplomacy impracticable.

Duedney goes on to question Kagan's policy recommendations for containment of the so-called autocratic states. He calls these counter-productive and self-fulfilling prophecies.

So far, so good.. Ikenberry and Deudney punched holes in some basic reasoning. Yet they dealt with their opponent according to gentlemanly rules of engagement. A tap on the wrist for "exaggerations" is too mild if the opponent is willfully dishonest, as Bacevich was intimating. I propose now to proceed further with the task at hand, and pick up where Bacevich left off. Let us consider Kagan's intellectual integrity as revealed in the sources he has chosen for expert knowledge of the parts of the world central to his argument on autocracy, and in how he uses or abuses these sources.

METHODOLOGY

The main arguments in Kagan's book are that Fukuyama was wrong about the 'end of history,' that the road ahead in international affairs is one of rivalry between world powers which may not be ideological but is nonetheless about ideas, and especially about autocracy versus democracy. This particular dichotomy is essential to Kagan because, whatever his current infatuation with *Realpolitik*, he has never abandoned one of the key articles of faith in the Neoconservative creed, the notion that a country's domestic political structure determines its behavior towards other nations. In this value system, one can expect nothing good from autocracies.

And so, notwithstanding the pretence of surveying the world at large and devoting several pages each to powers like Japan, India and Iran, the entire thesis of this book rests on Kagan's understanding of two powers, Russia and China, which he sets up as the embodiments of autocracy in our day.

I now propose to consider for a moment one of these countries, Russia. Kagan has never claimed to be an expert on Russia. Therefore when he repeatedly cites in the Notes a couple of sources, it pays to examine where and how he is mining his information.

One of Kagan's sources on Russia is Dmitri Trenin, who was at the time the Deputy Director of the Carnegie Moscow Center, a prestigious Western NGO whose events attract the serious attention of world media. Trenin's curriculum vitae indicates that most everything about his education and previous career was similarly prestigious, beginning with his bachelor's degree from the Military Institute, his Ph.D. from the Institute of USA and Canada in 1984 and his service as research fellow at home and abroad.

The works cited by Kagan are Trenin's article 'Russia Leaves the West' published in the July/August 2006 issue of *Foreign Affairs* magazine, and his book *Getting Russia Right*, published in 2007. Both works may be described as level-headed, describing unattractive features of today's Russia yet also calling out the positive. What Kagan has done is to extract from Trenin the negatives and ignore the positives.

Kagan picks up Trenin's references to the *tsarist* precedents for Russia's present behavior in the great power manner and his mention of the authoritarian ways of the Kremlin. He omits Trenin's emphasis that Russia should be viewed 'as an emerging capitalist society rather than a failed democratic polity,' that we may expect 'serious tension, and even conflict between Russia and the West, although nothing like a return to the Cold War.' Trenin concluded in his *Foreign Affairs* article that '[i]n light of Russia's new foreign policy, the West needs to calm down and take Russia for what it is: a major outside player that is neither an eternal foe nor an automatic friend.' Calming down about Russia is not at all what Kagan has in mind.

The second prominent source is a report entitled *A Power Audit of EU-Russia Relations* published in November 2007 by the European Council on Foreign Relations. Kagan quotes at length from them in one of his footnotes (18), though in fact he has borrowed a good deal more from its authors than he lets on.

Power Audit is the very first work of the ECFR, which was launched a month earlier. The book presents Russia in a highly unfavorable light as an undemocratic country living in the pre-modern age which is using its energy dominance and business machinations to pursue a policy of 'divide and rule' vis-à-vis the European Union. This tendentiousness suits Kagan's purposes admirably.

The co-authors of *Power Audit* are ECFR Director Mark Leonard and Nicu Popescu, ECFR Policy Fellow. Between the two, Leonard is the non-specialist journalist, described on the ECFR website as a 'prolific writer and commentator' while Popescu is the scholar with knowledge of Russian. Both have previously traveled in the same social milieu as Kagan: Leonard was a Transatlantic Fellow of the German Marshall Fund of the United States; Popescu was a Research Fellow of the (Soros) Open Society Institute in its Brussels office.

The Brussels-based European Council on Foreign Relations has a very impressive list of Council Members, a veritable who's who of the great and the good of the European Union. However, I would venture to say this is just window dressing. George Soros sits on the Board. The Soros Foundation Network is one of its key sources of support. And *Power Audit*, co-authored by one of his former staff in OSI, perfectly expresses one of George Soros's most deeply held convictions today: that Europe must unite against a Russian threat.

If the scholarly sources of Robert Kagan's Russian studies leave something to be desired, that is not necessarily a black mark. In current history, as we have seen while examining the writings of some of the great authorities of our day, analysts fairly often base their books on articles from the daily newspapers and non-specialized periodicals.This leaves us with another methodological issue: Kagan's habit of reversing cause and effect when it serves his purposes.

CAUSE AND EFFECT

'The mood of recrimination in Russia today is reminiscent of Germany after World War I...' This key assertion by Kagan in *The End of History* was well calculated to set off alarm bells in Whitehall, on the Quai d'Orsay and… in Foggy Bottom, Washington, D.C. A vengeful, resurgent Russia, flush with oil and gas earnings and rebuilding its once vast military spells a return of Cold War troubles.

However, the statement totally misrepresents the psychology of the Russian leadership, which is precisely restrained, unemotional and focused on what can be done to defend the country against an encroaching, meddling and ill-disposed United States which, whether by design or simple indifference to Russian interests while pursuing its own agenda of worldwide leadership, has been, de facto, undermining Russia's vital military and economic security interests. The Russian policies over the past decade have been almost entirely reactive, defensive and proportionate to the threats detected.

I do not propose to take the reader's time here with a detailed list of the American and European misdeeds of commission and omission to which Russians have been responding ever since newfound prosperity enabled them to find their voice, to speak and to act, beginning in 2006. I send the reader to the same primary source which Kagan himself cites repeatedly in the latter part of his book: then President Vladimir Putin's remarks at the 43rd Munich Security Conference in February, 2007.

The speech was more than 20 minutes long, just over 10 pages in typed format. Yet the world's media carried only two lines from the speech in which the Russian President rebuked the United States for violating the basic principles of international law. He also patiently described the way the United States had violated its promises going back to 1990 that Russian withdrawal from Eastern Europe would not lead to NATO troops at its borders He explained Russian misgivings over the way the United States was cancelling arms control agreements dating from the Cold War and post-Cold War periods and how it and its NATO allies had not ratified the Conventional Forces Europe treaty for bogus reasons while holding the Russians to account for implementing what were now one-sided conditions. The list of issues goes on and on.

Virtually the same grievances over double-dealing, double-talking and containment could be identified on the Chinese side. Of course, the Chinese almost never allow themselves the luxury of giving voice to these concerns publicly.

What Kagan gives us in *The End of History* can be likened to the childish antics that go on in primary school classes. When the teacher's back is turned, one student kicks another, who then rises to return the favor and is caught by the teacher and sent off to the principal's office for bad conduct.

Kagan is a Neoconservative. One of the points in the credo of Neoconservatives is that the domestic structure of nations determines their policies towards the outside world. This is a fundamental belief which Kagan reiterates in the book at hand. However, as we well know, the international landscape also shapes domestic policies and indeed political structures. Wartime powers turn the most progressive of democracies into repressive dictatorships of their executive and/or parliament.

It is disingenuous, to say the least, for Kagan to ignore the possibility that the 'tightening of the screws' domestically that characterized the latter part of Vladimir Putin's time as President was reactive – a direct response to the pressure being applied to Russia by the Western powers under US leadership.

It is wonderful to see in this book how Kagan puts responsibility for the 'color revolutions' in the Ukraine, Georgia, and Kyrgyzstan at America's door, for the way it financed NGO's and the 'democratic forces' in these countries at Russia's border. But it is then unacceptable for him then to speak of the Kremlin's reaction as if it were Dracula quaking before the sign of the cross. It is patently false to present Russia today as if it were the member in good standing of the anti-revolutionary Holy Alliance of the first half of the 19th century.

Kagan has every right to his interpretation. He has every right to be tendentious. And he has every right to be dead wrong.

THE RULE OF FAIRNESS

Some of Kagan's propositions are simply fantastic distortions of reality, not mere 'exaggerations,' for example:

"The billions of dollars in foreign assistance the West provided to Russia in the 1990s were a far cry from the huge sums the victorious powers tried to extract from Germany after 1918.'

The Cold War ended not in a military defeat and victory procession down the capital of the vanquished enemy but in a voluntary withdrawal from

Eastern Europe by a country which, under its remarkable statesman Mikhail Gorbachev, did the decent thing and declined to exercise military force against the sovereign wills of its captive nations. Though Russia withdrew and closed down bases, it fully retained its capacity for destroying the world dozens of times over if it so chose thanks to a vast residual arsenal even after strategic arms reductions agreements put in place in 1993.

As for the billions in aid send Russia's way, that argument flies in the face of the consensus view in the community of professional Russia watchers that if anyone 'lost Russia' it was the West's failure to put up real money to help Russia when it was flat on its back in the mid-1990s.

Regrettably, similarly misleading half-truths are sprinkled through a great many pages of Mr. Kagan's short book. I will call attention here only to one further shocking example of the manipulation of facts, the question of military spending of the would-be great powers per Robert Kagan.

In *The End of History*, he speaks of Japanese, Russian, Chinese, Indian spending relative to the U.S. or in relation to past budgets of these countries. Yet, as he knows full well the military spending of none of these countries represents more than 5% of the U.S. defense budget.

All sides, even Mr. Kagan, understand that what he describes as autocracies are pre-modern systems of governance which cannot be compared with totalitarianism in their hold on their citizenry. He admits that Russia, like China, is well on its way along a capitalist course. Consequently he has to sing and dance up a storm to insist on the resilience of their authoritarian regimes as an advancing economy necessarily promotes political pluralism.

I will not be drawn here into the controversy over Russia's supposed loss of democracy under Vladimir Putin. I contend there was no democracy to lose, and that the political liberalism Robert Kagan claims for the Yeltsin years was largely the invention of his Western backers. Indeed, the Yeltsin years were a chaotic transition period characterized by license not liberty.

Kagan and 'post-modern Europe'

I give all due credit to Robert Kagan for charm and wit as essayist. These gifts were especially evident in his 2003 work *Paradise & Power*. It is not for nothing that the book was a bestseller on the *New York Times* list for 10 weeks. And according to his official biography posted online, that book was also a bestseller in the U.K., France, Germany, Spain, Italy and The Netherlands, and it has been translated into more than 25 languages.

Yet, in that book, just as in *The End of History*, Kagan played loose and fast with causality. He abused his superior knowledge of the European political scene when addressing his presumably ignorant, primarily American readership.

Paradise & Power was written just before the US unleashed its attack on Iraq in 2003 when there was a hullabaloo in U.S. relations with the Continent. Kagan came forward to explain in a cogent way why Old Europe and the US were at odds over the impending invasion.

In the book, Kagan told us why Europe was from Venus and the United States was from Mars: in his terms 'post-modern' Europe embodied the Kantian ideal world of liberal democratic states who abjured great power rivalries and indulged in the belief that their consensual, rules-driven governance of international relations was the new model for the 21st century. The result is that Europe was spending too little of its GDP on defense, taking too much vacation time and was physically unable to project force abroad, whereas the United States was in its prime as the world's only remaining superpower and both could and would respond to threats in a unilateral fashion, if need be. When you have a hammer of military might, like the U.S., he said, then, rightly or wrongly, every problem looks like a nail. And when you don't have a hammer (Europe), then you don't want to see nails and deny the existence of threats to the peace of the international order.

Kagan's description of the European Union was a caricature. As someone on the ground in Brussels and well integrated into the diplomatic community here, Kagan had to know that the absence of a common European foreign and defense policy had real world, material causes as opposed to being driven by intellectual infatuation with ideas coming to us from Kant. Among these many factors was interference by the U.S. in internal EU affairs to frustrate the creation of a combined military force of core EU countries without U.S. participation in what was supposed to become a two-speed Europe. These American efforts to put a spanner in the works received active support from Europe's best military force, the United Kingdom, which systematically worked against any consolidation of defense capabilities on the Continent.

Of course, there are other factors strictly internal to Europe which also played their role. To begin with, there is the still very shallow integration of the European nation-states generally, their jealous retention of sovereignty precisely in the domains of foreign and military policy. Add to that the structure of domestic political institutions in the various Continental nations with coalition, multi-party governments resulting from the respective laws on parliamentary elections. These various technical features of the democracies have ensured that foreign policy and military issues virtually never figure in national elections. The European electorate gets a say in these matters if at all only at the periodic MEP elections or in referendums on EU constitutional reform like the Lisbon Treaty. In these circumstances, to speak of democratically formulated "European" policies on defense, to deal with Europe as if it were a unified nation-state as Kagan does repeatedly and to chastise Europeans for living in a Kantian never-never land is very misleading.

In conclusion, in the person of Robert Kagan we have an impressive Neoconservative polemicist who keeps his audience's attention with wit and style. He knows the classics of political philosophy and he marshals his arguments well. And in the spirit of a debater, he makes no pretence at being open-minded or fair. Winning is all that counts.

Noam Chomsky:

Failed States, Hegemony or Survival and Interventions

By any standard, Chomsky's many works exposing the lies and deception of American imperial myths are inescapable reading for serious students of U.S. foreign policy in the post-Cold War period. Captions on the cover of his recent books show that even media which feel the lash of his whip freely acknowledge his cult status. *The New York Times* says of him: "Chomsky is a global phenomenon…perhaps the most widely read voice on foreign policy on the planet." The *Observer* calls him "the world's greatest public intellectual." And *The Guardian* characterizes Chomsky as "a towering intellect."

Professor emeritus in MIT's Department of Linguistics and Philosophy, aged 81, Noam Chomsky has been a major contributor to the discourse on U.S. foreign policy ever since the 1960s when he became actively involved in the antiwar movement. The list of his of articles and books published year after year since then up to the present day shows remarkable political commitment as well as the uninterrupted accumulation of factual evidence to support his beliefs.

In this essay we shall examine three of his books published within the post-Cold War period. My summary of what these books are about will be brief, because, in effect, Chomsky's books are a continuum. Each new volume may be called a later edition of the foregoing work rather than a self-standing new monograph. By constantly repeating himself and reusing much of the same documentary material, Chomsky's writings are immediately identifiable.

The books under examination here are:

Hegemony or Survival: America's Quest for Global Dominance (2003)

Failed States: The Abuse of Power and the Assault on Democracy (2006)

Interventions (2007 expanded edition)

Hegemony was written shortly after the US attack on Iraq and is emotionally the hottest on this list. We occasionally sense Chomsky's anger and frustration. The book has many arguments rather than a single thesis and the author jumps around a great deal in time and space to drive home his points.

The argument which gives the book its title is that the policy of permanent United States' hegemony set out in the 2002 National Security Strategy which prepared the way and eventually justified the invasion of Iraq is merely a more explicit restatement of what been the underlying principle of the country's foreign policy ever since the early days of WWII. The objective has been: "to construct a world system open to US economic penetration and political control, tolerating no rivals or threats." As part of this policy, America must call to order any country seeking independence from its domination, if necessary by military means, so as to stamp out the 'virus infecting others,' whatever risks to world peace may ensue. Indeed, America's reliance on absolute military superiority has the contradictory result of encouraging the proliferation of weapons of mass destruction among nations seeking to counterbalance the hegemon, and thereby sows the seeds of ever greater insecurity in the world.

Within this volume, Chomsky tears asunder the building blocks of Wilsonian idealism or 'exceptionalism,' i.e., the notion of a country which is uniquely good, noble and fit to lead the world. He reminds us of the neocolonial behavior of the good President Wilson himself in America's backyard, the Caribbean. And he explains at length how in our own day, the selfless ideal of humanitarian intervention to save countries from the scourge of human rights abuses, even genocide, has, on the one hand, been abused, as in Kosovo, to serve ignoble purposes of pulling together an outdated military alliance (NATO) rather than its stated aims and, on the other hand, has been practiced very selectively, ignoring flagrant abuses and state-inflicted suffering on citizens when the responsible state is friendly or strategically important (Turkey and its Kurdish minority or Indonesia in East Timor). Thus, the self-congratulatory media attention to a 'new era of enlightenment' is nothing more than self-delusion or state propaganda.

In his excursion through America's hall of fame, Chomsky takes no hostages. He explains to us how the United States has gotten along with states that maintained order and were deemed good for business even if morally reprehensible throughout the 20th century. This went straight back to an accommodation with fascism in the 1930s, first in Italy and then in Nazi Germany under FDR.

Contempt for democracy has been a long-accepted American foreign policy practice. Donald Rumsfeld's notorious differentiation between Old and New Europe was only a new manifestation of this old pattern: the good European leaders (New) are those who ignored the overwhelming preferences of their people and backed the US intervention in Iraq, while the bad Europeans (Old – Germany, France) are those who listened to the popular will and resisted the American rush to war.

In *Hegemony,* Chomsky deals with much else. The only commonality is to overturn the generally accepted interpretation of cause and effect, of positive and negative values in American actions on the international arena across the board. We are told about America's largely negative influence on the Israeli-Palestinian peace process resulting from its unqualified support for Israeli expansionism and military solutions to political issues. We are given a quick lesson in American-sponsored state terrorism in Latin America during the 1980s. We are taught why the American bombing of Afghanistan after 9/11 was not the 'just war' nearly all Americans supposed it to be but actually a war of aggression given the lack of conclusive evidence to support military action when it was undertaken or even 9 months later. And we learn that the missile defense system rolled out under Bush II is in fact an offensive program intended to give America a first-strike capability. We read that the United States' pursuit of the militarization of space in unilateral manner and its ongoing development of biological weapons only increase the likelihood of WMD proliferation.

Failed States picks up many of the themes from *Hegemony* and updates them while offering the reader a more concentrated focus on the three or four elements which political scientists use to characterize 'failed' or 'rogue states' and which Chomsky argues are all present in spades in today's United States. Like 'failed states,' the United States is unable or unwilling to protect its citizens. Instead it exposes citizens to nuclear Armageddon by its irresponsible pursuit of new weapons systems in space and increases their vulnerability to terrorism by measures such as its war on Iraq which only serve to recruit radical Islamists to Al Qaeda. Like failed states, America views itself as beyond the reach of international law. It flouts the Geneva Conventions on use of torture and war crimes such as attacks on hospitals and other civilian targets. It makes a mockery of the Charter of the United Nations and other international conventions by waging preventive war in Iraq and or unleashing a humanitarian intervention in Serbia without the sanction of the United Nations. And it refuses to acknowledge the jurisdiction of the International Court of Justice. Finally, like failed states, the United States suffers from a 'democracy deficiency,' whereby the clearly documented popular will in favor of more social welfare and less defense appropriations is systematically ignored. Elections avoid issues and marginalize the population. Government public relations campaigns and industrial advertising techniques spread deceit which undermines democracy. In the end American voters feel powerless and become apathetic.

Not content to highlight the discrepancy between noble words on the promotion of human rights and the reality of US support for bloody dictators, which many would label hypocrisy or 'double standards,' Chomsky drives a stake through the heart of the monster by telling us there is only a single standard at work in American foreign policy: "what Adam Smith called the 'vile maxim of the masters of mankind…All for ourselves, and nothing for other people."

Interventions differs from the other two works under consideration here in that it is a collection of op-ed articles each limited to 1,000 words which Chomsky sold to the New York Times Syndicate for publication. In effect, these essays were picked up by regional US papers and abroad. They appeared in print during the period 2002-2007. We see here exactly the same themes and the same positions as Chomsky develops in his books though in the given space there is no room for self-indulgence and so he is more sparing in his proofs.

The invariable Mr. Chomsky

In our earlier examination of 'great thinkers' who had also been foreign policy practitioners during the Cold War and whose writing careers spanned decades prior to 1993, we were obliged to ask what had changed in their views to take into account the altered landscape of international affairs in the new era. In the case of Noam Chomsky that issue does not arise. One might say he was never taken in by the Cold War. For Chomsky, the ideological stand-off between the United States and the USSR was merely incidental to his understanding of the nature of governments anywhere and everywhere.

Chomsky's essential point is the continuity of lines in US foreign policy from the very foundation of the Republic which converge into bipartisan agreement on foreign policy ever since WWII. Unlike many thinkers on the Left, Chomsky was never enamored with Communism, was never 'mugged by reality,' and has remained to this day with the anarchist-syndicalist and radical libertarian views that he held at the time he first moved outside his professional specialty in linguistics and ventured into the political forum.

The issue before us as we contemplate Chomsky is whether gathering vast quantities of data and citations from responsible sources to support your contentions is enough to be a player in the political science debates. This will prepare us to answer at the end of our survey the question of why the political science profession does not appear to take Chomsky seriously and whether that is only because his heart is in the right (wrong) place.

Chomsky makes depressing reading.

Americans are by and large an optimistic people. The other nine authors in our survey tend to leave the reader with a vision of the future and possibly an action program for him or her to get involved. At a minimum, readers of their works will find bumper sticker issues to affix to their car. Reading Chomsky gives the American patriot no emotional *frisson*, just a feeling of depression. One blogger-reviewer aptly wrote of Noam Chomsky's *Failed States*: "If only one quarter of the offences contained in Noam Chomsky's book are true, the outlook for American democracy is more than bleak; it is utterly hopeless." (Charles Marowitz writing in *Swan's Commentary*, swans. com, 9 October 2006)

From Chomsky we learn about misdeeds of US foreign policy in relation to Haiti, Nicaragua, Iraq, Indonesia and dozens of other states. On every page we are shown the vast discrepancy between ideals pronounced by American leaders to explain their actions and the dismal reality on the ground. Interspersed with the mountains of description there is an occasional remark on causality, but the reader finds nothing resembling a full-blooded analytical framework. And Chomsky provides no detailed roadmap to a new and sustainable world order. We find only a few sketchy recommendations which we will examine further on.

Why is this so? Surely the reason is to be found in Chomsky's political philosophy, which is well known outside the books under review. He is an anarchist. He believes government exists to enforce property relationships and to protect the wealthy from the envy of everyone else. In the case of the United States, he reminds us that this was the openly avowed conviction of the nation's founders, Madison and Hamilton.

Chomsky's a world view becomes particularly awkward when the author is asked to give road directions to the planet's greatest power. It is as if we are in the company of a dedicated vegetarian and are awaiting his recommendations on preparing some fine meat dishes for a convention of hunters and trappers.

In *Failed States*, Chomsky tells us who exactly is running the U.S. government today and to what purpose. They are the 'reactionary statists,' pro-business politicians who are serving the interests of big international corporations and are constantly centralizing power.

What we have is the corporate state. This, together with a penchant for foreign aggression to deflect attention from an anti-democratic domestic economic policy, which Chomsky also lays at the door of the recent Republican administrations, would constitute key elements of what political scientists generally call fascism. It is curiously inconsistent that Chomsky refrains from using the 'F' word when talking about his homeland.

It must be stressed that for an author who otherwise nails down his every assertion with numerous mainstream references, his skimpy overview of what is going on and why is rendered as bald, unsubstantiated authorial assertion. Moreover, the author makes no attempt to differentiate between the objective results of the policies of the American political class on both sides of the aisle, which may or may not match his generalization, and the subjective intent of its members, the level at which most of us, except for the occasional Machiavelli of our day like Karl Rove, live and breathe. In that sense, Chomsky is dealing in caricatures.

Besides telling us that the U.S. government basically serves the interests of big business, Chomsky offhandedly mentions oil as the dominant driver in the recent U.S. invasion of Iraq. But here and in his discussion elsewhere about the evolution of the U.S. interest in controlling the Middle East, oil and energy resources generally are not an economic factor so much as a geopolitical factor: the United States wants to be the supreme gatekeeper of energy resources not for its own use but because of the political weight this brings in relation to the other world power centers, Japan and Europe, which are directly dependent on Middle Eastern energy. What is at issue is 'strategic power' and 'critical leverage' to maintain America's global hegemony for the more general reasons outlined above.

Chomsky and the mainstream: the American Empire

Chomsky's editors suggest and most of his readers seem to believe that Chomsky brings to the public facts and views which are otherwise unavailable. However, an inspection of his Notes makes it plain that Chomsky is not an original researcher and is doing little more than an impassioned reader of current events can do for himself from readily available sources. Much of Chomsky's factual material comes from the newspapers of record. Most of his interpretations are taken from specialized periodical literature dealing with foreign policy and defense issues. They are all highly authoritative and chosen by the author precisely because they make his conclusions so compelling. At most, Chomsky is drawing lines between dots of material by recognized experts who perhaps are averse to making sweeping statements or judgments.

At the same time, Chomsky uses *fewer* publicly available sources than a properly educated and motivated follower of international affairs might do for himself: it is absolutely fascinating to discover that all of Chomsky's sources are in English. This falls in line with a criticism sometimes directed against him that he is comparing America only to its own stated values and not to the world at large or that he does not consider other states as independent actors. But this English-only policy has special piquancy when one considers that Professor Chomsky is one of the world's best known linguists. Is this brilliant polymath language-deficient?

Equally important, much of what Chomsky says about the American Empire and its modus operandi is not merely accepted by his opposite numbers on the other side of the political spectrum but is put forward by them in a totally unapologetic if not boastful manner. In recent years, imperialism has come out of the closet and shows off its plumage. In 2006 the leading Neoconservative foreign policy thinker Robert Kagan devoted a book to the proposition that the US has been seen as a 'dangerous nation' from its very founding.

Meanwhile the middle ground of American politics has also discerned imperial features in both the institutions and the behavior of Washington today.

The debate centers on the fine points of indirect control versus physical occupation of its dependencies abroad. Boston University professor of U.S. diplomatic history Andrew Bacevich, who describes himself as a moderate conservative and belongs to the *realist* school of foreign policy, spent a volume demonstrating how America did not stumble upon its present vocation as world hegemon, was not drawn there by the invitation of others but moved steadily into the role from a tradition of national self-assertion beginning in the 19th century as manifest destiny.

Both Bacevich and Kagan are cited by Chomsky. The question is what value you assign to this imperial reality. For Chomsky it is all black. For Kagan, it is shining white. For Bacevich, the record became problematic in the 1960s and later when American expansionism began to subtract from rather than add to national prosperity.

In our examination of Zbigniew Brzezinski and Joseph Nye, we asked whether these *idealist* authors are also moral or ethical. In the case of Chomsky, it is clear that he wears his heart on his sleeve. He is judgmental in approaching men of state. He holds their deeds up to their fine words on every page of his writing.

Supporters and admirers of Noam Chomsky, of whom there are many, believe that he is on the side of the angels. But then again so do the many admirers of Robert Kagan and the Neoconservative movement that is diametrically opposed to Chomsky's value system if not to his description of reality

Good people, bad leaders?

In the recent writings of Zbigniew Brzezinski and Leslie Gelb, we have seen the view expressed that there is something wrong with the American people, that they have become consumerist, lazy and unready to sacrifice as needed to project their country's power on the world stage in the manner recommended by its foreign policy establishment.

By contrast, Chomsky is telling us there is something wrong with the American political elites – on both sides of the aisle. The Democrats are as culpable as the Republicans. The will of the American people is being subverted. The elites have turned the country into a rogue state.

Chomsky justifies his 'good people, bad government' beliefs by reference to public opinion polls, which he suggests are more valid indicators than electoral balloting. The polls repeatedly show that a substantial majority of Americans want to work in harmony with the United Nations and share the burden of world governance with others rather than act unilaterally, that they want a cutback in defense and a reallocation of resources to social needs.

There are several basic issues implicit in this approach which Chomsky does not deal with. First, there is the question of representative government in general versus plebiscites to resolve questions of state, large and small. Just how responsive government should be to the quickly changing tides of popular opinion has always been contentious. Should political leadership be out in front of the public on issues of foreign affairs? on issues of domestic policy? or should it 'lead from behind' as Chomsky is proposing?

In the given instance, Chomsky is very comfortable with the popular view on conduct of international affairs that the pollsters are reporting back to him. In the run-up to WWII would he have been be so comfortable to follow the isolationist lead that dominated American public opinion and which Franklin Delano Roosevelt overcame only by the kind of anti-democratic chicanery which Chomsky denounces in our day. Or in domestic policy, would Chomsky have accepted with similar enthusiasm the majority views which prevailed until very recently on such matters as racial discrimination, sexual harassment and the like? Or are those areas where he would look to enlightened (and un-democratic) leadership to provide suitable direction? If the golden mean is somewhere between these extremes, at what percent dissonance between government policy and popular will do we say *basta*, the people must have their way?

Let us approach the question of 'good people, bad government' from another angle. Civic engagement takes many forms in addition to the ballot box. It has long been argued that American baby-boomers have turned in on their private lives and forsaken most forms of public activism in ways that have nothing to do with phony or rigged elections. This phenomenon was widely publicized in Robert Putnam's opus *Bowling Alone* (2000).

Nor is it sufficient to blame state propaganda and advertising gimmickry for public ignorance about international affairs and U.S. foreign policy. Chomsky chooses not to explore the possibility of willful ignorance. *The New York Times* news reports on torture and human rights violations with U.S. complicity which Chomsky uses are read very widely and do not seem to rouse people to his conclusions or to the behavior of protest.

If the public can be hoodwinked in national elections, the same is not true of primaries and caucuses. The 2008 presidential campaign saw the candidacy of one Democrat with a foreign policy program genuinely at odds with the political elites and close to the notions Chomsky espouses. Before stepping down, Dennis Kucinich garnered merely 1% of the votes in his party. This leads me to ask how valuable Chomsky's poll figures really are. Politics is about mobilizing people to act on their preferences, not just express them.

In the same regard, we have to ask where were/are the popular protests against government policies that are so out of line with Chomsky's poll data. In several of the op-ed essays in *Interventions*, we see Chomsky's early misjudgment about the extent of antiwar protest in the US as the country headed into its invasion of Iraq and shortly afterwards. For a brief period, he was heartened by the antiwar turnout, which he contrasted with the silence back in the early 1960s when John Kennedy launched the war in Viet Nam.

In a March 2003 essay, Chomsky wrote:

"Today there is large scale, committed and principled popular antiwar protest all over the United States and the world. The peace movement acted forcefully even before the new Iraq war started. This reflects a steady increase over these years in unwillingness to tolerate aggression and atrocities, one of many such changes worldwide. The activist movements of the past forty years have had a civilizing effect."

At the very least, his later disappointment with the public's fall back into silence should have prompted Chomsky to reconsider his views on the guiltless American people and its cruel elites.

Chomsky's road map to a better world

Chomsky is not totally indifferent to his readers' likely demand for some hope, some guidance on the way out of the picture of moral despair he has drawn. At the very end of *Failed States*, he acknowledges, "One commonly hears that carping critics complain about what is wrong, but do not present solutions." In the half page which follows, he comes as close as ever to sharing his views on what would make for a better world:

1) accept the jurisdiction of the International Criminal Court and the World Court

2) sign and carry forward the Kyoto protocols

3) let the UN take the lead in international crises

4) rely on diplomatic and economic measures rather than military ones in confronting terror

5) keep to the traditional interpretation of the United Nations Charter

6) give up the Security Council veto and respect the opinion of mankind

7) cut back sharply on military spending and sharply increase social spending

However, he gives us no indication of how such a radical change in US foreign policy is going to come about without a revolution given the entrenched beliefs of the nation's political elite and the control which big business exerts over the levers of the federal government in his view.

The book ends on a positive note, congratulating us all for 'substantial progress in the unending quest for justice and freedom in recent years, leaving a legacy that can be carried forward from a higher plane than before.' He urges his readers on to greater public commitment and day-to-day educational work to promote democracy at home.

Without substantiation in a manner similar to his foregoing exposé of the nation's ills, these soothing words appear to be pasted on and enjoy no credibility.

Looking at his previous work, *Hegemony*, we similarly find words of encouragement at the very end. He claims to see a rising popular protest against the 'corporate globalization project' taking shape in the nations of the South which will create grassroots alliances in the wealthy industrial societies of the North. And so, he concludes: "We see two trajectories in current history: one aiming toward hegemony, acting rationally within a lunatic doctrinal framework as it threatens survival, the other dedicated to the belief that 'another world is possible,...' challenging the reigning ideological system and seeking to create constructive alternatives of thought, action, and institutions. Which trajectory will dominate, no one can foretell."

At this level of generalization, there is something formulaic in the rose-tinted dawn Chomsky offers his expectant readership.

Chomsky's critical standing

In January, 2005, John H. Summers published an article in the *History News Network* under the tantalizing title: "Why Do Historians Ignore Noam Chomsky?" in which he reminded us that Chomsky had published more than 30 books over the past three decades yet none of them had been reviewed in the professional journals, the *American Historical Review* and *Reviews in American History*. Though the author failed to provide any convincing reasons for the phenomenon, the identification of the issue was helpful. Indeed, given the extent of his readership in America and worldwide, it is curious how little scholarly attention Chomsky gets, not just in history but more broadly in the disciplines of political science where one might expect a critical response.

If I may hazard a guess as to why this is so, the answer lies in the genre in which Chomsky is toiling: though his books have all the trappings of scholarship, in particular Notes amounting to 10% of his overall text, he is in fact practicing *journalism* rather than academic scholarship. Moreover, given that all his 'research' is derivative, supported by if not simply drawing from the works of others, his journalism is of the popularizing as opposed to investigative variety.

In making this determination, I am using a simple rule: description is journalism; prescription is an essential attribute of academic scholarship in the political sciences. It is precisely the absence of theoretical structure in Chomsky's writings about foreign policy which have placed his work outside the interests of academic political science irrespective of the size of his audience or influence in the general public.

Due to his awkward political bias, Chomsky also tends to be ignored by the mainstream American press, though occasionally he gets his due. One such example is the well balanced and thorough review of *Failed States* which appeared in the Sunday Book Review magazine of *The New York Times* on 23 June 2006.

The article summarized masterfully Chomsky's achievements in demonstrating the vast discrepancy between words and deeds of the American leadership, to the point where Chomsky exposed 'the rot of the shining city on a hill, from its foundations to its steeples." At the same time the reviewer judiciously called out some of the key shortcomings of Chomsky's polemicist style: dense writing style and excessive quotations from his sources, failure to see those outside the United States as acting independently and for the sake of their own interests, prejudicial selection of materials, overly mechanistic view of politics and….providing only two paragraphs of solutions in a 260-page book of critique.

Nonetheless, the reviewer congratulated Chomsky on showing people that they are in a wilderness and he forgave the prophet for not pointing the exact way out. He ended with a sincere and positive 'buy' recommendation: "It's hard to imagine any American reading this book and not seeing his country in a new, and deeply troubling, light."

It was surely no accident that *The New York Times* selected as its reviewer not an American but Jonathan Freedland, an editorial page columnist for *The Guardian of London*, a newspaper with a readership solidly based in the British teaching establishment and politically liberal in the libertarian sense. By placing his essay in the Sunday Book Review magazine, the publishers were exceptionally generous: Freedland had 1200 words at his disposal, just enough to do his job properly.

It is a sign of how extraordinary an event this kind of review is in the American mainstream press that the newspaper was subsequently congratulated by readers on taking Chomsky's point of view seriously. As Joseph Barbato commented in his Letter to the Editor published on 16 July 2006: "The fact that such a straight-talking review appeared in The Times must have left Chomsky dumbfounded."

More commonly, the reviews of Chomsky's works in the United States turn up in marginal political action websites, private blogs and sites sponsored by booksellers. These are usually nothing more than a brief summary of some of the recurrent points in Chomsky's latest opus and an uncritical, friendly push to sales.

However, as usual, the amazon.com portal attracts many contributors and can be said to serve as a proxy 'voice of the people' on Chomsky and his writings.

First, in what must be a compliment to Chomsky and his ability to send out an unmistakably clear message, the readers of Chomsky understand very well what he is trying to do and love him or hate him accordingly. There is no confusion here to match what we saw in amazon.com reviews of more subtle and complex works such as Henry Kissinger's *Diplomacy*.

Out of the 280 reviews of *Hegemony or Survival* posted on the amazon portal on the day I inspected it, 137 readers gave Chomsky a top rating of 5 stars while 65 gave a condemnatory 1-star listing. At both sides of the spectrum of opinion, it is obvious the readers are passionate.

The naysayers seem to ignore or willfully distort what Chomsky is saying to place him in a preconceived bin of America-haters who should depart the home of the free and the brave at the earliest opportunity. As for the fans, what moves them is the facts Chomsky sets out to expose American misdeeds, imperialism and the anti-democratic reality of a government serving only big capital.

Time and again, the readers praise Chomsky's 'impeccable research,' his overwhelming and irrefutable documentation. They see in Chomsky 'a thorough and responsible academic mind." The leading critique by a contributor in Oregon which 71 of 80 readers found helpful provides a colorful overview of what attracts readers to Chomsky:

"As you read, you'll say, 'Wow, is that really true?' and flip to the footnotes. You'll find credible sources every time. You'll shake your head, wondering how you could have missed such important information."

Readers credit Chomsky's core professional skills as a linguist with helping him to penetrate the 'idealizing and utopian language' of those in power. The skimpy analytical framework and absence of any roadmap to a better world do not trouble these readers. As one reader remarks: "..come on, the guy's not the Savior. If you want change, that's up to you."

Outside the United States, Chomsky enjoys the status of 'American dissident' and gets somewhat more attention from the intellectual classes than in his homeland. However, contrary to what one might suppose, he is not the beneficiary of anti-American currents.

Indeed, in France, the country where one might expect him to rank with other iconic American personalities on the fringe like Woody Allen or Michael Moore, Chomsky is the butt of often vitriolic criticism from some of the country's leading intellectuals and mainstream press, including not only *Le Figaro,* the voice of French business interests, but also nominally left-leaning *Libération* and *Le Monde.*

As Jean Bricmont pointed out in his April 2001 article in *Le Monde diplomatique* ("The Bad Reputation of Noam Chomsky"), the French anti-Establishment generation of '68, which once saw in Chomsky a fellow traveler, made a U-turn to the Right during the '80s and '90s following disillusionment over Third World liberation movements they had once espoused and now found the unchanged and still anti-imperialist Chomsky to be an embarrassment, 'a bizarre and dangerous anachronism."

Though he does not say it directly, what Bricmont is describing about France's writers and thinkers parallels the changes in political bedfellows of comparable media like *The New York Review of Books* in New York in the same time frame and the development of Neoconservativism in the United States from among former Liberals and Communist sympathizers. Like their American counterparts, the (nominal) French Left has taken up the cause of human rights and supported unquestioningly the US-led humanitarian interventions of the 1990s in Kosovo and elsewhere. Here they come directly in the sights of Chomsky and his exposé of the drive for dominance and hegemony hiding behind the phony altruism of political leaders in Europe as in America.

In France Chomsky has endured the calumny of allegedly defending the Pol Pot regime of Cambodia when all he attempted to do was to liken the rightfully condemned genocide of the Khmer Rouge to the murderous policies of the Indonesian government in East Timor with Western complicity during the same time period. Chomsky's name has also been associated in France with the despised denier of the Holocaust, professor of literature at Lyon University Robert Faurisson whose right to self-expression Chomsky defended in a highly principled if maladroit way.

It is interesting to note that Bricmont concluded his analytical article with the kind of bouquet Chomsky rarely gets from academics in his homeland: "After years of hopelessness and resignation, a global challenge to the capitalist system appears to be reborn. It can only profit from the combination of lucidity, courage and optimism which marks the work and the life of Noam Chomsky." It is also true that, like Chomsky, Bricmont's scholarly authority is in an area well removed from the subject matter at hand: he holds a professorship in physics at the French-speaking University of Louvain.

Conclusion

The works examined in this book employ a variety of methodologies, reflecting the diverse training of the authors within what might be called a 'big-tent' discipline. . Whether the authors are promoting a political philosophy going back to Plato, off-the-shelf paradigms from a century ago or totally new theoretical formulations of their own making, political scientists love abstractions.

And yet the end product of their work takes the shape of concrete policy recommendations. Not everyone gets to be National Security Advisor, not to mention Secretary of State. But most of the political scientists working at the level of the authors we have reviewed are summoned to the nation's capital to provide expert advice to the executive or legislative branches of the federal government. Their priority audience is those in government who formulate policy and implement it.

Therefore it is highly relevant to recall that we have observed a disconnect between the theoretical parts of their writings and the practical policy recommendations they put forward for US foreign policy. Some of the best advice given by Huntington in the late 1990s has little or nothing to do with the *civilizational* theory that made him famous. We saw how Henry Kissinger did not necessarily fulfill his own generalization about realist policy-makers being well grounded in history as they make case-by-case calls. If your knowledge base is weak and your views are trite, as would seem to be the case of Kissinger on Russia, then it should come as no surprise that your concrete policy recommendations will not differ significantly from those of idealist liberal hawks or idealist Neoconservatives, however much you disdain such people.

What brings together the observations and advice of people as disparate as Leslie Gelb, Henry Kissinger, Joseph Nye in their recommendations of caution and criticism of doctrinaire approaches is a certain mature wisdom of people who have seen a great deal of foreign policy formulation and implementation from the inside.

Then there are others, like Zbigniew Brzezinski, who seem not to have mellowed from their life experience and who harbor distorting prejudices and hidden agendas which overrule what realism whispers in their ears.

I have noted already that professional readers tend to look past the theoretical work of fellow political scientists and to go straight to the bottom line of policy recommendations to see where the authors' feet are pointed. The reviewers of the books we have examined almost never speak of methodology, not to mention factual competence. Is this because it is self-evident to those who know the métier from inside that the conclusions will not follow from the philosophizing and show of plumage which precedes them?

In a way, what we have seen among these scholars-political activists parallels what goes on in the business world. However much mouth honor is given to the objective skills framed in an MBA degree, the reality in the board room is that very often decision-making is based on gut feelings and intuition of the chief executive, not on the splendid slide shows of their subordinates. In the end, though a number of the authors under examination here would protest, management of foreign affairs, like management of business or of people generally, is very much an art rather than a science.

This is not to say that fact-based decision making is unachievable. But then the facts should come from primary sources, not from news clippings in the US media. And those interpreting them should have a solid expertise in a given country, a given region and not serve up the world in 300, 600 or even 900 pages

* * *

That still leaves us to ponder what should be the profile of those who implement the foreign policy recommendations of our thinkers on international relations.

In his recent landmark work *Know Your Enemy: The Rise and Fall of America's Soviet Experts,* David Engerman reminds us how in the years before World War II, the State Department's Foreign Service had little interest in theorizing. He cites the well known diplomat and historian. George Kennan who wrote as late as 1950 that "the judgment and instinct of a single wise and experienced man, whose knowledge of the world rests on the experience of personal, emotional, and intellectual participation in a wide cross-section of human effort, are something we hold to be more valuable than the most elaborate synthetic structure of demonstrable fact and logical deduction."

This view soon was deemed inadequate to the challenges of the emerging Cold War, and area studies programs were set up across the nation to ensure that future policy-makers and implementers would be properly equipped with the facts and the theories to anticipate and master the threats to American security.

John Kennedy gave the professionalization of foreign policy implementation a mighty boost when he brought his brain trust of largely Harvard-affiliated scholars into government and the White House. This approach henceforth enjoyed bipartisan support. The culmination of the process came when Henry Kissinger was promoted from National Security Advisor to Secretary of State under President Richard Nixon. It has remained an unchallenged canon ever since.

In his memoirs, Dr. Kissinger distinguished himself from all his lawyer predecessors in the post who had come to the job with what he called condescendingly an 'inbasket-outbasket' mentality as opposed to his own deeply conceptual thinking. It was not for nothing that Dr. Zbigniew Brzezinski used the metaphor of a chessboard to describe his approach to foreign policy.

In light of both the strengths and the weaknesses in the reasoning processes and the value systems of the leading lights of the profession of political science/international relations whom we explored in this volume, I leave the reader to decide whether management of foreign policy should be left to the experts, our eminent political scientists and historians. Judging by the emphasis which the current administration in Washington has given to putting properly 'credentialed' persons into key ambassadorial and State Department posts, the question remains very topical.

About the Author

Gilbert Doctorow is a professional Russia watcher and actor in Russian affairs going back to 1965. He is a magna cum laude graduate of Harvard College (1967), a past Fulbright scholar, and holder of a Ph.D. with honors in history from Columbia University (1975). After completing his studies, Mr. Doctorow pursued a business career focused on the USSR and Eastern Europe. For twenty-five years he worked for US and European multinationals in marketing and general management with regional responsibility. From 1998-2002, Doctorow served as the Chairman of the Russian Booker Literary Prize in Moscow.

A number of his early scholarly articles on Russian constitutional history under Nicholas II drawn from his dissertation remain 'in print' and are available online. Mr. Doctorow has also been an occasional contributor to the Russian language press including *Zvezda* (St Petersburg), *Russkaya Mysl (La Pensée russe,* Paris) and *Kontinent* (a journal sponsored by Alexander Solzhenitsyn) on issues of Russian cultural and political life. He regularly publishes analytical articles about international affairs on the portal of the Belgian daily *La Libre Belgique.*

Mr. Doctorow's current research interest is trends in U.S. area studies programs. He is a Visiting Scholar of the Harriman Institute, Columbia University during the 2010-2011 academic year.

Mr. Doctorow is an American citizen and a long-time resident of Brussels, Belgium.

www.ingramcontent.com/pod-product-compliance
Lightning Source LLC
Chambersburg PA
CBHW062143280526
45788CB00001B/284